LEBANON IN MODERN TIMES

A. J. Abraham

University Press of America,® Inc.
Lanham · Boulder · New York · Toronto · Plymouth, UK

Copyright © 2008 by
University Press of America,® Inc.
4501 Forbes Boulevard
Suite 200
Lanham, Maryland 20706
UPA Acquisitions Department (301) 459-3366

Estover Road
Plymouth PL6 7PY
United Kingdom

Library of Congress Control Number: 2008924048
ISBN-13: 978-0-7618-4071-8 (clothbound : alk. paper)
ISBN-10: 0-7618-4071-0 (clothbound : alk. paper)
ISBN-13: 978-0-7618-4070-1 (paperback : alk. paper)
ISBN-10: 0-7618-4070-2 (paperback : alk. paper)

♾™ The paper used in this publication meets the minimum
requirements of American National Standard for Information
Sciences—Permanence of Paper for Printed Library Materials,
ANSI Z39.48—1984

THE PHOENICIANS CIVILIZED IT
THE GREEKS HELLENIZED IT
THE ROMANS LATINIZED IT
THE ARABS ARABIZED IT
MANKIND HAS PLAGIARIZED IT
AND, SCHOLARS HAVE IDEALIZED IT
THE LEBANON

CONTENTS

CONTENTS

PREFACE

Mounting interest in the modern history of Lebanon has continued unabated since the end of the recent conflict. That growing interest has prompted the completion of this survey, at this time, the close of the twentieth century.

This study, however, is not a detailed history of Lebanon that would require several volumes. It is an attempt to sketch the political history and meaningful events in the history of modern Lebanon. It is a chronicle of events in the emergence of the Lebanese state from the great Ottoman conquest (1516) to the present. It is also, to some extent, my interpretation and thoughts on the significance of Lebanon's political history stressing its internal-external linkages.

This narrative focuses on several themes. The first major theme is the proto-national identity of the Lebanese communities and how they act as semi-independent mini-states within a larger entity called Lebanon. The second theme explores the psychological pre-disposition among Lebanese communities and groups to seek autonomy and independence from their rapacious neighbors and the World Powers, or to use them at specific times to their own advantage. The third theme is drawn from their sectarian interrelations with one another, as well as, the intra-relations within each community or sect that often results in misinterpretations, misunderstandings, and conflict. And, lastly, the fourth theme highlights the identity crisis that permeates Lebanese communities and has maintained the high level of instability in the era of independence, including the recent civil war (1975-1982). The book concludes with prospects for the future.

Lebanon's contacts with the rest of the world has always been central to its evolution, and, thus, the foreign policy of that tiny state and the independent foreign policies of its sects, groups and communities will surely have some significance and relevance for the new century. That factor, and the fact that Lebanon represents a microcosm of the entire Middle East, makes the study of modern Lebanon and its communal relations and conflagrations important for the future.

The prototype manuscript of this study has been used for both undergraduate and graduate courses on Modern Lebanon, and the book is designed for use in classrooms. In over twenty-five years of teaching the history of Lebanon and doing research on that nation, I have, indeed, benefited greatly from the many suggestions of my Lebanese and non-Lebanese students, as well as a host of American and international politicians, diplomats, scholars, businessmen, and travelers to the area; and, of course, some of their impressions are inscribed in the pages of this text.

In composing this book, I had to sift through a staggering amount of material on Lebanon; the problem of what to use and what to leave out was monumental. I decided, in the interest of brevity and clarity, to exercise my own judgment in selecting sources and studies concerning the subjects, periods, and episodes to maintain the thematic view of the work while doing justice to the history of Lebanon. Unfortunately, some important studies were unavailable and others were destroyed in the recent conflict. In all cases, I have relied upon my insights and understanding to fill any gaps. And, I do hope that a younger generation of scholars on Lebanon will carry this study far into the twenty-first century.

The intended audience for this book includes scholars and laymen; I have translated and transliterated key words to facilitate a smooth reading. And, I am solely responsible for any errors of fact or opinion expressed in this work.

ACKNOWLEDGEMENTS

This book owes its genesis to several scholars, two of them are no longer with us, having left a void that can not be filled: They are Professor Philip K. Hitti of Princeton University, and Professor R. Bayly Winder of New York University, both of whom suggested and encouraged this study of modern Lebanon.

This work also owes its evolution to other scholars, men of great insight and inspiration: They are Professor Pierre Oberling of Hunter College and Professor C. Max Kortepeter of New York University.

And, there were still others as well whose personal support and expertise in Arabic and Middle Eastern History made this study possible. They are Dr. Kamil H. Taha and Dr. Kadri El-Arabi, both of the United Nations. Dr. Taha's extensive knowledge of Lebanon and the Arab World clarified numerous complex issues for me.

I also owe a tremendous debt of gratitude to Mr. John A. Cardello, a life-long friend, whose expert editorial skills and constant encouragement are deeply appreciated.

Lastly, my wife Esther was the pillar of strength needed for the completion of this project.

INTRODUCTION

Lebanon is truly a Temple of Janus; it is a door to the Arab-Islamic World and a window to Western-Christian Europe. Lebanon embraces and straddles two worlds at once; it is a Mediterranean society with a bi-cultural way of life. An inscription at the mouth of the Dog River boasts of several conquering nations, eastern and western, that have claimed Lebanon as part of their empires and civilizations, but they have long gone, whereas Lebanon remains. No doubt, all those nations have influenced Lebanon in many ways, and Lebanon has left its indelible mark upon their cultures as well. To the present time, the ebb and flow of cross cultural influence and tensions continues to impact upon Lebanon.

Lebanon is also a microcosm of the entire Near and Middle East; and, it has clearly been the beacon of the West on eastern landscapes. Some scholars say that Lebanon is more than just another country, nation or state in the region; it is a way of life and an idea - a center of humanism in an intolerant and hostile part of the globe - different from the nations around it, and the foreign states that have claimed it at one time or another; Lebanon has a personality of its own. It has been the home of numerous peoples, Christian and Moslem, as it stood watch over the crossroads of the world. And, in modern times, its prominence has grown as a column of progress and modernization for the entire region. Lebanon truly remains the only modern Arab or Moslem state in the Near East.

But, Lebanon is no fairy-tale land; it has its own, often hidden, ambiguities, along with its charm and uniqueness. It had and still has some serious problems that keep it unstable in both its domestic and foreign affairs. Some scholars trace the internal conflicts in Lebanon to the sacred while others seek causes in the profane. One group sees Lebanon's constant communal strife as a product of religious bigotry (a traditional view), while the others see it in more modern Marxist terms, as a product of class struggle (the have versus the have nots), or of an economic *"neglect,"* or *"marginalization,"* or *"victimization,"* of one sect or community at the hands of the others, producing a social or class conflict. These worn-out and out-dated theories still have some superficial significance for us today, in analyzing Lebanon's past.

But, Lebanon's recurring instability and communal conflicts, from early modern times (*the 1500's*) to the present, evolved largely from an unresolved identity crisis that is aggravated by communal relations with foreign powers that propagate a host of alien ideologies that often affect the Lebanese people and particularly their view of themselves.

This identity crisis manifests itself in communal and sectarian tensions which, in the long run, break-out as civil wars, or revolts for autonomy and independence, forcing the groups in Lebanon to seek out like-minded foreign allies.

xi

Also, each group, community or sect in Lebanon holds on to its own proto-national identity and often generates its own foreign policy with outside groups and nations (*the foreign powers*) to strengthen themselves. The result of these activities weakens the central government or source of national power and unity and produces protracted social conflicts (*PSC's*) or protracted inter-communal conflicts (*PIC's*) which have continued from generation to generation, over the past centuries.

This book is in part a study of the political history of modern Lebanon emphasizing the evolution and impact of the above tendencies on The Lebanon.

CHAPTER 1

THE LORD OF THE LAND: AMIR FAKHR AL-DIN AL-MANI II
AND THE DRUZE REVOLT

The Ottoman Empire, heir to Byzantium, stood like a mighty colossus astride the Bosphorus, gazing upon the Arab lands of West Asia. Soon it would add them to its powerful state.

The year was 1514 when the military forces of Sultan Salim, the grim, undertook a venture destined to bring the entire Arab World under Ottoman occupation for the next four hundred years. On the plain of Chalderon (*Chaldiran*) between Tabriz and Lake Urmia, on the twenty-fifth of April, 1514, Shah Ismail's Persian Army was utterly routed, and Salim prepared to press on against the Persian Empire. He occupied Ismail's capital, Tabriz; but, then the weary Janissary troops of the Sultan objected to any further penetration of Persian territory. Salim, consequently, turned his forces south against his one time ally, the Mamluks of Egypt, to protect his new conquests.[1]

The Mamluk Empire had been greatly weakened in its struggle with the Mongols and its rulers remained unable to rejuvenate their state as a result of their internecine conflicts. With the Ottoman Empire casting covetous eyes towards their eastern possessions, the Mamluks had sought a treaty with Shah Ismail who was only too happy to add their potency to his. As the Ottoman Army moved against the Persian forces, the Mamluk Sultan, Qansawh al-Ghawri, left Cairo for northern Syria with a powerful force to encounter Selim I with whom he had broken a previous treaty.[2] The Mamluk force comprised approximately 13,000 troops including mercenaries recruited along the way.[3]

On the morning of August 24, 1516, the Mamluk Army stood facing the Ottoman forces at Marj Dabiq, north of Aleppo. In the face of Ottoman artillery, long range weapons, and newly acquired muskets, some of al-Ghawri's troops defected;[4] and during the first charge, Khair Bey, the governor of Aleppo, deserted with his auxiliary [5] forces. Thereafter, victory quickly fell to the Ottoman Turks.

To the conquering Turkish army, Hamah capitulated on the twentieth of September. Hims fell on the twenty-second of September and Damascus surrendered on the ninth of October.[6] In Cairo, in April of that year, the last of the Mamluk sultans, Tuman Bey, was executed by Salim.[7] Thus, the Mamluk Empire was eclipsed forever and the Arab lands prepared themselves for a new master.

As the new lords of Syria, the Ottoman Empire was hailed as a deliverer, from Mamluk rule and, for the most part, met little resistance.[8] Ottoman rule had only slight effect on the ethnic, cultural or lingustic composition of the region;[9] the Hanifite law remained in effect[10] and that pleased most of the Moslems. For administrative purposes, Syria was divided into three provinces (*walayahs*): Damascus, Aleppo and Tripoli; later, Sidon was added[11] and a cadastral survey was prepared for the area. Apparently the sultan decided not to impose direct rule over Syria and Lebanon for he left the local authorities in charge of certain regions.[12] When Salim I departed in 1516, the administration of Lebanon had changed little from what it had been in Mamluk times.[13] The Ottoman impact on Lebanon, which was less direct than it was on Syria, produced hardly any change in that province.

During Sultan Salim's brief stay in Damascus, he was able to receive and entertain a delegation of princes (*amirs*) from Lebanon. The group was headed by Fakhr al-Din al-Mani I of al-Shuf, Jamal al-Din al-Tanukhi of al-Gharb, and Assaf al-Turkumani of Kisrawan.[14] At Marj Dabiq, Amir Fakhr al-Din I followed a prudent policy awaiting an indication of the outcome of the battle before joining the winning side.[15] Having gained favor in the sultan's eye, Fakhr al-Din I as leader of the delegation offered an eloquent prayer of praise to honor the sultan, and won the title "lord of the land" (*amir a-barr*) from him.[16] Although at that time the Shuf may have produced other contenders for the sultan's favor such as Qurqumas ibn Yunus or Alam al-Din Sulayman,[17] Fakhr al-Din I was clearly recognized as the most prominent Lebanese amir. In any case, the sultan confirmed the Lebanese amirs in their respective positions leaving them with the same privileges and autonomy they had had under Mamluk rule.[18] Thus, by appearing in the sultan's camp at a decisive moment, the Lebanese amirs retained autonomy and home rule for themselves and their posterity. The sultan remained content to control them indirectly through neighboring governors (*walis*).

In 1544, Fakhr al-Din I died leaving his son, Qurqumas, as successor. Forty years later, the Lebanese amirs found themselves in conflict with the sultan when a convoy destined for Istanbul was looted at Jun Akkar, thus forcing Sultan Murad III to send an expedition from Egypt commanded by his son-in-law, Ibrahim Pasha, to punish the Druze.[19] Ibrahim was reported to have killed 600 Druze at Ayn Sawfar and, later, another 60,000 of them in southern Lebanon.[20] Qurqumas, whose father had been killed by the Ottomans, now feared for his own life and fled from Ibrahim Pasha only to perish shortly afterwards.[21] The sultan imposed a payment of tribute on Lebanon after that incident.[22]

Although friendly at first, the attitude of the Druze towards the Ottoman Empire after the Ayn Sawfar event deteriorated into one of suspicion and mistrust; and, the heavy handed policy of the Turkish regime alerted the other inhabitants of Lebanon to the danger confronting them. Consequently, in the years following those events, it would not be surprising to find the Druze taking the lead in launching a policy seeking alliances within Lebanon or in Europe against the Ottoman Empire. One legacy of the Ottoman punitive expedition was to kindle in the hearts of the Druze of Lebanon the desire to go beyond the limits of local autonomy. For increased security, they sought a united Lebanon under Druze rule. Therefore it is easy to understand the willingness of the Maronites and other groups and sects to accept and cooperate with Fakhr al-Din II's political policies when he came to power.

Fakhr al-Din al-Mani and his brother Yunus were raised under the diligent eye of Maronite Shaykh Abu Nadir al-Khazin, to whom their mother had entrusted them to avoid death at the hands of the Egyptian governor, Ibrahim Pasha.[23] The personal relationship between the Maronite Khazins and Fakhr al-Din II cemented their ties not only socially but politically as well. In 1592, Fakhr al-Din and his uncle took a political initiative by presenting a gift to Murad Pasha, the governor of Damascus; in return, Fakhr al-Din was recognized and confirmed as the successor to Qurqumas.[24] Soon after, Fakhr al-Din began plotting the downfall of his enemies and planning for the independence of Lebanon. With the backing of the Maronites who had suffered under the rule of Yusuf ibn Sayfa,[25] Amir Fakhr al-Din took his revenge against the Sayfa's whom he blamed for the incident at Jun Akkar, resulting in the death of his father. After several military engagements Fakhr al-Din decisively defeated Yusuf ibn Sayfa and, shortly afterwards, he began a policy of creeping annexation in order to extend his political domain. The final battle, in 1607, placed Kisrawan within the amir's reach.[26] Later, his marriage to Yusuf ibn Sayfa's daughter united the political parties in Lebanon;[27] and his tolerant politics brought the Shi'ite banu Harfush of Balabakk and the bedouins of al-Biqa' as far as Galilee under his rule.[28] Fakhr al-Din's major political venture occurred in 1607 when he sided with Ali Junblat (*Jan Bulad*), the Kurdish chief of Aleppo, to balance the power of both the Sayfa's and the governor of Damascus, al-Hafiz Pasha.[29] The elimination of the military power of the Sayfa's brought the Lebanese amir into conflict with the Ottoman authorities, and his policies of religious tolerance, economic development, and military modernization increased the suspicions of the Porte.

If the psychoanalysts have been correct in asserting that the early stages of life leave deep impressions on an individual's behavior, perhaps, Fakhr al-Din's first policy of religious toleration and freedom grew out of his relationship with the Christian Khazins. Under Fakhr al-Din's rule, religious freedom became a norm. Christians could walk proudly in the streets with their heads raised and churches could be rebuilt and repaired.[30] His lack of fanaticism as well as his open mindedness permitted Christian missionaries to enter Lebanon and build churches and convents.[31] He raised the status of the Khazin family and he used many Christians in his administration.[32] Fakhr al-Din II brought the Maronites and the Druze into closer and more cordial relations when he permitted and even encouraged the migration of Maronites from the north into the predominantly Druze districts of South Lebanon.

In an atmosphere of congeniality, Fakhr al-Din II sought to encourage prosperity for all those who came under his rule. His plans for the economic progress of Lebanon included the modernization and improvement of agricultural techniques. The Lebanese amir encouraged the planting of olive and mulberry trees and he promoted local industry for flax and silk production.[33] To improve transportation towards the coast, he built four bridges along the four major river roads and caravanserais for foreign merchants.[34] Sidon rose in prominence as the residence of both the French consul and the Franciscan missionaries, as well as a seaport. The Lebanese ports of Sidon and Beirut were visited by vessels from France and Italy bringing new products to the east and taking back the fruits of Lebanese agriculture and crafts.[35] In 1608, Fakhr al-Din II signed a commercial treaty with Ferdinand I, the Medici Grand Duke of Tuscany, which included a secret military article against the Ottoman sultan.[36] From Tuscany, he received agricultural experts, architects and engineers.[37] While the agricultural experts contributed directly to a rise in the standard of living, the architects and the engineers were put to work on Lebanese fortifications. With unity and economic prosperity at hand, Fakhr al-Din opted for the creation of a totally independent Lebanon. No doubt, unity and prosperity were not only pursued for the happiness of his subjects, but also to support his military machine.

Internal security was needed before any attempt at independence could bear fruit. Thus, Fakhr al-Din not only set about to repair and rebuilt the fortifications of Lebanon, but he established garrisons at key points, introduced military patrols, and used carrier pigeons for communications.[38] The Lebanese amir imported artillery from Europe; his huge standing army included both the Druze and the Maronites and reached approximately 40,000 troops.[39]

Feeling confident of his prowess, Fakhr al-Din II began a more active policy of expansion. He sent Shaykh Abu Mulhim to Istanbul in 1609 to secure a decree (*a firman*) appointing his son as governor of Ajlun[40] and, encouraged by his success, the amir decided to widen his horizon. But, as long as Murad Pasha, the Ottoman grand vizir, was alive and in office Fakhr al-Din II could not proceed without fear. When Murad died in 1611, the new grand vizir, Nasuh Pasha, became even more suspicious of Fakhr al-Din's policy and his well equipped forces.[41] Indeed, Nasuh Pasha was no fool, and he quickly arrived at the conclusion that Fakhr al-Din was too dangerous. Meanwhile, the enemies of the Manis in Lebanon had corresponded with Nasuh Pasha in Istanbul,[42] and Ahmed Hafiz Pasha, the new governor of Damascus, was alerted to Fakhr al-Din's intentions. When Fakhr al-Din and Ahmad Hafiz Pasha clashed over claims to two districts (*sanjaks*), Nasuh Pasha began to mobilize an army to place at Hafiz Pasha's use against the Lebanese amir.[43]

Fakhr al-Din struck the first blow against his Ottoman suzerain. With the aid of his ally, Ali Junblat (*Jumblat*), the Lebanese amir raised the standard of revolt against Ottoman rule in 1613, by storming Damascus forcing it to surrender and pay a ransom.[44] At the same time, Fakhr al-Din intensified his negotiations with his Italian ally, through Italian traders and merchants in Beirut, hoping to obtain additional military weapons and to assure continued supply and support from Europe.[45] The Lebanese were prepared to hold out for five years of siege; but soon after the revolt began Fakhr al-Din's hopes were dashed when his Italian ally could not actively support him.

Meanwhile, the Sublime Porte could no longer tolerate the Lebanese amir's affront to the sultan's dignity; the Ottoman Empire began to prepare a force to defeat the rebellious amir. In 1614, when a force of 50,000 troops recruited from 50 districts converged on Damascus, and galleys blockaded the Lebanese coast so as to isolate the amir from foreign aid, Fakhr al-Din was pushed into an untenable position.[46]

Realizing his position was hopeless, the Prince of Lebanon decided on a self-imposed exile hoping to placate the sultan and to save Lebanon from an Ottoman invasion. Fakhr al-Din quickly called for a meeting which included his brother, Prince Yunus, his mother, the Shihabis of al-Shuf and the Khazins informing them of his plans. He asked them to remain united and to protect Lebanese autonomy in the face of the Ottoman threat[47] and then, he sent for two ships from France and one from Holland; on October 25, 1614, Amir Fakhr al-Din departed from the port of Sidon for the Italian port pf Leghorn (*Livorno*).

Soon after his arrival in Italy, Fakhr al-Din II was escorted to Pisa[48] and his safe arrival was communicated to both his brother and his family. He wrote to them as well as several other notables beseeching them to keep their promise of maintaining their hold on the castles and to continue to work for the independence of Lebanon:[49]

> I started negotiations with the leader of Tuscany concerning a European pact to help us get our independence and to evict the Ottoman forces from our country...I therefore advise you to depend upon yourselves, above everything else, if you desire to achieve a secure independence with a respectable position among nations.

In another letter Fakhr al-Din wrote:[50]

> Having set before our eyes a goal towards which we shall unswervingly move, the goal being the full independence of our country and its sovereignty, we are resolved that no promise of reward or threat of persecution shall in the least affect us.

While Fakhr al-Din II was in Messina, at that time still under Spanish rule, the amir sought permission to visit his homeland.[51] The Duke of Tuscany, Cosmo II, allowed him passage on a three ship pirate convoy which landed in Lebanon; thus the exiled prince met with his brother and other leading notables, on board the ship.[52] The ship departed for Malta where the Lebanese rebel spent three days, then they set sail for Palermo. While he was in southern Italy, the king of Spain offered Fakhr al-Din an estate and possessions greater than his former holdings if he would convert to Christianity.[53] The Lebanese leader politely refused the generous offer saying that if his presence as a Moslem offended them, he would be glad to return home.

At approximately the same time, a ship from Sidon arrived carrying a letter from Fakhr al-Din's mother saying that she had been released from prison, and that she wished to see him for she was advancing in years.[54] Once again, the amir requested a ship from his host and the request was favorably received. Fakhr al-Din's departure, however, was delayed when the duke was told that Fakhr al-Din could inform the sultan of Cosmo's military weakness.[55] After Fakhr al-Din reassured the duke that he had no intention of plotting against him with the Turkish leader or even visiting Istanbul, he was permitted to depart for Lebanon.[56]

The way for Fakhr al-Din's return had been prepared by his brother Amir Yunus. With the death of Nasuh Pasha in 1614,[57] Amir Yunus affected a peace with the new governor of Damascus who released Fakhr al-Din's mother from prison as a gesture of good faith; thus, Fakhr al-Din's return was not opposed.

After five years and two months of self-imposed exile, the Lebanese prince returned to Lebanon in 1618; he was warmly greeted by both his friends and some of his former enemies. While he had been in exile, Lebanon had drifted into chaos resulting from a breakdown in authority within the Druze community. Under Fakhr al-Din's strong rule, the Druze of both the Qaysite and Yamanite parties were united. With his exile, the unity of the two groups or parties, who trace their animosity to a north-south struggle in Arabia,[58] collapsed. Hence, Fakhr al-Din's presence appeared necessary to regain stability in the Druze camp.

Prince Yunus surrendered the reigns of government to his brother and, shortly afterwards, Fakhr al-Din II initiated action against his enemies. First he struck against the Sayfas storming and destroying Qalat al-Hisn and their palaces in Akkar and Tripoli; he used their stones to build his new palace in Dayr al-Qamar.[59] Then he turned against the Ottoman governor of Damascus, Mustafa Pasha, in an attempt to regain the two provinces he had previously lost. In 1623, he defeated Mustafa's forces and took him prisoner, but later the Lebanese amir released him.[60] Once again, encouraged by his military success, Fakhr al-Din undertook a policy of expansion. In the following year (1624) Fakhr al-Din II held sway from Aleppo to Jerusalem and he was recognized by Sultan Murad IV as the "lord of Arabistan,"[61] a vague title. A decree (an *imperial firman*) was issued to confirm the amir's position, and he later received the governorship of Tripoli in 1627.[62] Beirut became his capital in 1632.

In 1633, Fakhr al-Din grew ill, and it has been said that at that time he converted to Christianity, being baptized by Father Adrian De Labras.[63] Whether or not that is true, when Fakhr al-Din recovered from his illness, he found a new crisis awaiting him. His main ally, the Qaysite Tanukhs had been massacred by the Alam al-Din clan.[64] Weakened by that loss; the amir's position became somewhat precarious.

Sultan Murad IV was well aware of Fakhr al-Din's internal problems and had been fearful of his ambitions in northern Syria. Consequently, he ordered Kuchuk Ahmad Pasha of Damascus to march against the Lebanese amir with full Ottoman support.[65] Fakhr al-Din's enemies had informed the sultan that the amir intended to declare his independence.[66] Of all his former allies, only the Shihabis stood by his side, during that critical moment.[67] Khalil Pasha, the grand vizir, assigned Kuchuk Ahmed Pasha the task of leading the Ottoman army supported by 22 galleys under Jafar Pasha which could blockade and bombard the Lebanese coast.

One of Fakhr al-Din's sons commanded the Lebanese defense forces, and he was killed defending the region of Subayah, in Wadi al-Taym.[68] In desperation Fakhr al-Din again attempted to get aid from his Italian ally, but the 6,000 troops he had been promised were never dispatched, as a result of the thirty years war.[69] Betrayed on all sides; blockaded by sea, and facing an estimated 80,000 man army,[70] Fakhr al-Din II decided to flee the scene with his sons from Qalat Niha to a near by cave where he hoped to avoid detection for a while, and then try to escape to Europe. However they were captured in the cave near Jazzin, taken to Damascus, and later sent to the Ottoman capital.[71]

Fakhr al-Din met his sovereign face to face in Istanbul and he was well received. The Lebanese rebel defended his actions adequately. Nevertheless, the sultan continued to be suspicious of him. Partly because of his conversion to the Christian faith and partly because Mulhim ibn al-Amir Yunus's activity against the Porte, Fakhr al-Din finally lost favor at court.[72] Soon afterwards, the grand mufti declared him an apostate from Islam. With little hope for his survival, the Lebanese amir faced death bravely making the sign of the cross[73] before his execution, in 1635. Soon after his death, three of his sons were also put to death leaving one son, Husayn, who in fact became the Ottoman ambassador to India. After Fakhr al-Din's death, anarchy prevailed in Lebanon for no strong ruler could be found among the Manis who followed Fakhr al-Din al-Mani II.

In several studies Fakhr al-Din has been described as a greedy dictator[74] and the unity he achieved in Lebanon has been called dynastic rather than a prelude to modern nationalism.[75] No doubt, at times during his reign, Fakhr al-Din was forced to increase taxes substantially, but he did so because funds were needed for regional defense. He faced only slight opposition from the general public when taxes were collected, and he seems to have put the funds to good use by improving Lebanon's economic capabilities. He improved Lebanese ports, increased public work projects, and the taxes he spent on modernizing the agricultural system directly contributed to the welfare of those who worked the land. Perhaps Fakhr al-Din could have been more frugal, yet in no way did he squander the people's taxes. By going into self-imposed exile, the Lebanese prince showed concern for his own safety as well as concern for the welfare of his people. A greedy tyrant might have attempted to hold on to his possessions rather than surrender them and go into exile in a foreign land.

From his refuge in Italy, the Lebanese amir's concern for the autonomy of his homeland remained paramount. In his correspondence with his brother and some of the other notables he beseeched them to hold on to and protect their autonomy; and he cited full independence as his goal.[76] His secret alliance with the Grand Duke of Tuscany was in essence a declaration of independence from the Porte. If Fakhr al-Din had wanted to establish a dynasty to rule Lebanon, that fact in no way negates his desire for Lebanese independence. The unity he sought among the Lebanese could have served both his dynastic ambitions and his struggle for Lebanese independence equally well. In no way did the two desires of the prince produce mutually exclusive conditions. One need only to reflect upon the European dynasties to see that dynastic ambitions do not weaken drives for national autonomy or independence. Thus, Fakhr al-Din al-Mani II may still be considered the founder of modern Lebanese nationalism.

1. R. H. Davison, *Turkey*, New Jersey: Prentice Hall, 1968, p. 35.

2. Zeine N. Zeine, *Arab-Turkish Relations and the Emergence of Arab Nationalism*, Beirut: Khayat's Press, 1968, p. 10.

3. C. H. Churchill, *Mount Lebanon: A Ten Years Residence 1842-1852*, London: Bernard Quaritch, 1853, vol. 1, p. 331.

4. Davidson, *Turkey*, p. 35; P.K. Hitti, *Lebanon in History*, New York: St. Martin's Press, 1967, p. 351.

5. Hitti, *Lebanon in History*, p. 351.

6. Hitti, *Lebanon in History*, p. 351; Zeine, *Arab-Turkish Relations*, p. 11.

7. Hitti, *Lebanon in History*, p. 352; Zeine, *Arab-Turkish Relations*, p. 12.

8. Hitti, *Lebanon in History*, pp. 351-352.

9. A. H. Hourani, *Syria and Lebanon: A Political Essay*, London: Oxford University Press, 1946, p. 24.

10. Hitti, *History of Syria Including Lebanon and Palestine*, New York: The Macmillan Co., 1951, p. 664.

11. Hitti, *Lebanon in History*, p. 359; Hourani, *Syria and Lebanon*, p. 24.

12. George Haddad, *Fifty Years of Modern Syria and Lebanon*, Beirut: Dar al-Hayat, 1950, p. 29; Zeine, *Arab-Turkish Relations*, p. 11.

13. C. G. Hess and H. L. Bodman, "*Confessionalism and Feudality in Lebanese Politics*," MEJ, vol. 8, #1, 1954, pp. 10-11.

14. Hitti, *Lebanon in History*, p. 357; Hitti, *History of Syria*, p. 665; Zeine, *Arab-Turkish Relations*, p. 12.

15. Hitti, *Lebanon in History*, p. 357; Hitti, *History of Syria*, p. 665; I. I. Maluf, *Ta'rikh al-Amir Fakhr al-Din al-Thani*, Juniyah: Matba'at al-Risalah al-Lubnaiyah, 1934, pp. 23-24.

16. Churchill, *Mount Lebanon*, vol. III, p. 337; K. S. Salibi,"Fakhr al-Din," *E.I²*., p. 749; J. Catafago, "Histoire Des Emirs Maan, Qui ont Gouvernee Le Liban Despuis l'anne 1119 de J. C.Jusqu'a 1699," Journal Asiatigue, Sixieme Serie, vol. III, Paris,1964, p. 272; D. Urquhart, *The Lebanon: (Mount Souria) A History and a Diary,* vol. 1, London: T. C. Newly, 1860, p. 82; Hitti, *Lebanon in History*, p. 357; Hitti, *History of Syria*, p. 666; Zeine, *Arab-Turkish Relations*, p. 12.

17. K. S. Salibi, "The Secret of The House of Ma'n," *IJMES* vol. 4, no. 3, 1973, pp. 278-281.

18. Hitti, *Lebanon in History*, p. 357.

19. Hitti, *Lebanon in History*, p. 372; Urquhart, *The Lebanon*, p. 82.

20. Hitti, *Lebanon in History*, p.373; B. Qarali, *Fakhr al-Din al-Ma'ni al-Thani Hakim Lubnan*, vol. II, Rome: Realte Accademia d'Italia, 1928, p. 116.

21. Qarali, *Fakhr al-Din al-Ma'ni*, p. 116.

22. Urquhart, *The Lebanon*, p. 84.

23. Churchill, *Mount Lebanon*, vol. III, p. 343.

24. Maluf, *Ta'rikh al-Amir Fakhr al-Din*, p. 61.

25. Churchill, *Mount Lebanon*, p. 344; Salibi, "Fakhr al-Din,"*E.I.²*, pp. 749-750

26. Churchill, *Mount Lebanon*, pp. 344-345.

27. Hitti, *Lebanon in History*, p. 374.

28. Hitti, *History of Syria*, p. 680.

29. M. Chebli, *Une Histoire du Liban L'epoque des Emirs, 1635-1841,* Beirut: Imprimerie Catholique, 1955, p. 31.

30. Hourani, *Syria and Lebanon*, p. 25.

31. P. M. Holt, *Egypt and the Fertile Crescent, 1516-1922,* London: Longmans, 1966, p. 120; Hourani, *Syria and Lebanon*, p. 29; P. K. Hitti, *The Origins of The Druze People and Religion,* New York: Columbia University Press, 1928, p. 7.

32. Hitti, *Lebanon in History*, p. 377.

33. Hitti, *Lebanon in History*, p. 376.

34. Hitti, *Lebanon in History*, p. 376.

35. Hitti, *Lebanon in History*, p. 376.

36. Hitti, *Lebanon in History*, p. 376; Maluf, *Ta'rikh al-Amir Fakhr al-Din*, p. 91.

37. Holt, *Egypt and the Fertile Crescent*, p. 119.

38. Hitti, *Lebanon in History*, p. 376; I. Al-Duwayhi, "Tarikh al-Azminah 1095-1699 A.D.," *Al-Mashriq*, Beirut, 1951, vol. XLIV, pp. 303-304.

39. Holt, *Egypt and the Fertile Crescent*, p. 119; Hitti, *Lebanon in History*, pp. 376-377.

40. Maluf, *Ta'rikh al-AmirFakhr al-Din*, p. 92.

41. Salibi, "Fakhr al-Din," *E.I.* [2], p. 750.

42. Maluf, *Ta'rikh al-Amir Fakhr al-Din*, p. 101.

43. Salibi, "Fakhr al-Din," *E.I.*[2], p. 750.

44. Churchill, *Mount Lebanon*, p. 345.

45. Maluf, *Ta'rikh al-Arnir Fakhr al-Din*, p. 103.

46. Hitti, *Lebanon in History*, pp. 377-378; Churchill, *Mount Lebanon*, p. 346.

47. Al-Duwayhi, "Tarikh al-Azminah," p. 304.

48. Churchill, *Mount Lebanon*, p. 353.

49. Maluf, *Ta'rikh al-Amir Fakhr al-Din*, p. 130; Hitti, *Lebanon in History*, p. 379; Aziz al-Ahdab, *Fakhr al-Din al-Kabir*, Beirut: Dar al-Kitab al-Lubnani, 1984, p. 157; Anis al-Nusuli, *Rasail al-Amir Fakhr al-Din min Tuskana*, Beirut: n.p., 1946, pp. 16-17.

50. Hitti, *Lebanon in History*, pp. 379-380.

51. Maluf, *Ta'rikh al-Amir Fakhr al-Din*, pp. 146-147.

52. Maluf, *Ta'rikh al-Amir Fakhr al-Din*, pp. 147-149.

53. Maluf, *Ta'rikh al-Amir Fakhr al-Din*, p. 160.

54. Maluf, *Ta'rikh al-Amir Fakhr al-Din*, pp. 160-161.

55. Maluf, *Ta'rikh al-Amir Fakhr al-Din*, p. 162.

56. Maluf, *Ta'rikh al-Amir Fakhr al-Din*, p. 162.

57. Salibi, "Fakhr al-Din," *E.I.* [2], p. 750.

58. Hitti, *Origins of The Druze People*, p. 8.

59. Hitti, *Lebanon in History*, pp. 380-381.

60. Hitti, *Lebanon in History*, pp. 380-381; Adel Ismail, *Histoire du Liban du xvii Siecle a Nos Jours,* 5 vol., Paris: G. P. Maisonneune, 1955-1958, vol. 1, p. 8; Urquhard, *The Lebanon*, p. 88.

61. Hitti, *Lebanon in History*, p. 382.

62. Maluf, *Ta'rikh al-Amir Fakhr al-Din*, p. 194.

63. Maluf, *Ta'rikh al-Amir Fakhr al-Din*, p. 200.

64. Salibi, "Fakhr al-Din," *E.I* [2], p. 751.

65. Hitti, *History of Syria*, p. 684; Catafago, "Histoire Des Amirs Maan," p. 281; Salibi, "Fakhr al-Din," *E.I* [2], p. 751.

66. Maluf, *Ta'rikh al-Amir Fakhr al-Din*, p. 202.

67. Maluf, *Ta'rikh al-Amir Fakhr al-Din*, p. 203.

68. Salibi, "Fakhr al-Din," *E.I.* [2], p. 751; Hitti, *Lebanon in History*, p. 384.

69. Maluf, *Ta'rikh al-Amir Fakhr al-Din*, p. 207.

70. Hitti, *Lebanon in History*, p. 383.

71. Hitti, *Lebanon in History*, p. 384; Hitti, *History of Syria*, p. 685.

72. Maluf, *Ta'rikh al-Amir Fakhr al-Din*, p. 212.

73. Maluf, *Ta'rikh al-Muir Fakhr al-Din*, p. 213

74. Salibi, "Fakhr al-Din," *E.I* [2], p. 751.

75. Holt, *Egypt and the Fertlie Crescent*, p. 115.

76. Hitti, *Lebanon in History*, p. 380.

CHAPTER 2

THE SHIHABI AMIRATE (EMIRATE) I:
NEUTRALITY IN THE ERA OF NAPOLEON AND AHMED AL-JAZZAR
PASHA

The Mani dynasty, which had sky rocketed to dazzling heights in the seventeenth century, plummeted into oblivion in 1596 when Amir Ahmad al-Mani died leaving no heir.[1] Thus, Lebanon was thrown into confusion; but in the following year the Lebanese notables called for a general assembly to meet at Simqaniyah to elect a leader who could hold the reigns of government as steadily as the previous dynasty. The assembly elevated the Sunnite Shihabi family of Rashayya into the limelight of Lebanese politics and Amir Bashir al-Shihabi I (1697-1705) was elected to the amirate of Lebanon; the governor (al-hakim) of the mountain.[2] The Shihabi family derived some prestige from their membership in the Quraysh tribe of which the Prophet Muhammad was a member.[3] However, Bashir I election did not go uncontested and, until the emergence of Amir Bashir al-Shihab II, the Shihab family faced a continual struggle to maintain their hold on Mount Lebanon.

The Porte opposed the decision of the notables at Simqaniyah, and with the influence of Fakhr al-Din's sole surviving son, Husayn, opted in favor of Haydar al-Shihab.[4] The Lebanese, however, almost unanimously supported Bashir al-Shihab I for he promised not to increase taxes.[5] Although the Ottoman Empire had given the Lebanese amirs considerable freedom by instituting indirect rule in Lebanon, the Porte wanted to retain a degree of control over the autonomous regions. When Bashir attempted to uphold the authority of the notables, what might have been a local dispute appeared to have taken increased significance because it pitted the authority of the Lebanese amirs against their sovereign in Istanbul, and challenged his authority over them. Almost from the onset, Shihabi rule found itself championing the cause of Lebanese autonomy.

Amir Bashir I rule was short lived. In 1705, he was poisoned either by an agent of the sultan or a cousin from Hasbayya who had supported Amir Haydar's claim;[6] shortly afterwards, Amir Haydar was appointed hakim (1706-1730). Although his rule began in a tranquil fashion, Haydar was unable to control the local Qaysite and Yamanite political factions. Conditions continued to deteriorate until they reached a head when Haydar favored the Qaysite party and decided to take advantage of the situation before his right to rule was further threatened. In 1711, at Ayn Darah, Haydar struck a devastating blow at the Yamanite party almost totally eliminating their political power.[7] Creating unity by force of arms, Amir Haydar established hegemony over Lebanon; and the hakim reorganized the feudal family structure to place his supporters in power and then he centralized economic functions among them. After the Ayn Darah incident, peace and prosperity reigned until Haydar's death in 1731.

Amir Haydar's son, Amir Mulhim, was next in the line of a succession and ruled until 1753 or 1754 when he resigned.[8] (Originally Sunnite Moslems, the Shihabi family is today part Christian and part Moslem. Conversion to Christianity, it is said, began with one of the Sons of Amir Mulhim.) Amir Mulhim pursued a policy of expansion which added al-Biqa' and Beirut to his possessions;[9] he defeated Asad Pasha of Damascus at Barr Ilyas as well as his supporter, the lord of Balabakk of the Harfush family.[10] In 1743, the Lebanese prince brought the rebellious Matawilah (Shi'ite Moslems) under his control.[11] His reign launched the Shihabis along the road to conquest and unity in the mountain, until his abdication. In 1753, Amir Mulhim's hand was pierced by a thorn from a cactus plant and he became ill.[12] Shortly afterwards, the mountain prince became too weak to carry out his governmental functions and was quickly confined to bed.[13] Unable to fully recover, the hakim abdicated in favor of his two brothers, Ahmad and Mansur; then he departed for Beirut where he studied Islamic theology until his demise.[14] The unity Mulhim sought to establish collapsed with his abdication and, under the rule of his two brothers; Lebanon reverted to a condition of internal strife and discord.

Amir Mulhim's brothers, Amir Ahmad and Amir Mansur, were supported by rival political factions splitting Lebanese unity into two major parties; the Yazbakis and the Junblats.[15] The instability lasted until Amir Yusuf, Amir Mulhim's son, succeeded both of his uncles, after Amir Mansur stepped down. Thus, partial unity was reestablished in the Mountain. Almost as soon as he succeeded to power, Amir Yusuf expanded his hold to Dayr al-Qamar and he defeated opposition by the Matawilah in 1771.[16] However, Yusuf continued to face the hostile Druze factions and thus he sought the aid of the Christians to bolster his position. His guardian was a Maronite named Sad al-Khuri[17] whom Bashir I had appointed as an official advisor and confidant to the hakim. Even with Christian support, Yusuf continued to face the relentless hostility of the Junblat faction which refused to accept his authority. In 1788, in a major battle at Qabb Ilyas, Yusuf's forces were routed and he was compelled to sponsor Bashir al-Shihab II for the office of hakim.[18]

Bashir al-Shihab II won the support of the notables as well as the common people but his right to rule did not remain unchallenged. With the aid of the governor of Acre (Akka), Ahmed al-Jazzar Pasha, the sons of Amir Yusuf began a conspiracy against the hakim,[19] which poisoned Bashir's relationship with his neighboring wali in Acre. Nevertheless, the plot served as a warning to Bashir for his suspicions alerted him to the covetous intentions of al-Jazzar. Clearly, from the onset of his reign, Bashir II sought to maintain his hold on Lebanon, unify the region, and steer it clear of involvements or entanglements with the rapacious Ottoman governors he had for neighbors.

In the early part of the nineteenth century, the Ottoman Empire had no successful method which could control the varied ambitions of its walis. Hence, in the primary stage of his rule, Bashir attempted to preserve Lebanese autonomy by playing off the surrounding walis against one another and by his attempt to keep Lebanon neutral. Within the Lebanese province, Bashir played a dual Moslem-Christian role: His palace had both a chapel and a mosque in it and he worshiped in both. It has been said that Bashir II was a "Christian by baptism, a Moslem by matrimony, and a Druze prince to his subjects." His true beliefs, however, may remain obscured, for all communities have claimed him.

Ahmed al-Jazzar Pasha kept a watchful eye on the internal developments in Lebanon hoping to find an opportunity to interfere in Lebanese affairs. Bashir was fully acquainted with al-Jazzar's behavior and he quickly grew fearful of him. On three occasions, in 1793, 1794, and 1798, Bashir was deposed by al-Jazzar and the sons of Amir Yusuf (Husayn, Sad al-Din, and Salim) were elevated to Bashir's position resulting in a great deal of disorder in Lebanon.[20]. Consequently, Bashir saw al-Jazzar in the light of his actions as an outside element interfering in the local body politic. But, Ahmed Pasha's attention was immediately deflected from his ambition in Lebanon when Napoleon Bonaparte launched a campaign to capture the Near East, a project which brought him to the walls of Acre in Palestine.[21] Thus, Ahmed al-Jazzar, who had once supported Bashir II against the Druze, had to come to terms with both Bashir II and the Druze in the face of a powerful new enemy.[22] Yet, stability on his northern border did not enhance Ahmed Pasha's military position against the French incursion. When al-Jazzar asked Bashir for help, the Lebanese hakim told him that he could not help him because Lebanon was not under his control.[23] To a great extent Bashir was responding accurately for the Christians of Galilee and the Maronites of Lebanon openly supported independence from the Ottoman Empire and the French incursion.[24]

When British aid reached al-Jazzar, Napoleon's position became difficult and, consequently, he sought assistance from Bashir II; but he was rebuffed by the Lebanese amir on at least two occasions.[25] Ahmed Pasha, no doubt, learned of Bashir's refusal to aid the French general and the news temporarily placated the Pasha of Acre. Finally, British aid to Ahmed al-Jazzar and the spread of the plague in the French camp brought defeat to the world famous French general forcing him to retreat from Palestine.[26] Yet before Napoleon's defeat, Bashir II had taken precautionary steps to maintain Lebanon's autonomy regardless of the outcome of the war in Palestine. To insure the security of Lebanon from al-Jazzar's ambitions, Bashir attempted to befriend Sir Sidney Smith, the Admiral of the British fleet in the area, and Sulayman Pasha who had been sent from Istanbul with a powerful army to confront Napoleon.

Admiral Smith's acquaintance with the Lebanese hakim had resulted from an accidental occurrence. A Christian wine merchant taking wine to the French troops was captured by the British in Beirut and he informed the British of Bashir's rejection of Napoleon's plea for aid.[27] Admiral Smith and Bashir began an exchange of messages and gifts which mutually served the purposes of both men, to al-Jazzar's discomfort.[28] No doubt, Bashir sought to use the British as an ally against Ahmed Pasha, while the British wanted stability in the Near East in the face of Napoleon's threat. Sir Sidney met with Bashir II and promised him that he would not let the Pasha of Acre take advantage of him.[29] Then, the admiral asked al-Jazzar to improve his relationship with the Lebanese hakim, but Ahmed Pasha flatly refused.[30]

Meanwhile, Bashir's keen knowledge of Ahmed al-Jazzar proved to be extremely useful to him. Bashir had no intention of having his fate dangle on the whims of al-Jazzar or upon Britain's flexible policies. The Lebanese amir decided to take matters into his own hands in order to insure continued autonomy. Bashir knew of the advance of the Ottoman grand vezir, Yusuf Pasha, to aid and bolster al-Jazzar position and, consequently, he sent him gifts and a letter describing Ahmed Pasha's misrule.[31] When the grand vezir arrived in Damascus, he found more gifts awaiting him and military supplies for his troops.[32] Thus, Bashir had opted to play two sides against the Pasha of Acre but, after Napoleon's withdrawal, Ahmed al-Jazzar Pasha was in no way content to be passed over in favor of Bashir II.

With his major fear allayed, Ahmed Pasha had no intention of sitting tight in his principality south of Lebanon. Truly infuriated by Bashir's initiatives against him, al-Jazzar Pasha began to concern himself with Lebanese affairs and thus he was prepared to take advantage of Bashir's internal difficulties and to utilize them to his own advantage. In many respects, al-Jazzar was a master of Ottoman diplomacy to suit his own purposes. Later, with the grand vezir out of the picture after Napoleon's defeat, al-Jazzar moved against Bashir who faced local opposition which caused him to lose control over the Lebanese amirs.[33] With approval of the Lebanese notables, Ahmed Pasha appointed the sons of Amir Yusuf to the hakimate. No doubt, the Pasha of Acre foresaw the confusion that it would create, thereby enabling him to intensify his interference in Lebanese politics. Bashir of course also realized that, but he had no support within Lebanon at that time. Apparently, the other Lebanese amirs were deceived by al-Jazzar who had created the impression that he had liberated them from the dictates of Bashir II. Ahmed al-Jazzar Pasha's plans might have succeeded had Admiral Smith not come to Bashir's relief.

Hearing of Bashir's misfortunes, Admiral Smith was prompted to make an on the scene appearance; he promised the deposed hakim his total support.[34] Bashir, who had fled to Damascus, made a hasty return to Lebanon and, then, he left with Sir Sidney Smith on a British vessel.[35] While Bashir was in temporary exile, Admiral Smith arranged a meeting between the ex-hakim and the Ottoman grand vezir who was camped at al-Arish [36] on his way to encounter the French forces still in Egypt.[37] Through the quick intercession of the grand vezir, Bashir al-Shihab was returned to power and took up his residence at Dayr al-Qamar while Amir Yusuf's Sons retained a hold on Jubayl.[38]

Bashir al-Shihab II was welcomed by the people who complained bitterly about al-Jazzar's heavy handed behavior and the rule of the sons of Amir Yusuf.[39] Clearly, al-Jazzar Pasha lost the final round with Bashir II when the Lebanese hakim won the support of both the Porte and the admiral of the British fleet. The death of Ahmed Pasha on April 23, 1804 removed Bashir's major obstacle to power,[40] for the Lebanese amir believed that Ahmed al-Jazzar Pasha was the major force interfering in Lebanon's autonomy.[41]

Al-Jazzar Pasha was of Bosnian origin and seemed to care little for the people who came under his rule. Apparently, his main concern was his own aggrandizement and, hence, he embarked on an expansionist policy infringing upon Bashir's authority in the Lebanese province. Unlike al-Jazzar, Bashir was a native of the province he ruled and he had close ties with his subjects. The Lebanese hakim was not interested in expanding his authority outside Lebanon for his main concern was Lebanon's autonomy and, clearly, he championed that autonomy and won his battle against the Pasha of Acre. In his rejection of aid to both al-Jazzar and Napoleon, Bashir II sought to steer clear of Ottoman political entanglements. He sought the aid of the Grand vezir and Admiral Smith but he did so without compromising Lebanon's autonomy. Bashir utilized both men to retain his hold on Lebanon knowing that either of them could alter the situation if they mistrusted him or if Bashir were to pose a threat to the Ottoman Empire or to British interests in the Near East. Consequently, Bashir's policy in the early stages of his rule was defensive in character, later, to be replaced by a more aggressive commitment in search of total independence from the sultan's hold. But before Bashir could inaugurate a more forceful policy on behalf of his Lebanese subjects, he had to consolidate his rule within Lebanon.

1. Hitti, *Lebanon in History* p. 387; T. Al-Shidyaq, *Kitab Akhbar a fi Jabal Lubnan* Beirut: al-Jami'at al Lubnaniyah, 1970, p. 48; H. Al-Shihab, *Lubnan Fi Ahd al-Umara al-Shihablyin,* Beirut: al-Jami'at al-Lubnaniyah, 1969, p. 3; W. I Polk, *The Opening of South Lebanon,* 1788-1840 Boston: Harvard University Press, p. 11; Hitti, *Origins of The Druze People,* p. 7.

2. Hitti, *Lebanon in History,* P. 387; H. Al-Munayyir, "Al-Durr al-Marsuf fi Ta'rikh al-Shut," *Al-Mashriq* vol. 48, 1954, pp. 672-673.

3. A. Abu Khattar, "Mukhtasar Ta'rikh Jabal Lubanan," *Al-Mashriq,* vol. 46, 1952, part III, p. 334; B. F. Sfeir, *Al-Amir Bashir al-Shihabi,* Beirut: Dar al-Tiba'ah wa al-Nashr, 1950, p. 19.

4. Hitti, *Lebanon in History,* p. 387.

5. Polk, *The Opening of South Lebanon,* p. 11.

6. Al-Munayyir, *"Al-Durr al-Marsuf,"* vol. 48, 1954, p. 679; Al-Shidyaq, *Kitab Akhbar al-Ayan,* p. 48.

7. Hitti, *Lebanon in History,* p. 390; Hitti, *History of Syria* pp. 686-677; Al-Munayyir, *"Al-Durr al-Marsuf,"* vol. 48, 1954, pp. 676-677; Churchill, *Mount Lebanon,* p. 29.

8. Holt, *Egypt and the Fertile Crescent,* p. 123.

9. Hitti., *History of Syria,* p. 687.

10. Hitti, *Lebanon in History,* p. 391.

11. Al-Munayyir, *"Al-Durr al-Marsuf,"* vol. 48, 1954, p. 678.

12. Al-Shihab, *Lubnan fi Ahd al-Umara,* p. 43.

13. Al-Shihab, *Lubnan fi Ahd al-Urnara,* p. 43.

14. Al-Shihab, *Lubnan fi Ahd al-Umara,* p. 43, 49; Hitti, *Lebanon in History,* p. 392.

15. Al-Shihab, *Lubnan fi Ahd al-Umara,* p. 57.

16. Al-Munayyir, *"Al-Durral-Marsuf,"* vol. 49, 1955, pp. 264-266.

17. Holt, *Egypt and the Fertile Crescent,* p. 123; Hitti, *Lebanon in History,* p.393.

18. Hitti, *Lebanon in History,* p. 397; Sfeir *Al-Amir Bashir al-Shihabi* p. 33; Hitti, *History of Syria,* p. 691.

19. Hitti, *History of Syria,* p. 691.

20. K. S. Salibi, *The Modern History of Lebanon,* New York: Frederick A. Praeger Publishers, 1965, pp. 20-21; Urquhart, *The Lebanon,* pp. 116-118.

21. A. Al-Aynturini, "Kitab Mukhtasar Ta'tikh Jabal Lubnan," *Al-Mashriq,* vol. 47, 1953, p. 64; Salibi, *The Modern History,* p. 21.

22. Al-Munayyir, *"Al-Durr al-Marsuf,"* vol. 50, 1956, pp. 432-436, 448.

23. Al-Shidyaq, *Kitab Akhbar al-Ayan,* p. 369; Al-Shihab, *Lubnan fi Ahd al-Umara,* p. 192.

24. A. L. Tibawi, *A Modern History of Syria, Including Lebanon and Palestine,* London: Macmillan and Co., 1969, p. 37; Salibi, *The Modern History,* p. 21.

25. Al-Shihab, *Lubnan fi Ahd al-Umara,* p. 193; Chebli, *Une Histoire du Liban,* p. 207; A. DeLamartine, *Souvenirs, Impressions, Pensees et Paysages un Voyage en Orient,* 1832-1833 Paris: Hachette et Cie-Furne, 1835, vol. I, p. 240.

26. Al-Shihab, *Lubnan fi Ahd al-Umara,* p. 193; Hourani, *Syria and Lebanon,* p. 28.

27. Al-Shihab, *Lubnan fi Ahd al-Umara,* p. 193.

28. Chebli, *Une Histoire du Liban,* pp. 208-210; Al-Aynturini, *"Kitab Mukhtasar Ta'rikh Jabal Lubnan,"* vol. 47, 1953, p. 64; Al-Shidyaq, *Kitab Akhbar al-Ayan,* p. 369.

29. Al-Shihab, *Lubnan fi Ahd al-Umara,* p. 194; Al-Munayyir, *"Al-Durr al-Marsuf,"* vol. 51, 1957, p. 445.

30. Al-Shidyaq, *Kitab Akhbar al-Ayan,* p. 369; Al-Shihab, *Lubnan fi Ahd al-Umara,* p. 194.

31. Al-Shihab, *Lubnan fi Ahd al-Umara,* p. 194; Al-Munayyir, *"Al-Durr al-Marsuf,"* vol. 51, 1957, p. 443.

32. Al-Shihab, *Lubnan fi Ahd al-Umara,* p. 195; Al-Munayyir, *"Al-Durr al-Marsuf,"* vol. 51, 1957, p. 444

33. Al-Shidyaq, *Kitab Akhbar al-Ayan* p. 372; Al-Shihab, *Lubnan fi Ahd al-Umara*, pp. 196-197; al-Munayyir, *"Al-Durr al-Marsuf,"* vol. 51, 1957, p. 446.

34. Al-Munayyir, *"Al-Durr al-Marsuf",* vol. 51, 1957, p. 446.

35. Al-Munayyir, *"Al-Durr al-Marsuf,"* vol. 51, 1957, p. 447; Al-Shihab, *Lubnan fi Ahd al-Umara,* p. 201; Al-Shidyaq, *Kitab Akhbar al-Ayan,* p. 373; DeLamartine, *Souvenirs, Impressions*, p. 243.

36. Al-Shihab, *Lubnan fi Ahd al-Umara*, p. 201; Al-Munayyir, *"Al-Durr al-Marsuf,"* vol. 51, 1957, p. 447.

37. Al-Shihab, *Lubnan fi Ahd al-Umara,* pp. 203-204.

38 Al-Shidyaq, *Kitab Akhbar al-Ayan*, p. 375; Salibi, *The Modern History*, p. 22; Al-Munayyir, *"Al-Durr al-Marsuf,"* vol. 51, 1957, p. 453.

39. Al-Shihab, *Lubnan fi Ahd al-Umara,* pp. 207-209.

40. Hitti, *Lebanon in History,* p. 414.

41. Sfeir, *Al-Amir Bashir al-Shihabi,* pp. 36-37.

CHAPTER 3

THE SHIHABI AMIRATE (EMIRATE) II:
LEBANON AND THE EGYPTIAN INVASION

In the early part of Bashir II's rule he had successfully defended Lebanon's autonomy by skillfully negotiating alliances with the Porte's representative and the Commander of the British fleet. When Ahmed al-Jazzar Pasha died in 1804, Bashir set in motion the forces which he hoped would enable him to free Lebanon from Ottoman rule. His first step was designed to consolidate Shihabi power in Mount Lebanon, and then to negotiate an alliance with Muhammad Ali, the Viceroy of Egypt, which could have led to an independent Lebanon, allied to an independent Egypt.

With the death of Ahmed al-Jazzar, the population of Damascus revolted against his agent, Hashim Aga,[1] while many of the Lebanese amirs who had betrayed Bashir II attempted to reaffirm their allegiance to him.[2] Nevertheless, Bashir al-Shihab quickly moved to eliminate his dangerous rivals; he struck first at the sons of Amir Yusuf putting them to death.[3] Then, systematically, he eliminated the power of the Abu Nakad shaykhs; the Arslani shaykhs, the Talhuq shaykhs, the Imadi shaykhs, and the Abd al-Malik family.[4] In that process, Bashir devastated Druze political power leaving the Maronite lords almost untouched. As a result of this stringent policy Bashir unified Lebanon by centralizing authority in his hands and by banishing the major Druze notables who had opposed his rule.

Although Bashir opposed the Druze notables, he was in no way anti-Druze or a religious bigot. He treated the Druze population fairly and with great respect because he needed their support to retain his grip on Lebanon; his opposition to Druze power proved to be highly selective. When the Druze leaders of Aleppo revolted against Ottoman rule, they sought refuge in Lebanon.[5] Almost 15,000 families found safety and, later, prosperity in Lebanon. When the governor of Sidon threatened Bashir for not punishing the Druze, the Lebanese hakim replied that they were not in Lebanon.[6] His defiance was based upon his belief that he was acting justly on their behalf. Bashir al-Shihab, on another occasion, offered a similar hospitality to Malkites of Aleppo when they were persecuted by the Ottoman authorities.

Although Bashir II opposed the Ottoman walis at times, the amir found himself supporting Ottoman rule in Syria when the province was threatened by the Wahhabis, a militant religious movement based in Arabia. In 1810, the Wahhabi forces led by Alayyan advanced towards Hawran in Syria and its governor requested Bashir's aid to defend the city of Damascus.[7] Bashir recruited approximately 15,000 troops and led this powerful force towards Tiberias to join the grand vezir's Turkish troops. As the combined armies approached the Wahhabi warriors, the Arabian forces withdrew[8] from Syria avoiding a major battle. In the same year, Bashir found himself marching back towards Damascus when Yusuf Kanj Pasha challenged the Lebanese hakim's control over the Bekka Valley (*al-Biqa'*).[9] However, Yusuf Pasha relinquished his claim and fled to Egypt shortly afterwards enabling Bashir to flex his military muscle with little to fear from the other local walis; from 1810 until 1819, Bashir al-Shihabi's hold on the Lebanese province remained impregnable.

In 1819, Sulayman Pasha, Bashir's ally, died and the hakim lost one of his major supporters. Meanwhile, internal unrest intensified within Lebanon so that by 1820, Bashir II found himself unsupported and facing a major crisis. To sustain his military posture and ventures, Bashir had doubled taxes and enforced their collection.[10] This forced the Lebanese amirs to revolt launching the first ammiyyah or popular uprising against Bashir al-Shihab. Based at Lahfid, the revolt spread to Jubayl, Batrun and Kisrawan;[11] it was led by Monsignor Yusuf Istifan and Shaykh Fadil al-Badawi al-Khazin.[12] Bashir soon found himself facing an insurmountable obstacle; the whole population in revolt. Thus, he found it prudent to ease his demands in order to retain his hold on the Lebanese province.

The newly established stability in Lebanon, however, did not last long. When Bashir opposed the sultan's will and threatened Damascus by supporting Abd Allah Pasha in a conflict with Darwish Pasha, the sultan's man, Bashir II was deposed.[13] A short while later, Abd Allah Pasha won favor at the sultan's court and he was reappointed. Soon after, Bashir supported Abd Allah in a local dispute with Bashir Junblat, and Bashir al-Shihab was reinstated prior to the execution of Bashir Junblat in 1825.[14] And, once again, Bashir II found himself in power in Lebanon with his hold on the Lebanese tighter than ever before.

During Bashir al-Shihab's earlier sojourn or exile to Egypt while he was out of favor with the Ottoman authorities, he had met with Muhammad Ali Pasha, the Ottoman Viceroy for Egypt,[15] and his son, Ibrahim Pasha; and, a friendship quickly developed. Bashir had planned to take an initiative in part of a future expedition that was destined to change the Levant; the Egyptian invasion of Syria. The hakim had arranged to play a major role in that event and to take an aggressive policy aimed at the total and complete independence of Lebanon.

Muhammad Ali had intervened in local affairs in Lebanon to reinstate both Abd Allah Pasha and Amir Bashir and, therefore, the sultan could be sure that the Pasha of Egypt looked east to satisfy his territorial ambitions. In 1825, the sultan's fears would have been easily corroborated because the French consul in Sidon had informed his ambassador in Istanbul that French agents had known of Muhammad Ali's preparations to extend his authority over Syria.[16] The sultan, however, did not act against the Pasha of Egypt for he believed that Muhammad Ali could not proceed with his plans as long as Great Britain supported the Porte, even if France gave its whole hearted backing to Muhammad Ali and Ibrahim Pasha. Also, the sultan was in no position to attempt an invasion of Egypt to oust his potentially rebellious wali. The Ottoman forces had encountered heavy losses in the Greek War for independence and on the Russian front[17] and, consequently, they were incapable of effectively countering the intentions, the plots and ploys, of Muhammad Ali. Hence, Muhammad Ali could bide his time and prepare himself adequately for a large scale venture. The adventurous Ibrahim Pasha had already demonstrated Egyptian military might against the Greeks and the Wahhabis of Arabia; and, no doubt, he felt confident that he could thwart or defeat Ottoman power in Syria. Bashir II's assistance came as a welcomed surprise and perhaps advanced Ibrahim's schedule.

Bashir's meeting with Muhammad Ali Pasha helped set the stage for the Egyptian invasion of Syria giving Ibrahim Pasha a powerful ally in the heart of the Ottoman Empire's Arab possessions. It has been said that the Viceroy of Egypt told Bashir II that Syria was looking for a rightful ruler to replace the misrule of the Ottoman Turks and that he hoped to fill the role.[18] Also, it has been suggested that Muhammad Ali requested Bashir II's aid and that he informed the Lebanese amir that he harbored no intention of implementing direct rule over Lebanon;[19] and, that he would guarantee Lebanon's independence from the Ottoman Empire.[20] Whether or not an agreement was reached between Muhammad Ali and Bashir al-Shihab at that time, it seems highly likely that Bashir would co-operate with the Egyptians since they had a common enemy encroaching on their prerogatives; the Turkish Empire. Bashir, however, remained cautious in his involvement with the Viceroy of Egypt.

On October 29, 1831, Ibrahim Pasha's forces invaded Syria on the pretext of an argument with Abd Allah Pasha.[21] As the 11,000 man Egyptian army advanced towards Acre on November 26, Bashir was called upon to prepare himself to fulfill his part of the obligation, presumably in accordance with their previous meeting.[22] At the same time, Abd Allah Pasha, the governor of Acre, called upon his ally, Bashir II, to help him resist the Egyptian advance.[23] Bashir's reply was evasive;[24] he had found himself trapped between his two friends and allies, but fortunately for him, he pleaded inability to act resulting from civil strife in Mount Lebanon. The Druze knew of Bashir's alliance with the Egyptians and revolted against the hakim in favor of the Porte.[25] Ibrahim Pasha wrote to Muhammad Ali informing him of Bashir's refusal to aid him, and the Egyptian Viceroy threatened Bashir II with the destruction of Lebanon.[26] At first, Bashir al-Shihab attempted to enter the conflict as a neutral seeking a cease-fire but soon he sought Abd Allah Pasha's capitulation to Ibrahim Pasha.[27] The war resumed and Ibrahim was victorious.

In the closing days of the battle in Palestine, Bashir threw his lot in with Ibrahim Pasha and supported him with troops and supplies.[28] Bashir, thus, committed Lebanese forces to the campaign to conquer Syria and the hakim's powerful forces took part in the campaigns for Tripoli, Hims, Aleppo, Zahlah and Damascus. Amir Bashir, his son Khalil, and Ibrahim Pasha entered Damascus victoriously, and it was not long before the Egyptian troops reached the Taurus and struck at the heart of the Ottoman Empire. Bashir II's assistance to Ibrahim Pasha made him one of the principle architects of Ibrahim's rapid victory and, in return, in August of 1832, Ibrahim Pasha conferred upon Bashir al-Shihab authority over Lebanon and Damascus with its plains.[29] Nevertheless, Bashir remained content to rule only over an independent Lebanon. He had no imperialistic designs on territories outside Lebanon, but it was apparent that by restricting his authority to Lebanon, Bashir hoped to avoid any conflict with Ibrahim Pasha whose rule in Syria found extensive support.[30]

Clearly, Ibrahim Pasha inaugurated his regime in Syria by winning the confidence and respect of most of its population. He reorganized the provincial districts centralizing authority under Egyptian rule and, consequently, freed the people from the vicissitudes of the Ottoman provincial governors.[31] He won the support of the notables[32] who had resented Ottoman interference in what they thought were their prerogatives. The religious minorities also found their condition vastly improved under Egyptian rule. Ibrahim Pasha allowed the Christians to ride horses and enter into new fields formally forbidden to them, thereby eliminating the old restrictions placed upon them.[33] Ibrahim selected a Christian, Hanna al-Bahri, as his secretary of finance.[34] In general, the masses supported the Egyptian Pasha because they believed that he would eliminate the abuses of the Ottoman regime, especially when he terminated the heavy taxes imposed upon them, and when he brought greater justice to all.[35] Ibrahim's popularity, however, was short lived. What began as a just and tolerant rule deteriorated.[36] Once he felt secure in Syria, the Egyptian Pasha began thinking of further conquests which required a much greater acquisition of Syrian resources and public taxes. Thus, the people he liberated turned against him.

Ibrahim Pasha began to reorganize the economic life of Syria along Egyptian lines, as established by Muhammad Ali. The monopolization of key economic resources adversely affected the economic life of the Syrians and the establishment of a corvee system planted the seeds of dissatisfaction among some of them.[37] Furthermore, many Moslems resented and were unwilling to accept Ibrahim's policy of total equality for the Christians. When he weakened the authority of the notables through centralization, they began to plot against him.[38] Then, Ibrahim raised the taxes by introducing a new head tax (al-fardah), payable by all males between the ages of fifteen and sixty at the rate of twelve percent; and he undertook a policy of disarmament and conscription of the Druze which resulted in a revolt against his authority.

No doubt, the major insurrection came from the Druze who flatly refused conscription into Ibrahim's army. The Christians, however, were not subject to military draft and the Druze resented this. When attempts to disarm the Lebanese failed,[39] Ibrahim instructed Bashir II to draft both the Maronites and the Druze, but the Maronites objected and threaten to seek French intervention, if any attempt to draft them took place. Although France supported the Egyptian invasion of the Arab East, it was obligated to support the Maronite Catholics in that instance and to act as a mediator in the dispute. Clearly, the Maronite Christians preferred to remain allied to the Egyptians but did not wish to be drafted into the Egyptian army, so that they could retain their autonomy. The Druze objected to the draft because it would create a shortage of man power among them, and because mixing with Ibrahim's Sunnite Moslem troops might result in a repudiation of Druze beliefs among some of the new recruits.[40] No doubt, the methods used for conscription were severe[41] and, finally, in 1838, the Druze was forced into open revolt against the Egyptians.

The major insurrection began in Hawran and quickly spread to the rocky area of al-Laja.[42] The Druze, assisted by some Bedouins, inflicted heavy casualties on the Egyptian troops.[43] Ibrahim's forces were stalled by the ferocious resistance of the Druze of Lebanon and Syria forcing him to ask Bashir al-Shihab to send him reinforcements capable of defeating the Druze mountain warriors. Bashir responded by sending Ibrahim 4,000 Maronite warriors who did succeed where the Egyptians had failed.[44] The Maronites were given 16,000 weapons for their use, and they were permitted to retain their arms for themselves and for their descendents.[45] Defeated by the Maronites, the Druze surrendered to the Egyptians and were pardoned and forced to give up their weapons.[46] By 1839, the Maronite Christians were the most powerful military force in Lebanon having been able to accomplish military tasks that Ibrahim's famed Egyptian army could not achieve. Ibrahim Pasha, consequently, grew fearful of the Maronites but, at the same time, he needed them for he had to reckon with a far greater danger, his neighbor to the north.

Fearful of the unchecked strength of Ibrahim Pasha, the sultan attempted to reclaim his lost territory in Syria, in the summer of 1839. Ottoman troops crossed the Syrian border in full strength but were quickly routed at Nezib on June 24, of that year.[47] The road to Istanbul was now open to the ambitious Pasha from Egypt. But, more importantly, Ibrahim felt secure enough to focus his attention on the Maronites whose military skill left them as a major factor for consideration. Either because he no longer required their aid or because he feared them, Ibrahim Pasha decided to attempt to disarm that militant community. But, his plans were aborted by Sultan Abd al-Majid's new initiative. Early in 1840, the Porte opened negotiations with the Viceroy of Egypt, but the European powers were not content to see the Ottoman Empire capitulate to Muhammad Ali. With the aid of Ferdinand I of Austria, Nicholas of Russia, Frederick III of Prussia and Queen Victoria,[48] Sultan Abd al-Majid found a new lease for the life of his empire when the European powers decided to rescue the sultan from the impending disaster he faced. With Ottoman consent, the major European powers began to interfere in Lebanese affairs. (France was the only European power to support both Muhammad Ali and Ibrahim Pasha, understandably so.).[49]

Both British and Ottoman officials entered Lebanon and tried to win Amir Bashir to their cause.[50] When Bashir II rejected their advances, the British and Ottoman agents sought allies among the Lebanese sectarian groups. Richard Wood, a British agent of the Catholic faith, was sent to Lebanon to attempt to win the Maronites to the British-Ottoman effort but he proved to be more successful among the Druze.[51] The French found themselves in a far more critical predicament. Once again, France had two agents to support, both in opposition to one another. France could not support either Muhammad Ali or the Maronites whole heartedly in their conflict and, therefore, France chose to play the role of a mediator;[52] but towards the end of the conflict it supported the Maronites to off-set British influence among the Druze.[53] Meanwhile, Ibrahim Pasha took steps in Lebanon which consolidated the opposition of the Druze and the Maronites against him and the hakim. The ill feelings that existed between the Druze and the Maronites resulting from the insurrection at al-Laja appear to have faded away in the face of a common threat to the autonomy of both communities. Indeed, the Druze and the Maronites had many grievances against the regime of Bashir II which were further compounded by the interference of Ibrahim Pasha in Lebanese affairs.

The Druze needed no special event to trigger a revolt against Bashir al-Shihab and Ibrahim Pasha for they had sought the right moment to obtain revenge against them. The Maronites began to stir against Bashir and Ibrahim when the Egyptian Pasha sensed the danger awaiting him in Lebanon and ordered Bashir to disarm the Maronite community.[54] Perhaps of equal significance was the fear of the Maronites that they would be inducted into Ibrahim's army when they heard that some Lebanese Christians, studying in Cairo, had been drafted and that military uniforms were being sent to Beirut.[55]

By peaceful means Bashir tried to prevent the revolt and alleviate the fears of the Maronites or weaken the opposition. He went to the leaders of the revolt and told them that their actions were too dangerous and could lead to the destruction of Lebanon and that they should go home and obey the laws and not be remiss in their obligations.[56] Then, the hakim wrote to Muhammad Ali and Ibrahim Pasha informing them that he tried to carry out their wishes.[57] In the face of Bashir's efforts, both the Maronites and the Druze became increasingly suspicious of the hakim.

The Maronites, the Druze, and the other sects intensified their efforts by joining in a military and political convention held at the church of Antilyas, near Beirut, on June 8, 1840.[58] They listed their grievances against the regime of Bashir II which included a demand to end the corvee, to reduce taxes, to eliminate conscription, and to halt the confiscation of weapons.[59] The insurgents made a common appeal for revolt to obtain their freedom and in it they cited the success of the Greeks in their war for independence.[60] Al-Khuri Arsanus al-Fakhuri wrote to the governments of France, England, Austria and the Ottoman Empire seeking their immediate aid,[61] and Shaykh Francis al-Khazin took command of the Lebanese forces.[62] With the hope that aid would arrive shortly, the Lebanese began military operations against the Egyptians.[63] But, Ibrahim Pasha was not going to jeopardize his position in Syria and, consequently, he requested immediate reinforcements from his father in Egypt. On June 27, Abbas Pasha, Ibrahim's brother, arrived off the port of Beirut with a naval squadron.[64] Finally, due to insufficient weapons, the rebel forces were defeated and forced to temporarily disband while the leaders of the insurrection were exiled to Sennar in the Sudan.[65]

In August, the European fleet supported by British, Austrian and Ottoman troops appeared off the coast of Beirut. In all, thirty-one vessels (25 British, 5 Austrian, and 1 Ottoman) arrived under the command of Captain Sir Charles Napier and it proceeded to attack coastal installations and to disembark troops at the Bay of Juniyah to make contact with Lebanese guerrilla units[66] still operating against the Egyptians. On October 10, 1840, Ibrahim's forces were routed at the battle of Bharsaf in the Matn.[67] Two days later Bashir al-Shihab II went to Sidon to board a British ship to carry him to Malta, his chosen place of exile.[68] Upon his arrival on Admiral Stopford's ship, the Lebanese hakim was honored by a seventeen cannon salute.[69] (Although Bashir's authority as the hakim of the mountain was not always recognized by the Druze amirs, he was acknowledged as the hakim (hakim Lubnan) and the most prominent amir by the Ottoman authorities and the European powers.) From Malta, Bashir was permitted to travel to Istanbul where he remained until his death in 1851.

Bashir al-Shihab's role during the Egyptian interlude has shown him to be a Lebanese nationalist. When the British fleet arrived off the Lebanese coast in a show of strength, Bashir was informed in a letter from Richard Wood that if he defected to the British-Ottoman cause he could remain in office.[70] Shaykh Mansur al-Dahdah, a confidant of the hakim, advised Bashir to go over to the British side, but Bashir steadfastly refused.[71] Clearly, the hakim saw in Ibrahim's rule the methods for modernization, reform and independence[72] and, perhaps, the Lebanese amir hoped to plant the first seeds of Arab nationalism in the Near East.[73] Apparently, Bashir was fully prepared to become a co-partner in Ibrahim's plan to wrest the Arab East from the Ottoman Empire. Thus he supported the Egyptian campaign hoping that the Egyptian forces could hold off the European Powers until French aid or additional reinforcements from Egypt could arrive. With French support, Bashir II had good reason to believe that Ibrahim Pasha could have stalled the European incursion long enough to allow him to negotiate a peace with the sultan which might have resulted in the independence of Syria and Lebanon.

Furthermore, while Bashir opposed the alliance of Antilyas (1840), he did so in the attempt to maintain himself in power and to advance his national aspirations. Bashir II realized that the outcome of the Maronite-Druze national unity conference at Antilyas would have ephemeral results. The two major parties to the convention had two opposing European allies: France and Great Britain. Even if the Maronite-Druze unity had prevailed after the defeat of the Egyptians, the interference of the European powers would have destroyed the compact. Also, it should be remembered that Britain's partner was the Ottoman Empire hence; no true independence could have been achieved by the Maronites and the Druze in 1840. The Antilyas conference as an instrument of national unity has been somewhat overrated.

From Bashir's opposition to the Antilyas meeting the true motivations behind his staunch support for the Egyptians has emerged. While Bashir II supported Ibrahim Pasha's initiative, his main concern was the acquistion of independence for himself and the Lebanese province. Thus, he sought to find a third party to be involved in the political affairs of the Levant; a non-Ottoman, non-European power. He found his third party in the guise of the Egyptian army. Although France supported Ibrahim Pasha indirectly through Egypt, France was in no condition to threaten Lebanon's independence as either Great Britain or the Ottoman Empire could. In addition, Bashir could not deal as an equal with either the sultan or the major European powers, but he could deal equably with his friend and ally Ibrahim Pasha. Ibrahim did not covet control over Lebanon and the hakim repudiated any pretense to rule over Syria. Had the European powers not interfered in the Near East after the Ottoman defeat at Nezib (June, 1839), Bashir's dream of an independent Lebanese state might have been realized. But, Bashir's dream died a bitter death when the Egyptian Pasha's forces had to retreat from the Levant, due to a European ultimatum.

With the exile of Amir Bashir al-Shihab II, the office of hakim became vacant and the Maronites, the British and the Shihabi family sought to occupy it with another member of that illustrious family. The logical candidate was Bashir Qasim al-Shihab (*Bashir III*). On August 14, 1840 Bashir III had written to Commodore Napier informing him of his availability to join the conflict against Ibrahim Pasha.[74] Richard Wood supported his candidacy and, consequently, he was installed in office by an Ottoman decree (*a firman*) on September 3, 1840.[75]A good-natured man, Bashir III was known as the "flour giver," for at the beginning of his reign he distributed flour to the poor at his own expense.[76] But, Bashir III's rule was not as popular as his supporters had hoped it would be. The Greek Orthodox opposed his rule because they believed that he cared little for their welfare and that he was only a tool of the Maronite church.[77] Meanwhile, the Druze found his election offensive for it retained a Christian Shihabi in power.[78] The net result was that Bashir III proved to be a weak link in the chain of Shihabi power.[79]

1. M. Al-Dimishqi, "Ta'rikh Hawadith al-Sham wa Lubnan," *Al-Mashriq*, vol. 15, 1912, pp. 105-106.

2. Al-Shidyaq, *Kitab Akhbar al-Ayan*, p. 382.

3. Holt, *Egypt and the Fertile Crescent*, p. 233.

4. Polk, *The Opening of South Lebanon*, p. 17; Salibi, *The Modern History*, p. 22.

5. Al-Shihab, *Lubnan fi Ahd al-Umara*, vol. III, p. 595;Chebli, *Une Histoire du Liban*, p. 262; G. W. Chasseaud, *The Druze of Lebanon: Their Manners, Customs and History*, London R. Bentley, 1855, pp. 170-171.

6. Al-Shihab, *Lubnan fi Ahd al-Umara*, vol. III, p. 59.

7. Al-Shihab, *Lubnan fi Ahd al-Umara*, vol. III, p. 557; Salibi, *The Modern History*, p. 23.

8. Al-Shihab, *Lubnan fi Ahd al-Umara*, vol.111, p. 557.

9. A. J. Rustum, "Bashir Shihab II," $E.I.^2$, p. 1078.

10. Holt, *Egypt and the Fertile Crescent*, p. 233; Al-Shidyaq, *Kitab Akhbar al-Ayan*, p. 401; Al-Shihab, *Lubnan fi Ahd al-Umara*, vol. III, p. 685.

11. Al-Shihab, *Lubnan fi Ahd al-Umara*, vol. III, p. 685.

12. Al-Shidyaq, *Kitab Akhbar al-Ayan*, p. 401; Sfeir, *Al-Amir Bashir al-Shihabi*, p. 56.

13. Al-Shidyaq, *Kitab Akhbar al-Ayan*, p. 422; M. T. Al-Hattuni, *Nubdhah Ta'rikhiyah fi al-Muqataat al-Kisrawaniyah*, Beirut: n.p., 1956, p. 248; A. J. Rustum, *The Royal Archives of Egypt and The Origins of The Egyptian Expedition to Syria*, Beirut: American Press, 1936, p. 18.

14. Holt, *Egypt and the Fertile Crescent*, p. 234.

15. Polk, *The Opening of South Lebanon*, p. 23.

16. Polk, *The Opening of South Lebanon*, p. 83.

17. Rustum, "Bashir Shihab II," $E.I.^2$, p. 1078.

18. Churchill, *Mount Lebanon*, p. 347.

19. M. Le Baron D'Armagnac, *Nezib et Beyrouth*, Paris: J. Laisne, 1844, p. 251.

20. Sfeir, *Al-Amir Bashir al-Shihabi*, p. 61

21. Holt, *Egypt and the Fertile Crescent*, p. 234.

22. Hitti, *Lebanon in History*, p. 417, 421; Polk, *The Opening of South Lebanon*, p. 96; Al-Shidyaq, *Kitab Akhbar al-Ayan* , p. 444

23. Al-Shidyaq, *Kitab Akhbar al-.Ayan*, p. 444; Al-Shihab, *Lubnan fi Ahd al-Umara*, vol. III, p. 820.

24. Chebli, *Une Histoire du Liban*, p. 348.

25. Hitti, *Lebanon in History*, p. 421; Salibi, *The Modern History*, p. 28.

26. Al-Shidyaq, *Kitab Akhbar al-Ayan*, p. 444.

27. Al-Shihab, *Lubhan fi Ahd al-Umara*, vol. III, p. 832.

28. Polk, *The Opening of South Lebanon*, p. 97; Hitti, *Lebanon in History*, p. 421; Al-Shihab, *Lubnan fi Ahd al-Umara*, vol. III, p. 863; Hitti, *History of Syria*, p. 962; Al-Hattuni, *Nubdhah Ta'rikhiyah*, p. 263; A.J. Rustum, *Calendar of State Papers From The Royal Archives of Egypt Relating to The Affairs of Syria*, Beirut: The American Press, 1940-1943, vol. I, p. 217

29. M. Jouplain, *La Question du Liban*, Paris: A. Rousseau, 1908, p. 197; Chebli, *Une Histoire du Liban*, p. 351; 0. Douin, *La Premiere Guerre De Syrie*, Cairo: L'Institute francais d' archealogie orientale du Caire pour la soc. royal de geographie d'Egypte, 1931, p. 96.

30. Hitti, *Lebanon in History*, p. 423.

31. Holt, *Egypt and the Fertile Crescent*, p. 235.

32. A. J. Rustum, *Bashir Bayna al-Sultan wa al-Aziz*, Jubayl: Manshurat al-Jami'ah al-Lubnaniyah, 1966, p. 117.

33. Hitti, *Lebanon in History*, p. 423; Salibi, *The Modern History*, p. 30; Holt, *Egypt and the Fertile Crescent* p. 235.

34. Hitti, *Lebanon in History*, p. 423.

35. B. Qarali, ed., *Ta'rikh al-Amir Bashir al-Kabir*, Lebanon, n.p., 1922, p. 84; A. J. Rustum, *The Royal Archives of Egypt and The Disturbances in Palestine 1834*, Beirut: The American Press, 1938, p. 42.

36. George Antonius, *The Arab Awakening*, New York: Capricorn Books, 1946, p. 24; L. Meo, *Lebanon: Improbable Nation*, Indiana: Indiana University Press, 1965, p. 15.

37. Holt, *Egypt and the Fertile Crescent*, p. 235; Sfeir, *Al-Amir Bashir al-Shihabi*, p. 65; Qarali, *Ta'rikh al-Amir Bashir*, p. 84; Hitti, *Lebanon in History*, p. 423.

38. Rustum, *The Royal Archives of Egypt*, p. 47.

39. Holt, *Egypt and the Fertile Crescent*, p. 235; Rustum, *The Royal Archives of Egypt*, pp. 75-76.

40. Polk, *The Opening of South Lebanon*, p. 121; A. J. Rustum, "A New Page in The History of The Druze Revolution," *Al-Mashriq*, vol. 35, 1937, p. 490.

41. Anon., *Memoirs of Lady Hester Stanhope*, London: H. Colburn, 1845, vol. III, p. 115

42. Al-Shidyaq, *Kitab Akhbar al-Ayan*, p. 454; bit, *Egypt and the Fertile Crescent*, p. 235; Hitti, *Lebanon in History*, p. 424; Polk, *The Opening of South Lebanon*, p. 139; Al-Hattuni, *Nubdhah Ta'rikhiyah*, p. 267.

43. Qarali, *Ta'rikh al-Amir Bashir*, vol. II, p. 87; Urquhart, *The Lebanon*, p. 163; Rustum, 'Bashir Shihab II," *E.I.*[2], p. 1079.

44. Qarali, *Ta'rikh al-Amir Bashir*, vol. II p. 88; Salibi, *The Modern History*, p. 35; Al-Shidyaq, *Kitab Akhbar al-Ayan*, p. 454; Polk, *The Opening of South Lebanon*, p. 139; Rustum, *Bashir Bayna*, p. 142; Hitti, *Lebanon in History*, p. 424; Al-Hattuni, *Nubdhah Ta'rikhiyah*, p. 267

45. Hitti, *Lebanon in History*, p. 424; D'Armagnac, *Nezib et Beyrouth*, p. 233; Al-Shidyaq, *Kitab Akhbar al-Ayan*, p. 454; Holt, *Egypt and the Fertile Crescent*, p. 235.

46. Rustum, *Bashir Bayna*, p. 145; A. Laurent, *Relation Historique des Affaires de Syrie Depuis 1840 Jusqu'en 1842*, Paris: Gaume Freres, 1846, vol. I, P. 7.

47. Rustum, "Bashir Shihab II," *E.I.*[2], p. 1079; Holt, *Egypt and the Fertile Crescent*, p. 235; Salibi, *The Modern History*, p. 36; Hourani, *Syria and Lebanon*, p. 29.

48. Al-Hattuni, *Nubdhah Ta'rikhiyah*, p. 274; Al-Shidyaq, *Kitab Akhbar al-Ayan*, p. 457.

49. Rustum, "Bashir Shihab II," *E.I.*[2], p. 1079.

50. Rustum, "Bashir Shihab II," *E.I.*[2], p. 1079

51. Qarali, *Ta'rikh al-Amir Bashir*, vol. II, p. 91; A. Bruneau, *Tradition et Politique de la France au Levant*, Paris: F. Alcan, 1932, p. 143.

52. Ismail, *Histoire du Liban*, vol. IV, p. 78, 81.

53. C. G. Hess, "Confessionalism and Feudality in Lebanese Politics," *MEJ*, vol. 8, no. 1, 1954, p. 12.

54. Rustum, *Bashir Bayna*, p. 173; Salibi, *The Modern History*, p. 28; Sfeir, *Al-Amir Bashir al-Shihabi*, p. 66; Laurent, *Relation Historique*, vol.1, pp. 20-21; Holt, *Egypt and the Fertile Crescent*, p. 236; Hitti, *Lebanon in History*, p. 242; Henry Guys, *Beyrouth et le Liban, Relation d'un Sejour de Plusieurs Annees Dans ce Pays*, Paris: Imprimerie de W. Remquet et Cie, 1850, vol. II, p. 260.

55. Al-Shidyaq, *Kitab Akhbar al-Ayan*, pp. 457-458; Al Hattuni, *Nubdhah Ta'rikhiyah*, pp. 274-275.

56. Rustum, *Bashir Bayna*, p. 175; Laurent, *Relation Historique*, vol. I, p. 52.

57. Rustum, *Bashir Bayna*, p. 175.

58. Holt, *Egypt and the Fertile Crescent*, p. 236; Hitti, *Lebanon in History*, p. 424-425; Rustum, *Bashir Bayna*, p. 180.

59. Al-Hattuni, *Nubdhah Ta'rikhiyah*, p. 279; Salibi, *The Modern History*, p. 42; Al-Shidyaq, *Kitab Akhbar al-Ayan*, p. 459; Ismail, *Histoire du Liban*, vol. IV, pp. 42-54; P. and F. al-Khazin, *Majmuat al-Muharrarat al-Siyasiyah wa al-Mufawadat al-Dawliyah, Djounieh*, n.p., 1910, vol. I, pp. 2-3.

60. Albert Hourani, *Arabic Thought in the Liberal Age, 1798-1939*, London: Oxford University Press, 1962, p. 62; Hitti, *Lebanon in History*, p. 425.

61. Sfeir, *Al-Amir Bashir al-Shihabi*, p. 6; Al-Shidyaq, *Kitab Akhbar al-Ayan*, p. 468.

62. Hitti, *Lebanon in History*, p. 425; Sfeir, *Al-Amir Bashir al-Shihabi*, p. 67; Al-Shidyaq, *Kitab Akhbar al-Ayan*, p. 458.

63. Hitti, *Lebanon in History*, p. 425.

64. Laurent, *Relation Historique*, vol. I, p. 66; Al-Hattuni, *Nubdhah Ta'rikhiyah*, p. 277, 279.

65. Sfeir, *Al-Amir Bashir al-Shihabi*, p. 67; Al-Hattuni, *Nubdhah Ta'rikhiyah*, pp. 280-282.

66. Sfeir, *Al-Amir Bashir al-Shihabi*, pp. 67-68; Rustum, "Bashir Shihab II," *E.I.*[2], p. 1079; Salibi, *The Modern History*, p. 43; Al-Hattuni, *Nubdhah Ta'rikhiyah*, p. 283.

67. Salibi, *The Modern History*, p. 44; Rustum, "Bashir al-Shihab II," *E.I.*[2], p. 1079.

68. Salibi, *The Modern History*, p. 44; Al-Shidyaq, *Kitab Akhbar al-Ayan*, p. 471; Hitti, *Lebanon in History*, p. 425; Rustum, "Bashir Shihab II," *E.I.*[2], p. 1079.

69. Ismail, *Histoire du Liban*, vol. IV, p. 102.

70. Sfeir, *Al-Amir Bashir al-Shihabi*, p. 68; Rustum, *Bashir Bayna*, p. 184.

71. Rustum, *Bashir Bayna*, p. 184.

72. Rustum, *Bashir Bayna*, p. 184.

73. Rustum, *The Royal Archives*, p. 96.

74. Sir Charles Napier, *The War in Syria*, London, Parker, 1842, vol. I, pp. 38-39.

75. Salibi, *The Modern History*, p. 44; Sfeir, *Al-Amir Bashir Al-Shihabi*, p. 70; Hitti, *Lebanon in History*, p. 694

76. Sfeir, *Al-Amir Bashir al-Shihabi*, p.17.

77. C. Farah, *The Problem of Ottoman Administration in Lebanon 1840-1861*, unpublished Ph.D. Dissertation, Princeton, 1957, p. 117

78. Meo, *Lebanon*, p. 18.

79. Hourani, *Syria and Lebanon*, p. 31.

CHAPTER 4

THE MARONITE ESTABLISHMENT: INDEPENDENCE AND
THE MARONITE CHURCH

With the installation of Bashir Qasim al-Shihab (Bashir III) as hakim, the Maronite clergy intensified its efforts to dominate the political life of Lebanon. Although Bashir III filled the vacuum of power arising from his predecessor's political demise, he in fact only served as a tool of the Maronite church. From the Maronite point of view, Bashir's weakness proved to be ideal, for it enabled them to bring to fruition their cherished hope of uncontested power in Lebanon as leaders of a movement for independence.

In the period leading up to Bashir III's reign, the Maronite clergy had been organizing itself into a potentially powerful political force which contained the seeds of a successful revolt against Egyptian domination. By 1841, the Maronites were the only political force in Lebanon with foreign support, a romanticized ideology, charismatic leadership under the Maronite Patriarchs, organizational strength and military proficiency capable of challenging the Sublime Porte and its Lebanese allies, the Druze.

The eclipse of Crusader power in the Levant did not leave the Maronites of Lebanon isolated from the Christian west for long. Religious and commercial ties continued to flourish with Italy and France. When the trade agreements (the capitulations) were granted by Sulayman I to Francis I in 1534, both France and the Maronites stood to benefit greatly from them; and as early as 1569, the French flag could be seen in Lebanese ports establishing a base for French supremacy in the Levant.[1] From then on, both the French and the Maronites were drawn into a closer relationship with one another.

The promotion of trade obviously brought greater political responsibility. In 1616, Sidon was chosen as the site for the first French consul[2] but, by 1622, French diplomatic prestige required its relocation to Beirut. King Louis XIV, the French monarch, issued a proclamation on April 28, 1649 which extended French protection to the Maronites.[3] Six years later, Nadir al-Khazin (Abu Nawful) was appointed deputy French consul in Beirut[4] and shortly afterwards, the status of full consul was granted to the Khazin deputy. At a council held at Luwayzah near the Dog River in 1736, the Maronite church entered into complete union with Rome,[5] and in the following year, King Louis XV reissued the pledge of protecting the Maronites.[6] Gradually the Maronite Christians of Lebanon opened diplomatic relations with France; and by the sixteenth century, they could rely upon France to protect them if it became necessary to request French political or military assistance.

By the middle of the eighteenth century, the Maronites who had been looking at the West found the West staring back at them. Of all the patriarchs of the East, only the Maronite patriarchs looked to Europe for their investiture rather than Istanbul and, in doing so, they rejected recognition of the sultan's authority over the Maronite community[7] as well as the Ottoman conquest of Mount Lebanon. For almost three centuries, the Maronite clergy retained its autonomy and a degree of independence. By the middle of the nineteenth century the Franco-Maronite relationship took on a political coloration. In 1840, when France leaned towards the Maronites instead of Muhammad Ali, the Maronites intensified their efforts to reestablish a Christian Arab amirate in the Ottoman Empire, with the help of several European powers.[8] French diplomacy constantly supported the candidacy of Bashir al-Shihab III, the Maronite church, and the ascendancy of the Maronite population.[9] In fact, France could greatly enhance its position in the East by that policy and could have possibly posed a threat to Great Britain's hold on India. Thus, France found itself in an excellent position to support the Maronites and, apparently, the Maronite leadership believed they could rely on the full support of France when they would make their bid for total independence from the Porte. In order to prepare themselves and their followers more fully in anticipation of a clash with the Ottoman authorities, the Maronite clergy revived interest in the Maronite historical past and began to propagate their version of it.

Throughout their history the Maronites maintained an intellectual tradition, nurtured by their clergy, to defend the orthodoxy of their flock. The literature they produced evolved into an ideology and, by the nineteenth century, the Maronite clergy harnessed it to serve their nationalistic goal of complete freedom and independence for Lebanon. The Maronite clergy utilized their view of the Maronite historical past to awaken or stir latent or covert feeling of homogeneity among their co-religionists, as the Greek clergy had done to support their goal of independence from the Ottoman Empire.

Jibrail ibn al-Qilai was one of the first Lebanese writers of the Maronite sect to write a history of that community defending the orthodoxy of his church. His major works were entitled: *Madiha ala Jabal Lubnan (Praise On Mount Lebanon)* and *Tabkit kull man zagh an al-iman (The Status of Each One Who Deviated From The Faith)*; they were written when the Maronites were an isolated sect holding out from the Mamluk forces in the Lebanese highlands. He died in the year of the Ottoman invasion of the Arab lands (1516). Al-Qilai opposed the Jacobite (monophysite) tendencies infecting his church while emphasizing Orthodox Catholicism to his flock.[10] He wrote poems in vernacular Arabic (zajaliyah)[11] to depict historical events and to demonstrate their relationship to his theological precepts. But, he also wrote in classical Arabic for the highly educated clergy.[12] The nationalistic content of al-Qilai's work may be summarized as an appeal to the good old days when the Maronite community was unified by religious doctrine.[13] Al-Qilai maintains that Mount Lebanon was the home of the Maronites prior to the appearance of Islam and, as such, the Maronites had the right to rule its coasts and its highlands and to oppose the Moslem occupation of their lands.[14] Al-Qilai says that in the Crusader period the Maronites were allies of the West and he failed to distinguish between the Maronite lords and the Latin lords implying unity in faith as well as unified opposition to Moslem encroachments on Lebanon.[15] Thus al-Qilai accentuated religious and sectarian unity for his co-religionists; and he expressed his thoughts for both the educated elite and the common man. Clearly Jibrail ibn al-Qilai attempted to reject Moslem authority in the mountain as well as the right of any Moslem to reside there. Al-Qilai's work was continued by the historian Istifan al-Duwayhi (1624-1704).

Istifan al-Duwayhi has been called the father of Maronite historiography.[16] He wrote a history of the Maronite church emphasizing Lebanon's territorial unity, autonomy, and the orthodoxy of the Maronite sect.[17] Al-Duwayhi played down the struggle with Islam although he appealed to the Maronites in terms of the church's attempt to maintain itself in a sea of Moslems.[18] His major works include a history of the Maronite sect; a chronicle of Islamic events until 1703 and a chronicle and biographical sketch of the Maronite Patriarchs.[19] Like his predecessor, al-Duwayhi regarded the Maronites as the only legitimate inhabitants of the Mountain and considered the Druze aliens on their midst.[20]

The scholars who followed al-Duwayhi were describing more complicated events and towards the nineteenth century, they appeared to be more secular as implied in the works of Tanus al-Shidyaq,[21] as well as others. However, it must not be assumed that because the historiography of the nineteenth century became more secular in outlook that the Maronite population achieved secular tendencies or that their clergy approved or even supported secularism. Furthermore, the Maronite-Druze unity achieved during the reigns of Fakhr al-Din al-Mani II and Al-amir Bashir al-Shihab II were based upon the extraordinary qualities of both men as well as a product of the "infringements" upon Lebanese autonomy by the Porte and, later, by Ibrahim Pasha.

The average Maronite or Druze of the mid-nineteenth century continued to relate primarily to their own faith and their co-religionists. Al-Shidyaq put forth the Phoenician concept of Lebanese nationalism[22] as a secular geo-political entity as well as a rejection of Moslem and Druze right to rule or reside in Lebanon in any other capacity than as guests of the indigenous Phoenician people now Christianized and called Maronites. Thus, the Maronites began to recognize themselves as the descendents of the Phoenicians who could reject the political rights of any other group dwelling in their mountains or on Lebanon's coasts. The formation of the Maronite historical past was also shaped in part by the contact the Maronites had with Rome and with the establishment of the Maronite seminaries in Lebanon. It was in those seminaries that the Maronite clergy fashioned and developed its version of the Maronite nation.

The clergymen who molded the ideology of the Maronite church were graduates of western institutions in Europe and in Lebanon. In 1584, Gregory XIII established the Maronite College in Rome.[23] Often its students were sponsored by French clergymen operating in the Levant. Jibrail al-Qilai and Istifan al-Duwayhi had studied in Rome and, later, became Maronite Patriarchs. At Ayn Waraqah, Ghazir, and Zagharta schools were erected which served to create a highly educated clergy.[24] From those western styled educational institutions emerged the Maronite clergy of the nineteenth century prepared to take an active role in the government and leadership of the Maronite nation.

No doubt, the elite members of the Maronite church were distinguished by their scholarship and national and political awareness. Most of the major patriarchal figures of the period contributed to the enhancement of Maronite power either by the force of their personalities or by fostering changes in the church-state relationship. From the earliest times, the Maronite clergy had retained prerogatives over its pastoral flock and, consequently, the priests, bishops and patriarchs maintained both spiritual and secular authority over their followers.[25] At the Council of Luwayzah (1736), their authority was regulated to include questions of both civil and religious law; and, with the aid of some faithful followers, the priests, bishops and patriarchs kept a watchful eye on any socio-political change that might diminish their sway or control over their flock.[26] Through their contacts with the western clergy, notably the Jesuits in Lebanon,[27] the Maronite clergy began to reorganize their church along the lines of the Roman Catholic church; and with that reorganization, the clergy began to take stronger initiatives. The Maronite church, however, did not Latinize itself;[28] it continued to propagate Maronite nationalism in church-state affairs.

Throughout the nineteenth century, the Maronite clergy exhibited strong hierarchical and powerful disciplinary tendencies capable of taking a commanding position in church-state relations.[29] Until that time the Maronite clergy had been subservient to the major feudal families but they could threaten divine retribution against their opponents. However, the nineteenth century gave them greater independence from their own lords. It was clerical reorganization coupled to economic independence that gave the church its first step towards total freedom.

Subservience and obedience of the bishops to the patriarchs remained intact but decentralization and definition of function presented the clergy with a primary impetus towards independence.[30] Also, the Maronite clergy began to rely heavily on their own resources; the land upon which the Maronite institutions stood. The church began a campaign to extend their monastic institutions throughout Lebanon. By the middle of the nineteenth century more than 200 monasteries existed and were manned by poor Maronite farmers and the clergy creating an interlocking complex throughout Lebanon that was obedient to the patriarch or his representatives.[31] The monasteries' produce, the tithes collected, and the adult tax contributed to the independence of the church.[32] And, no doubt, the numerous religious endowments the church received made it economically powerful and stable.[33] Thus, the Maronite church became the most powerfully organized and extensively manned institution in Lebanon,[34] under the control of a dynamic clergy.

Of the most important patriarchical figures of the early nineteenth century with whom major reforms may be associated were Yuhanna al-Hilu (1809-1823) and Yusuf Habash (1823-1845). Yuhanna al-Hilu called for an assembly of notables to regulate economic affairs in Lebanon and he convoked a synod of bishops designed to instruct the clerics and to reorganize administrative districts by placing the bishops in their provinces.[35] The authority of the church was dispersed to cover a wider area, and thus, Yuhanna brought the Maronite masses into a more intimate relationship with their bishops. In return, the bishops were drawn into closer contact with local events and they could quickly channel information to their superiors. When Yusuf Habash was confirmed as patriarch by Rome, he faced a dual role of safeguarding the temporal authority of the church and preventing the defection of some members of his flock to a new threat, the Protestant missionaries.[36] He encouraged the study of Latin, theology, philosophy, and natural sciences to combat Protestant educational activity and, in 1840, Yusuf established a society of preachers to propagate to the general public.[37] He directed the clergy in the organization of the Maronites into a politically active force along national lines.[38] Under Yusuf's leadership, the Maronites of Lebanon were molded into a politically enlightened force capable of supporting the Patriarch's will. Thus, the archbishops, bishops, and even the village priests were functioning through a chain of command as the envoys of the patriarch in the propagation of church politics and clerical directives.[39] Clearly, the Maronite clergy was in almost complete control of its parishioners throughout the provinces and through the educational system and monasteries; no doubt, they were able to control the Maronite population with ease and efficiency. At the same time, the Maronite church undertook a political initiative to infiltrate the government of Bashir II at its highest level in order to prepare themselves against any revolution from above or below which could have weakened their political power.

From the Maronite educational institutions emerged as an educated elite destined to attempt to capture and control the Lebanese government. Those men moved into the public service by virtue of their knowledge and talents and often fostered the policy of the Shihabi amirs.[40] As early as 1825, with the eclipse of Druze power, the priests, bishops and patriarchs became the administrative aids and advisors to Bashir II.[41] When rational debate failed to obtain a patriarchical goal, the clergy could use its spiritual power to threaten the hakim with the "power of the keys" to which the Christian Shihabs had to bow.[40] When Bashir II found his political authority being strangled by the clergy, he strengthened his relationship with Ibrahim Pasha. At that point, the patriarch joined the open revolt against Bashir and his ally,[43] bringing the whole weight of the Maronite nation to bear upon the mountain prince. For his efforts, Yusuf Habash received a diamond medal and his leadership was recognized by the Ottoman Empire and the European Powers.[44] The patriarch knew he had little to fear from the Powers, the Porte or the religious sects within Lebanon, for the Maronites had received new arms and were capable of ruling all of Mount Lebanon.[45] Should his own military power fail, the patriarch could hoist the French flag from the churches and the monasteries and summon aid from France directly through the patriarch's delegate at the French court.[46] When the patriarch supported the candidacy of Bashir III, it was only a diplomatic ploy. He sought to have a controllable hakim in office and one who would be acceptable to the European

Powers and the Ottoman Empire in order to ward off their encroachments on Lebanon, at that time.

Clearly, by 1840, the Maronite establishment was the only major dynamic political force in Lebanon. It had energetic leadership, organizational strength, and mass support to carryout its objectives. Furthermore, the Maronites were the best equipped military force in Mount Lebanon; and, they had recourse to France in support of their policies. When Bashir III filled the role of hakim, he was a tool of the Maronite clergy. From 1840 until 1860, the Maronite establishment began to chart a course which inevitably led to a clash with the remnants of Druze power over total control of Mount Lebanon and, later, with the Ottoman Empire for the independence of the Lebanese province.

1. Hitti, *Lebanon in History*, p. 398; P. Masson, *Histoire du Commerce Francais Dans Le Levant au XVIII Siecle*, Paris: Librairie Hachette, 1911, p. 519; Hitti, *History of Syria*, p. 672.

2. Hitti, *Lebanon in History*, pp. 399-400.

3. Chibli, *Une Histoire du Liban*, pp. 50-51; Iliya Harik, *Politics and Change in a Traditional Society: Lebanon, 1711- 1845*, New Jersey: Princeton University Press, 1968, p. 85.

4. Chibli, *Une Histoire du Liban*, p. 56; Hitti, *Lebanon in History,* p. 400.

5. Hitti, *Lebanon in History*, p. 406; Hourani, *Arabic Thought*, p. 55.

6. Hitti, *Lebanon in History*, p. 398.

7. H. A. R. Gibb and H. Bowen, *Islamic Society and the West*, vol. I, part II, London: Oxford University Press, p. 230, 248; Albert Hourani, *A Vision of History, Near Eastern and Other Essays*, Beirut: Khayats, 1961, p. 67; Harik, *Politics and Change,* p. 19.

8. A. Bruneau, *Traditions et Politique de la France au Levant*, Paris: F. Alcan, 1932, p. 147.

9. Hess, *Confessionalism and Feudality*, p. 12.

10. Harik, *Politics and Change*, p. 129; K. S. Salibi, *Maronite Historians of Mediaeval Lebanon*, Beirut: AUB Publications of the Faculty of Arts and Sciences, 1959, p. 25.

11. Harik, *Politics and Change*, p. 129; Salibi, *Maronite Historians*, pp. 26-27.

12. Salibi, *Maronite Historians*, p. 26, 33.

13. Harik, *Politics and Change*, p. 129; Salibi, *Maronite Historians*, pp. 36-37.

14. Harik, *Politics and Change*, p. 129; Salibi, *Maronite Historians*, pp. 69-72.

15. Salibi, *Maronite Historians*, p. 69.

16. Salibi, *Maronite Historians*, p. 89.

17. Istifan al-Duwayhi, "Sisilat Batarikat al-Taifah al-Maruniyah," *Al-Mashniq*, vol. I, 1898, pp. 393-396; Hourani, *A Vision of History*, p. 61; Hourani, *Arabic Thought*, p. 58.

18. Harik, *Politics and Change*, p... 132.

19. Istifan al-Duwayhi, *Ta'rikh al-Taifah al-Maruniyah*, Beirut: Al-Matba'at al-Kathulikiyat, 1890. A brief description of his works "Ta'rikh al-Taifah al-Maruniyah;" "Ta'rikh al-Azminah;" and "Silsilat Batarikat al-Taifah al-Maruniyah" may be found in Salibi, *Maronite Historians*, p. 94, 98, 99.

20. Harik, *Politics and Change*, p. 134.

21. Salibi, *Maronite Historians*, p. 168; Hourani, *Arabic Thought*, p. 58; Harik, *Politics and Change*, p. 138.

22. Al-Shidyaq, *Kitab Akhbar al-Ayan*, p. 11, 14, 16. Harik, *Politics and Change*, p. 146; Chebli, *Une Histoire du Liban*, p 35.

23. Hitti, *Lebanon in History*, p. 402.

24. Hitti, *Lebanon in History*, p. 402; Frederick J. Bliss, *The Religions of Modern Syria and Palestine*, New York: C. Scribner's Sons, 1912, p. 102

25. F. Perrier, *La Syrie sous Le Gouvernement De Mehemet Ali, Jusqu'en 1840*, Paris: Arthus, Bertrand Librarie, 1842, p. 289; Bliss, *The Religions of Modern Syria*. pp. 108-109.

26. Churchill, *Mount Lebanon*, p. 59; DeLamartine, *Souvenirs, Impressions*, p. 271; Bliss, *The Religions of Modern Syria*, p. 109.

27. D. Chevallier, "Les troubles agraires libanais en 1858," *Annales, Economics, Societe, Civilisation*, 14 Annee, no. I, Janvier-Marc, 1959, p. 59.

28. Harik, *Politics and Change*, p. 102.

29. P. A. d'Orleon (Comte de Paris), *Damas et Le Liban*, London: W. Jeffs, 1861, pp. 70-71; Harik, *Politics and Change*, pp. 97-98.

30. Harik, *Politics and Change*, pp. 105-107.

31. DeLamartine, *Souvenirs, Impressions*, pp. 272-273; Chevallier, "Les troubles agraires" p. 59; Harik, *Politics and Change*, p. 711.

32. Bliss, *The Religions of Modern Syria*, pp. 108-109.

33. Harik, *Politics and Change*, p 112; d'Orleans, *Damas et Liban*, pp. 71-72; Richard van Leeuwen, *Notables and Clergy in Mount Lebanon, The Khazin Sheikhs and the Maronite Church (1736-1840)*, The Netherlands: E. J. Brill, 1994, pp. 148-151, 233-234, 239-241.

34. Harik, *Politics and Change*, p. 125.

35. Yusuf As'ad Daghir, *Batanrkat al-Maruniyah*, Beirut Matba'at al-Kathulikiyah, 1958, pp. 76-78; Chebli. *Une Histoire du Liban*, p. 155

36. Chebli, *Une Histoire du Liban*, pp. 155-156.

37. Daghir, *Batarikat al-Maruniyah*, pp. 79-80.

38. Harik, *Politics and Change*, p. 277.

39. Harik, *Politics and Change*, p. 239.

40. Salibi, *The Modern History*, p. 13.

41. Farah, *The Problem of Ottoman Administration*, p. 34.

42. Churchill, *Mount Lebanon*, p. 157.

43. Salibi, *The Modern History*, p. 38.

44. Harik, *Politics and Change*, p. 247; I. Daww, *Kitab Hadiqat al-Jinan fi Ta'rikh Lubnan*, Beirut: Al-Matba'ah al-Jami'ah, 1913, p. 310.

45. Polk, *The Opening of South Lebanon*, p. 192.

46. Polk, *The Opening of South Lebanon*, p. 222; Hourani, *A Vision of History*, p. 68.

CHAPTER 5

THE MARONITE INSURRECTION IN MOUNT LEBANON
(1841; 1845); THE STRUGGLE TO SECURE INDEPENDENCE

In the course of Lebanese history, the period between 1841 and 1860 was one of the darkest. It was a time of conflict and animosity so deep that it threatened Lebanon with almost complete disintegration and possibly the total extinction of the Maronite sect at the hands of the Druze and the Ottoman Empire. The period culminated in a massacre of the Maronite Christians when they made their bid for independence.

It would not be accurate to place the blame for the Maronite-Druze civil wars of 1841, 1845, and 1860 on any single group or cause. The conflict was in part motivated by many factors and all the inhabitants of the region contributed to the tensions which impinged upon the formerly cordial atmosphere in Lebanon. Also, the European Powers interfered in Lebanese affairs during that period and in doing so they contributed to the polarization of the religious factions which only served to create further unrest rather than stability. However, the nucleus around which the conflict revolved was the national aspirations of the Maronite church.

In the period lasting from 1841 until 1860, the Maronite establishment exhibited an unparalled zeal aimed at the acquisition of Lebanese independence from the Porte. The Maronites had emerged from the conflict of 1840 with their candidate in office, military support, organizational strength, an ideology and the charismatic leadership of their patriarchs which made them capable of leading a national revolt. No other sect or faction in Lebanon could have matched the Maronite establishment in its progressive drive towards independence. No doubt, the Maronite clergy was prepared to play a role similar to the role played by the Greek Orthodox clergy in their war for independence from the Ottoman Empire. Nevertheless, in part, Mount Lebanon was a "bi-national" home for both the Maronite and Druze sects and probably other sects as well. Therefore, the first step taken by the Maronite clergy was an attempt to gain a political foothold in the Druze districts partially inhabited by their co-religionists.

While the Maronite clergy planned its political expansion, the Druze objected to the Maronite hakim, Bashir Qasim al-Shihab III, partly because they believed he did not serve their political interests. Bashir's relations with the Druze started on a sour note and continued to deteriorate throughout his short term in office. At first Bashir attempted to exert his independence from the Maronite clergy[1] and to follow a more evenhanded political path by supporting the Ottoman plan for the establishment of a representative council (majlis).[2] The council was to consist of twelve members to be composed of 2 Maronites, 2 Druze, 2 Greek Orthodox, 2 Greek Catholics, 2 Sunnite Moslems and 2 Shi'ite Moslems (Matawilah).[3] The council would have equally represented all the faiths and it was designed to help the hakim administer the province more fairly. But the Druze leaders refused to cooperate or to send delegates to the council upon their return from exile in Cyprus, Istanbul, and the Sudan[4] for they believed that the council was a usurpation of their feudal rights to do as they pleased.[5] The refusal of the Druze leaders to join Bashir's government moved him closer to the Maronite community which appeared to be cooperating with him. Finally, Bashir's negotiations with the Druze amirs became insulting and hostile,[6] leaving him clearly within the Maronite political camp; Bashir began to rely on the Maronites for his aids[7] rather than the Druze; and he became more anti-Druze with each passing day. At the same time, the Maronite clergy began to exploit the situation to their favor by using and supporting the hakim against the Druze parties.

The Maronite-Druze relationship took on a turn for the worse in 1841 when Bashir III distributed Druze territory to his relatives, and the patriarch refused to help the Druze to regain it. A Druze delegation was sent to the patriarch, Yusuf Habash, to negotiate the return of the lost territory[8] but the patriarch's mediators supported the hakim's right.[9] Thus, the Druze became convinced that the patriarch was also involved in a plot against their privileges.[10] The final challenge to Druze authority came from the patriarch himself.

In 1841, Yusuf Habash took an even bolder step than the hakim had taken against the Druze. He issued a circular signed by several Shihabi and Lam'i amirs as well as other elites which called upon the Maronites in the mixed villages to reject Druze feudal authority and to elect two men in each town or village to act as agents of the patriarch and to assume local authority.[11] For the Druze feudal lords, the decree was a challenge to Druze rights within their own districts and an attempt to eliminate their political power.[12] At Dayr al-Qamar, the Christians received the decree with "much gaiety," singing and firing their weapons into the air while the Druze looked upon the scene with fear and bewilderment.[13] Nu'man Bey Janblat, from nearby Mukhtarah, was sent to the patriarch to negotiate an agreement, but he received an evasive reply from the Maronite leader.[14] While in the patriarch's residence, the Druze amir overheard threats against his people, should they not comply with the circular.[15] Upon returning home, Nu'man Bey Janblat began to prepare the Druze for an impending clash. At the same time, the patriarch received at least L20, 000 from France to continue his program of creeping annexation and to employ his agents in the Druze villages.[16]

The Maronite experience of 1840 had brought to their clergy ideals concerning national independence and, consequently, they embarked on a policy pressing for the liberation or annexation of the mixed districts inhabited by Druze lords and some Maronite peasants. The first step towards independence was the attempt to obtain Maronite unity by peaceful infiltration of the mixed districts. But the Druze chiefs who had returned from exile wanted to reclaim their lost prerogatives, and thus they resisted the Maronite initiatives. This led to the first clash!

On September 14, 1841, the first violent outbreak between the Maronites and the Druze occurred.[17] A Christian from Dayr al-Qamar shot a partridge on the property of a Druze from the Abu Nakad family in a field at Baqalin and, shortly afterwards, what might have passed for a local incident of trespassing blossomed into armed conflict.[18] The Druze attacked the Christian youth and the Christians called for help from their co-religionists.[19] A major clash was, however, averted at that time by the efforts of Colonel Hugh Rose, the British consul general in Beirut, and a local Druze chief.[20] Concurrently, the patriarch tried to avoid a wider conflict and upon hearing of the incident, he sent his representatives and wrote to the hakim asking him to intervene and restore order.[21] Also, the patriarch sent a special delegation of Khazin and Hubaysh shayks to the Shuf region to apologize for the clash. But as the Druze accepted the apology, they secretly prepared to obtain their revenge.[22] The first clash had left the Druze with sixteen dead and sixteen wounded; and the Maronites with five dead and eight wounded.[23] Clearly, the Maronites had won the battle, but the Druze were obliged to avenge their fallen brothers.

The Druze's opportunity for revenge came when Bashir III called for a peace conference at his residence in Dayr al-Qamar. He wrote to the Druze leaders to meet with him to discuss the unrest in the southern districts.[24] On October 14, 1841, the Druze army approached the town of Dayr al-Qamar while their agents infiltrated it to prepare an insurrection against the hakim.[25] When the large and well equipped Druze force reached the city, Bashir sent approximately 150 Christians there to forbid them entrance.[26] With the Maronite force outside the city, the Druze inside the city attacked the unarmed Christians there, killing about forty of them while losing only one shaykh from the Abu Nakad family.[27] Within hours the Druze became masters of the city and moved to dispose of Bashir III[28] who sought refuge in his family palace. By clandestine means,[29] Bashir sent messages to the Ottoman authorities and the Maronite Patriarch seeking help.

Prior to the receipt of the urgent message from the hakim, the patriarch had learned of the spread of the conflict in al-Shuf and al-Gharb encompassing the towns of Jazzin, Abayh, al-Shuwayfat, al-Hadath and Baabda.[30] The Druze shaykhs of the Janblat and Imad families had joined the Abu Nakad shaykhs in their offensive,[31] in October of 1841. The Ottoman forces took the Druze side and the patriarch took the offensive to relieve the hard-pressed Maronite population. The patriarch called upon the Maronites to come forward in defense of their co-religionists in the south and to save the hakim at Dayr al-Qamar.[32] Although the patriarch was ill at that time, he requested that he be carried in his bed with a cross and a gun to the battlefield, to raise the Maronite standard and morale by his presence.[33] He raised 6,000 combatants by the expedience of threatening to excommunicate anyone who refused to help and to close the churches in any town or village which would not send troops.[34] By those means the patriarch sanctioned and encouraged the war; and thus, the Maronites poured forth from the northern sections of Lebanon. The patriarch placed Antun Khaddar in charge of war finances.[35]

Since the Ottoman Turks had begun to actively intervene, the patriarch had no choice but to take the most effective measures available to him to defend his flock, and to attempt to unite the Lebanese in the mixed districts under his rule. The Ottoman irregular forces were attacking the Maronite refugees, robbing and looting them, as they attempted to make their way to safety near the city of Beirut.[36] The Turkish authorities had supplied both sides with some weapons but had vigorously supported the Druze; and, they knew of the Druze scheduled attack fourteen days before they had left for Dayr al-Qamar.[37] Finally, the hostilities ended on November 19, 1841 leaving the Maronites the victor in that their losses were less than half the number of troops lost by the Druze.[38] Even with the support of the Ottoman Turks, the Druze had been unable to defeat the Maronites. In its essence the conflict was not religious nor was it motivated solely by a political greed on behalf of the patriarch. The events that transpired indicate the varied motivations involved in the first civil war.

The alignment of forces in the 1841 conflict offers a clue to the complexity of the situation. While it was true that there were no Maronites fighting on the Druze side, nor were there any Druze fighting on the Maronite side, the roots of the conflict were not religious in a Moslem versus Christian sense. There was no unified Moslem faction operating against a unified Christian faction. While the Maronites and the Greek Catholics had joined forces in defense, the Greek Orthodox joined the Druze forces on several occasions.[39] Also, the Shi'ite Moslems joined the Maronite side in the warfare.[40] The Ottoman Turks supported both national groups, a process which would have served to enhance their control over Lebanon.

Nor was the cleavage between France and Great Britain a cause of the alignment of religious factions in that conflict. From 1840 until 1841, Great Britain attempted to win the support of the Maronites[41] and when the conflict was at its height, the Maronite Patriarch implored the British consul in Beirut to protect the Maronites.[42] But Great Britain's response was non-committal and the consul vaguely replied that they would help determine the course of justice.[43] Thus, the Maronites turned to their ally France for aid and they received money for relief purposes.[44] Consequently, the first round in the nineteenth century civil war was not inspired by foreign intrigues or by religious prejudices. In fact, the war was in part the result of the Maronite clergy's attempt to spread its authority into the mixed districts to unify the mountain area under one rule, the patriarch's. During the next few years, the Maronite clergy challenged the Ottoman authorities for the independence of the Lebanese province.

The Maronite challenge to the Porte's authority was in part due to its attempt to impose direct rule over Lebanon. The Ottoman government had realized that by instigating both sides in the conflict it was following an extremely dangerous path. While the Porte did, indeed, succeed in keeping Lebanon divided, proving that they were essential to maintaining order there, the Turkish Empire had also inadvertently opened the way for European intervention. Although the Porte had no intention of permitting Lebanese autonomy to go unchecked, it equally had no wish to create circumstances favorable for foreign intervention. In order to placate the two sides in the conflict, the Ottoman government sent a Turkish officer, Mustafa Pasha al-Nuri, with a peace keeping force of 2,000 Albanians to investigate the situation, restore order, and integrate Lebanon more fully into the Ottoman Empire.[45] Bashir Qasim al-Shihab III was deposed and sent to Istanbul thus bringing to a close the Shihabi rule over Lebanon.[46] To help bring Lebanon under more direct or intense Ottoman domination, Mustafa Pasha appointed Umar Pasha al-Namsawi, a Hungarian who was assigned to the Ottoman forces that had been sent to evict Ibrahim Pasha from the Levant, as the hakim at Bayt al-Din, on January 16, 1842.[47]

Umar Pasha's rule was short lived because both the Maronites and the Druze were hostile to foreign domination. At first the Druze were less hostile to Umar's rule because he was a Moslem but soon after he took office, the Druze combined with the Maronites to plan a revolt against him.[48] The Maronites had refused to recognize Umars authority for they maintained that he had been chosen by the falsification of Maronite signatures.[49] In an attempt to gain the support of the Maronites, Umar began to appoint some Maronites to high positions and, soon after, they became his most favored sect. Thus, when the Druze revolted against the Pasha, in November of 1842 under the leadership of Shibli al-Uryan, the Maronites withdrew their support from the Druze.[50] As the revolt grew in intensity, the Maronite Patriarch hoped that the conflict would weaken both his adversaries which would serve his political ambitions. He proceeded to inform the European Powers that the Maronites had never supported direct Ottoman rule in Lebanon, that any declaration to that effect was a forgery,[51] and that withholding support in the Druze revolt did not constitute any recognition of foreign control over Lebanon. Thus, not only did Umar Pasha fail to reintegrate Lebanon into the Ottoman Empire, but he failed to maintain peace during his brief tenure as hakim.

Throughout the period after the first civil war and the end of Umar Pasha's rule, the Maronite clergy remained extremely hostile to any attempt to impose direct Ottoman rule in Lebanon. With the dismissal of Umar Pasha, the patriarch was convinced that the Druze could not sustain another war against the Maronites; therefore, the Maronite establishment quickly moved to challenge the Druze and the Ottoman Empire.

The patriarch began a program to supersede the Porte's authority in the Lebanese province. Soon all the Maronites were prepared to follow the lead of the Maronite church; talk of revolt was heard in the slogan on every Maronite's lips, sometimes whispered in secret and at other times proclaimed aloud that "the Patriarch is our Sultan."[52] Indeed for the Maronites, that expression embodied their feelings and their support for the patriarch as the sole authority in regions where the Maronites lived. When several Protestant missionaries entered a Maronite village to preach, they were evicted by the local priest and, later, they complained to the Porte. The Ottoman authorities sent several officials to the village to obtain an apology for the losses the missionaries had incurred, but instead they were greeted by that slogan.[53] Clearly, that statement represented a major challenge to the Porte. Even earlier, the Maronites had declared that they were no longer willing to be subjected to Ottoman rule; during the civil war of 1841, the French flag could be seen flying above the Maronite convents.[54] By hoisting the French flag in the Lebanese province the Maronites had exceeded the limits of local autonomy or indirect rule. Those treasonable actions could only serve to infuriate the Porte and to draw the Ottoman officials closer to the Druze. Once again, the sultan's authority was being challenged by the Maronite establishment and its faithful followers. And, the Ottoman Empire sensed it!

Perhaps as a result of the Maronite challenge to Turkish rule, the sultan had the Maronite headquarters, at Jubayl, placed under direct Ottoman rule by attaching it to the Pashalik of Tripoli[55] so that the patriarch's freedom would be radically restricted by constant surveillance. In the years leading up to the second Maronite-Druze civil war, Lebanon was divided by Ottoman decree while a realignment of forces was taking place within the country.

When Umar Pasha was deposed, the Maronites insisted on the installation of a Shihabi amir as hakim, but the Porte sensed the danger and distrusted the Shihabis who had at one time cooperated with the Egyptian expedition.[56] Hence, they sought an alternative. Either the Austrian Chancellor, Prince Klemens von Metternich,[57] or Great Britain[58] offered a compromise plan for promoting a course of action that could avoid direct Ottoman rule or control over Mount Lebanon or the Maronite north. The plan called for the establishment of a dual qaim maqam (a subgovernor) dividing Lebanon into two parts separated by the Beirut-Damascus highway to be under the supervision of the governor of Sidon, Asad Pasha.[59] In January of 1843, the Maronite Patriarch chose Haydar Abu al-Lam'i as the Christian qaim maqam; the Druze shaykhs chose Ahmad Arslan as their qaim maqam.[60] Outwardly, the problem seemed to be solved but in reality this plan set back the patriarch's design for an independent Lebanon. Once again, Lebanon was divided and the patriarch began to lose control over the southern mixed districts which the Maronite establishment had fought so hard to gain. Also, the plan had no provision for Maronite rule over the Maronite subjects in the Druze districts. As far as the patriarch was concerned, the new arrangement was an obstacle to Lebanese independence because the qaim maqams were subject to Ottoman authorities.

The plan was destined to fail from its inception for it had inherent weaknesses. It had no provision for the Greek Orthodox (who had asked for their own qaim maqam)[61] or any other religious sect in Lebanon.[62] While the plan succeeded in separating the Maronite north from the Druze south it did not specify the authority of the qaim maqam nor did it have any provisions for the administration or legal representation of cases in the mixed districts.[63] (Thus, some Druze feudal chiefs began to loot and oppress some Christians under their rule.)[64] In a final attempt to rectify those conditions, the Ottoman Empire assigned Admiral Khalil Pasha to investigate conditions in the mixed districts and, soon after his arrival, he appointed two agents (wakils) responsible to the qaim maqam of their faith to try minor cases;[65] but, conditions continued to deteriorate in those regions. The Maronites refused to submit to an Ottoman or Druze authority, even through the auspices of a wakil of their own religion. Consequently, the Maronite establishment began to plan for a second campaign to liberate the mixed districts and to bring their co-religionists under the patriarch's control. Since the Ottoman Empire had supported the Druze in 1841, the Maronites had to challenge both the Druze and the Ottoman Empire. Before the first blow could be struck, both the Druze and the Maronites began to strengthen old alliances and form some new ones.

In the preparation for the second civil war the situation took on the appearance of a sectarian struggle. In reality, the conflict resembled a border war for political supremacy,[66] and national unity. Nevertheless, there was a religious realignment along Christian-Moslem lines which had a significant effect on the war. By 1843, the Greek Catholics and the Greek Orthodox has entered into a defensive alliance against the Druze.[67] In the first civil war, the Greek Orthodox had sided with the Druze for they were fearful that a Maronite victory might impinge upon the Orthodox Patriarch's religious prerogatives. The Greek Catholics had been allies of the Maronites and through skillful negotiations they won the Orthodox community to the Maronite Patriarch's cause for an independent Christian Lebanon. By 1844, all the Lebanese Christian sects had united behind the Maronite Patriarch when he called for a united Lebanon under either Maronite or Druze rule.[68]

Of all the Christian sects in Lebanon, only the Protestants were anti-Maronite and pro-Druze, because the Maronite prelates were hostile to Protestant missionary activity. But their opposition was not completely based on doctrinal grounds. At times, the Maronite priests and bishops acknowledged some truth in Protestant teachings;[69] they feared the weakening of their power as a result of any large scale conversions that might occur. Apparently, the patriarch could not tolerate conversions for it would weaken the Maronite nation as a whole. The Druze, on the other hand, were capable of winning the admiration of the Protestants with ease through the practice of dissimulation (taqiyyah) which deceived the Protestant missionaries into believing that they had succeeded in converting some Druze. When the Maronites forced the shut down of Protestant schools in the 1841 conflict, the Protestants were greatly offended as were their British sponsors and protectors.

Although the Maronites were supported by France, they were not anti-British. They regarded the British as true Christians and, as late as 1844, they appealed to them to support the Maronite establishment against the Druze,[70] for Ottoman favoritism towards the Druze was becoming increasingly manifest. The Druze was promised immunity from persecution as a heretical sect and the possible return of some territories that were lost to the Maronites, if they supported the empire against the rebellious Christians. Indeed, the ominous fact was that while the Ottoman government had remained hostile to the maintenance of a Druze nation as well,[71] they did enter into an unofficial agreement or alliance with them. Soon after, the Shi'ites came to fit the configuration when the Ottoman Empire promised them autonomy in religious affairs, since they were also considered a heretical sect by the militantly Sunnite Moslem Turks. By 1844, Lebanon had been realigned along sectarian lines in preparation for a new conflict.

By the following year, the Maronites and the Druze were prepared for the impending clash. On February 2, 1845, the Druze chiefs met at al-Mukhtarah to plan their strategy, while the Maronites gathered near Beirut to hear the plans of the patriarch and the veterans of the 1841 campaign.[72] Tensions heightened when Asad Pasha was dismissed and his successor, Wajihi Pasta, favored a Druze in a conflict with a Christian and ordered his troops to punish the Christians.[73] (Fearing such action in the previous year, the Maronites had elected local leaders, Shuyukh al-Shab, to store weapons for self defense or for an uprising.)[74] The news of the event infuriated the patriarch and he called for either Maronite or Druze supremacy saying that the party that would strike first would have twice the chance for success.[75] The clergy began to preach a "holy war" in their churches; and the bishops began to organize the first strike.[76]

In April of 1845, the Maronites struck at several Druze villages to put an end to the oppression of their co-religionist, to unite their nation, and to challenge the Ottoman Empire's hold on them. Led by Abu Samra Ghanim, a Christian from Jazzin, the Maronite forces pressed on to the seat of Junblat power in al-Mukhtarah.[77] In its initial phase the Maronites were successful; but, by the end of May, Ottoman intervention under Wajihi Pasha had put the Maronites on the defensive and the Druze troops on the offensive.[78] At Ras al-Matn, the Christian forces received a decisive defeat; and, soon after a general massacre of Christians began at the hands of the Druze warriors and the Ottoman irregular forces.[79] Churches and convents were destroyed by Ottoman artillery as the remnants of the Christian forces struck back at the Ottoman troops,[80] hoping to defend their homes and families. Colonel Hugh Rose with the support of some 700 Ottoman soldiers saved some Christians from imminent death; while Doctor Thomson, a prominent Protestant missionary, took a white flag to the Druze camp attempting to secure a cease fire.[81] At that time, the Greek Orthodox and Maronite bishops ordered their troops to protect the foreign missionaries.[82] Clearly, the second Maronite-Druze civil war proved to be a failure for the Maronites. The Druze was well prepared for the onslaught. They had organized outposts on the slopes of their mountains and, at constant intervals; messengers would traverse the area to bring the latest intelligence on the enemy to the Druze command.[83] Weak points in the Druze defenses were reinforced and Druze discipline and courage in the field was unfailing.[84] Thus, the Maronites were ready to terminate hostilities when the European Powers pressed the Ottoman Empire to restore order in Mount Lebanon.[85] The Ottoman foreign minister, Shakib Effendi, was immediately sent to Lebanon to investigate the disturbances and to establish tranquility, in that Ottoman province.[86]

The events that had transpired prior to the arrival of Shakib Effendi show that the Maronite-Druze conflict had strong national and sectarian overtones.

Unlike the civil war of 1841, in which there was a conflict between some Maronite feudal lords, who supported the privileges and prerogatives of the Druze feudal lords, against the increasing power of the Maronite Establishment; the conflict of 1845 involved religious alliances to a far greater extent, for religion was used as the cementing force to hold the Moslem and Christian coalitions together for both the Maronite and Druze leadership. And, on the Christian side, the Maronite Church paid their troops four piasters per combatant; threatened to excommunicate anyone who tried to stay aloof of the conflict; and they used their convents as magazines to store ammunition.[87] When the Druze and Ottoman forces attacked the convents and monasteries, they were operating against legitimate military targets; the sources of supply and propaganda. The role of the Ottoman Turks kept the anguish of the Maronites alive by their lack of action against Druze oppression as well as their constant military support for the Druze.[88] The Ottoman Turks, however, were not the only foreign power to meddle in Lebanese affairs, at that time.

Great Britain attempted to contain the situation through the influence of Colonel Hugh Rose. The Maronites had requested British aid as a symbol of religious alignment with Christian England and in an attempt to get Great Britain to come to their relief. Britain's secondary clients, the Protestant missionaries, had been put under the patriarch's protection which indicated that the Maronites showed little prejudice towards them, even though the Protestants favored the Druze. Thus, only the internal politics of Lebanon could give a definite clue to the motivations behind the conflict.

From the point of view of power politics, the Shihabi party attempted to maintain and enhance its hold on Lebanon, and, thus, they contributed to the prevailing instability. Both Great Britain and the Ottoman officials had indicated that the Shihabi party helped to crystallize the hostilities[89] hoping to have a Shihabi amir installed in the office of hakim, as the only family capable of controlling Lebanon's internal politics. The continued presence of Bashir III in Istanbul was cited as one factor that instigated the revolt,[90] and as an indication of the validity of the point, he was later exiled to a more remote place. Yet no matter how strong the Shihabi party might have been, it lacked sufficient force to control, organize or direct the Maronites in the civil war of 1845. Only the Maronite hierarchy could have undertaken a venture of that magnitude.

No doubt at least in part, the civil war of 1845 was an extension of the war of 1841. Although termed as a defensive struggle by both sides,[91] the Maronite clergy launched a campaign to relieve their co-religionists in the mixed districts.[92] But, the campaign undertaken by the Maronites was equally intent on eliminating Ottoman power in Lebanon which was intrinsically linked to the Druze attempts to contain Maronite encroachments on Druze territory. And, on numerous occasions the Maronites opened fire on the regular Ottoman forces. Also, the British diplomatic papers of the period point directly to the role of the Maronite clergy in the civil war as one which interfered with the temporal prerogatives of the sultan and actually defied his power and authority in Lebanon.[93] In 1841, the patriarch's ambition may have been limited to a campaign to liberate the mixed districts as the first step towards Lebanese unity and independence. But by 1845, the patriarch had come to challenge both the Druze and the Ottoman Empire. Unfortunately for the Maronites, the Ottoman-Druze military complex proved too tenacious for them; consequently, the Maronites were only too happy to accept the cease fire established by Shakib Effendi.

1. Daghir, *Batarikat al-Mawarinah*, p. 86.

2. Salibi, *The Modern History*, p. 48; Antun Dahir al-Aqiqi, (Trans. by M. H. Kerr), *Lebanon in The Last Years of Feudalism, 1840-1860*, Beirut: Catholic Press, 1959, p. 4; Al-Shidyaq, *Kitab Akhbar al-Ayan*, p. 478.

3. Al-Aqiqi, *Lebanon in the Last Years of Feudalism*, p. 4.

4. Jouplain, *La Question du Liban*, p. 252; Ismail, *Histoire du Liban*, p. 108.

5. Al-Aqiqi, *Lebanon in the Last Years of Feudalism*, p. 4; Salibi, *The Modern History*, p. 48.

6. Charles Henry Churchill, *The Druze and The Maronites Under Turkish Rule: From 1840-1860*, London: B. Quaritch, 1862, p. 37; H. Jessup, *Fifty Three Years in Syria*, N.Y.: Revell, 1910, p. 60.

7. Ismail, *Histoire du Liban*, pp. 127-128

8. Istifan Daww, *Kitab Hadiqat al-Jinan fi Ta'rikh Lubnan*, Beirut: Al-Matba'ah al-Jami'ah, 1913, p. 312; Al-Shidyaq, *Kitab Akhbar al-Ayan*, p. 478.

9. Al-Shidyaq, *Kitab Akhbar al-Ayan*, p. 478.

10. Harik, *Politics and Change*, p. 242.

11. Churchill, *The Druze and The Maronites*, p. 38; Ahmad Tarabayn, *Azmat al-Hukum fi Lubnan Mundhu Suqut al-Usrah Shihabiyah Hatta Ibtida Ahd al-Mutasarrifiyah, 1842-1860*, Damascus, n.p. 1966, pp. 58-59; Salibi, *The Modern History*, p. 48; Al-Aqiqi, *Lebanon in The Last Years of Feudalism*, p. 4; Farah, *The Problem of Ottoman Administration*, p. 9, 117; Frederick J. Bliss, *The Reminiscences of Daniel Bliss*, London: Fleming H. Renvell Co., 1920, p. 141; H. Jessup, *Fifty Three Years in Syria*, p. 160.

12. Churchill, *The Druze and The Maronites*, p. 38; Salibi, *The Modern History*, p. 48.

13. Churchill, *The Druze and The Maronites*, p. 39.

14. Churchill, *The Druze and The Maronites*, p. 40.

15. Churchill, *The Druze and The Maronites*, p. 40.

16. Churchill, *The Druze and The Maronites*, p. 40.

17. Laurent, *Relation Historique*, p. 279; Hitti, *Lebanon in History*, p. 434; Churchill, *The Druze and The Maronites*, p. 44.

18. Hitti, *Lebanon in History*, p. 434; Al-Shidyaq, *Kitab Akhbar al-Ayan*, p. 479; Daww, *Kitab Hadiqat al-Jinan*, p. 314; Salibi, *The Modern History*, p. 49; Churchill, *The Druze and The Maronites*, p. 44; Laurent, *Relation Historique*, p. 280; Churchill, *Mount Lebanon*, p. 306; Al-Hattuni, *Nubdhah Ta'rikhiyah*, pp. 294-295; Caesar E Farah, *The Politics of Interventionism in Ottoman Lebanon, 1830-1861*, London: I. B. Tauris, 2000, pp. 101-107.

19. Al-Shidyaq, *Kitab Akhbar al-Ayan*, p. 479.

20. Churchill, *The Druze and The Maronites*, pp. 45-46.

21. Al-Shidyaq, *Kitab Akhbar al-Ayan*, p. 479

22. Churchill, *The Druze and The Maronites*, pp. 45-46.

23. Al-Shidyaq, *Kitab Akhbar al-Ayan*, p. 479.

24. Al-Shidyaq, *Kitab Akhbar al-Ayan*, p. 478.

25. Salibi, *The Modern History*, p. 49.

26. Salibi, *The Modern History*, p. 49; Al-Shidyaq, *Kitab Akhbar al-Ayan*, p. 480.

27. Churchill, *Mount Lebanon*, p. 306; Salibi, *The Modern History*, pp. 49-50; Al-Shidyaq, *Kitab Akhbar al-Ayan*, p. 480.

28. Al-Hattuni, *Nubdhah Ta'rikhiyah*, p. 296; Salibi, *The Modern History*, p. 50.

29. A1-Shidyaq, *Kitab Akhbar al-Ayan*, p. 480.

30. Hitti, *Lebanon in History*, p. 434; Daww, *Kitab Hadiqat al-Jinan*, pp. 315-337.

31. Hitti, *Lebanon in History*, p. 434; Jouplain, *La Question du Liban*, p. 268; Churchill, *The Druze and The Maronites*, pp. 47-48.

32.Al-Shidyaq, *Kitab Akhbar al-Ayan*, p. 482; Al-Hattuni, *Nubdhah Ta'rikhiyah*, p. 296.

33. Laurent, *Relation Historique*, p. 325; Churchill, *The Druze and The Maronites*, p. 49.

34. Laurent, *Relation Historique*, p. 354; Narcisse Bouron, *Les Druzes: Histoire du Liban et de la Montagne Haouranàise*, Paris: Berger-Levrault, 1930, p. 204.

35. Al-Hattuni, *Nubdhah Tarikhiyah*, p. 296.

36. Hitti, *Lebanon in History*, p. 434; Churchill, *The Druze and The Maronites*, p. 52; Salibi, *The Modern History*, p. 52.

37. Jouplain, *La Question du Liban*, p. 272; Hitti, *Lebanon in History*, p. 434; Churchill, *The Druze and The Maronites*, pp. 55-56.

38. Farah, *The Problem of Ottoman Administration*, p. 129; Hitti, *Lebanon in History*, p. 435.

39. Bliss, *The Reminiscences of Daniel Bliss*, p. 141; Jessup, *Fifty Three Years in Syria*, p. 162; Salibi, *The Modern History*, p. 51; Al-Aqiqi, *Leban in The Last Years of Feudalism*, p. 7; Ismail, *Histoire du Liban*, p. 137.

40. Salibi, *The Modern History*, p. 51; Rene Monterde, *Precis D'Histoire de Syrie et du Liban*, Beirut: Imprimerie Catholique, 1939, p. 127.

41. Philippe Al-Khazin, *Lamahat Ta'rikhiyah*, Cairo: Matba'at al-Fajjalah, 1910, p. 22.

42. Laurent, *Relation Historique*, pp. 315-116.

43. Laurent, *Relation Historique*, p. 316.

44. Ismail, *Histoire du Liban*, p. 148; R. Anderson, *History of the Mission of The American Board of Missions to Oriental Churches*, Boston: Congregational Publishing Society, 1872, p. 253.

45. Churchill, *The Druze and The Maronites*, pp. 65-67; Salibi, *The Modern History*, p. 52; Ismail, *Historie du Liban*, p. 175; Al-Shidyaq, *Kitab Akhbar al-Ayan*, p. 490.

46. Yusuf Daryan, *Nubdhah Ta'rikhiyah fi Asl al-Ta'ifa al-Maruniyah*, Beirut: Al-Matba'ah al-'Ilmiyah, 1919, p. 245; Al-Shidyaq, *Kitab Akhbar al-Ayan*, p. 490; Salibi, *The Modern History*, p. 53; Holt, *Egypt and the Fertile Crescent*, p. 238.

47. Churchill, *The Druze and The Maronites*, pp. 76-79; Al-Aqiqi, *Lebanon in The Last Years of Feudalism*, p. 5; Al-Shidyaq, *Kitab Akhbar al-Ayan*, pp. 492-493; Daryan, *Nubdhab Ta'rikhiyah*, p. 294; Daghir, *Batarikat al-Mawarinah*, p. 88.

48. Holt, *Egypt and the Fertile Crescent*, p. 239; Hitti, *Lebanon in History*, p. 435; Al-Shidyaq, *Kitab Akhbar al-Ayan*, pp. 492-493; Farah, *The Problem of Ottoman Administration*, p. 134; Daryan, *Nubdhah Ta'rikhiyah*, p. 247; Daww, *Kitab Hadiqat al-Jinan*, p. 339.

49. Daghir, *Batarikat al-Mawarinah*, p. 88.

50. Churchill, *The Druze and The Maronites*, pp. 76-79; Al-Aqiqi, *Lebanon in The Last Years of Feudalism*, p. 5; Al-Shidyaq, *Kitab Akhbar al-Ayan*, pp. 492-493; Daryan, *Nubdhah Ta'rikhiyah*, p. 249; Daghir, *Batarikat al-Mawarinah*, p. 88.

51. Daghir, *Batarikat al-Mawarinah*, p. 88; Salibi, *The Modern History*, p. 55.

52. Churchill, *Mount Lebanon*, pp. 58-59; J. F. Scheltema, *The Lebanon in Turmoil: Syria and The Powers in 1860*, New Haven: Yale University Press, 1920, p. 22.

53. Churchill, *Mount Lebanon*, pp. 58-59.

54. *Le Moniture Universal*, September 4, 1841, p. 2042.

55. Meo, *Lebanon*, p. 22.

56. Daryan, *Nubdhah Ta'rikhiyah*, p. 249.

57. Salibi, *The Modern History*, p. 62; Tarabayn, *Azmat al-Hukum fi Lubnan*, p. 72.

58. Daghir, *Batarikat al-Mawarinah*, p. 89.

59. Salibi, *The Modern History*, p. 63; Meo, *Lebanon*, p. 21; Al-Shidyaq, *Kitab Akhbar al-Ayan*, p. 526; Hitti, *Lebanon in History*, p. 435; Holt, *Egypt and the Fertile Crescent*, p. 239; Harik, *Politics and Change*, p. 271. Farah, *The Politics of Interventionism*, pp. 247-249; Daghir, *Batarikat al-Mawarinah*, p. 89.

60. Salibi, *The Modern History*, p. 63; Daryan, *Nubdhah Ta'rikhiyah*, pp. 251-252; Daghir, *Batarikat al-Mawarinah*, p. 89; Al-Shidyaq, *Kitab Akhbar al-Ayan*, 526, 530; Hitti, *Lebanon in History*, p. 435; Harik, *Politics and Change*, p. 271.

61. Salibi, *The Modern History*, p. 64.

62. Al-Aqiqi, *Lebanon in The Last Years of Feudalism*, p. 7; Farah, *The Problem of Ottoman Administration*, p. 171; Daryan, *Nubdhah Ta'rikhiyah*, p. 252.

63. Salibi, *The Modern History*, p. 63.

64. Churchill, *The Druze and The Maronites*, pp. 82-83; Al-Shidyaq, *Kitab Akhbar al-Ayan*, p. 530.

65. Holt, *Egypt and the Fertile Crescent*, p. 239; Salibi, *The Modern History*, p. 66.

66. The Earl of Carnarvon, *Recollections of the Druze of Lebanon*, London: J. Murry, 1860, pp. 109-110; Anderson, *History of the Missions*, pp. 273-274.

67. Bliss, *The Religions of Modern Syria*, p. 164.

68 Bliss, *The Religions of Modern Syria*, p. 163.

69. *The Missionary Herold*, (Boston, 1857), p. 349.

70. *Correspondence Relative to the Affairs of Syria*, part I, 1844, (London; 1845), p. 35.

71. The Earl of Carnarvon, *Recollections of the Druze*, p. 116.

72. Salibi, *The Modern History*, p. 67.

73. Al-Shidyaq, *Kitab Akhbar al-Ayan*, p. 531.

74. Al-Shidyaq, *Kitab Akhbar al-Ayan*, p. 531.

75. Churchill, *The Druze and The Maronites*, p. 83; Farah, *The Politics of Interventionism*, p. 381.

76. Churchill, *Mount Lebanon*, p. 309; Churchill, *The Druze and The Maronites*, p. 90.

77. Hitti, *Lebanon in History*, p. 436; Salibi, *The Modern History*, p. 69.

78. Salibi, *The Modern History*, p. 69; Churchill, *Mount Lebanon*, p. 307.

79. Salibi, *The Modern History*, pp. 69-70; Pere Antoine Rabbath, *Documents Inedits Pour Servir a L'Histoire Du Christianism en Orient*, Paris: A. R. Picard et Fils, 1911, pp. 151-166.

80. *The Times*, (London), June 5, 1845, p. 5.

81. *The Times*, (London), June 5, 1845, p. 5; Jessup, *Fifty Three Years in Syria*, p. 61; Farah, *The Politics of Interventionism*, pp. 395-398.

82. Jessup, *Fifty Three Years in Syria*, p. 61.

83. Churchill, *Mount Lebanon*, p. 310.

84. Churchill, *Mount Lebanon*, p. 310.

85. Al-Khazin, *Lamahat Ta'rikhiyah*, p. 36.

86. Al-Khazin, *Lamahat Ta'rikhiyah*, p. 36; Salibi, *The Modern History*, pp. 70-71; Hitti, *Lebanon in History*, p. 436.

87. *Correspondence Relative to the Affairs of Syria*, part II, 1845, p. 161.

88. *Correspondence Relative to the Affairs of Syria*, part II, 1845, p. 161, 112, 106.

89. *Correspondence Relative to the Affairs of Syria*, part I, p. 112; part II, p. 98.

90. A1-Shidyaq, *Kitab Akhbar al-Ayan*, p. 538.

91. *Correspondence Relative to the Affairs of Syria*, part II, 1845, p.25.

92. *Correspondence Relative to the Affairs of Syria*, part I, 1845, p. 112; part II, 1845, p. 25, 132, 159-161.

93. *Correspondence Relative to the Affairs of Syria*, part II, 1845, pp. 111-112.

CHAPTER 6

THE MARONITE-DRUZE CIVIL WAR OF 1860: A DECADE OF CONFLICT AS THE OTTOMAN EMPIRE ATTEMPTED TO REINTEGRATE LEBANON TIGHTLY INTO THE PORTE'S EMBRACE

When the Maronite-Druze hostilities ended in 1845, the Ottoman Empire sent Shakib Effendi to the Lebanese province to investigate conditions there and to tighten the Porte's control over its Lebanese subjects. As an official inspector (mufattish), Shakib initiated reforms in the qaim maqam and, in keeping with the reorganization (tanzimat) policies of his day; he attempted to weaken local forces in order to reintegrate the Lebanese province more tightly under Ottoman control.

Upon his arrival on the scene, Shakib Effendi moved to quickly restore order; during his temporary occupation, Shakib attempted to collect weapons[1] but he was not very successful. As an official of the Porte, Shakib offered an indemnity as compensation to the Christians,[2] and, then, he drafted an organic law known as the Reglement of Shakib Effendi,[3] hoping to avert a recurrence of the Maronite-Druze conflict. In its essence, the law called for a continuation of the dual qaim maqam and wakil representation but it also added a council (majlis) to each qaim maqam consisting of Maronites, Druze, Sunnite and Shi'ite Moslems, Greek Orthodox and Greek Catholics.[4] The new regulation served to bring Lebanon under more complete control; weaken foreign influence, and reduce local authority.[5] The council reported to the qaim maqams and its members were provided with salaries and held authority over taxation and judicial reviews.[6] The reglement resulted in a temporary peace between the Maronites and the Druze but, at that time, both sects were undergoing internal problems.

Although the Druze and the Ottoman Empire had co-operated against the Maronites in 1845, their co-operation could be regarded as a marriage of convenience. The Ottoman Empire had no desire to see the rise of an independent Maronite or Druze nation and, consequently, an antagonistic undercurrent continued to underline the Ottoman Empire's divide and rule policy in Lebanon. The Druze chiefs had formed a confederation of parties allied to Great Britain and when the Ottoman officials tried to conscript them in 1852, a revolt broke out against the Turks.[7] The Porte sought the aid of the Maronites resulting in a few localized clashes but by 1852, the Druze was again on good terms with the Turks and a contingent of 3000 Druze fought in the Crimean War as volunteers.[8] The Druze continued to harbor resentment towards the Maronites; and, the clashes of 1852 reinforced and intensified their distrust and hatred of the Maronites. While the Druze community found a few years of contentment between 1853 and 1860, the Maronites of northern Lebanon faced internal convulsions which only served to weaken their power.

The Maronite north, particularly Kiserwan (*Kisrawan*), found itself in the grips of a class struggle between the Maronite lords and the commoners. The Maronite feudal lords, led by the Khazins, challenged the authority of the Abu Lam' qaim maqam whom they considered inferior to themselves, and they attempted to increase their control over the peasant population.[9] In 1859, a full scale agrarian revolt against the Khazins occurred and the Khazins appealed to the British, the Druze, and the Ottoman governor of Beirut, Khurshid Pasha, for aid.[10] That act totally alienated the Maronite peasants and clergy from their lords and, thus, the Khazins were ousted and their property was either confiscated or burned by the peasants, under the leadership of Tanyus Shahin, who proclaimed a peasant republic in Kiserwan as Shaykh al-Shab.[11] The Maronite clergy lent its support to the struggle.

At first the Maronite church supported the revolutionary forces and the patriarch, Bulus Masad (*Mas'ad*), a commoner, was cheered as the patriarch of equality, freedom, and justice.[12] To a considerable extent, the revolt was led by the priests for the patriarch believed it would release him from the last vestiges of responsibility to the lords.[13] Yet even though the patriarch and the Maronite clergy aided the revolt in its early stages, they soon began to act as mediators to limit the rebellion's destructive effects on Maronite unity.[14] When the Khazin lords appealed to Khurshid Pasha for help, he sent some troops under the command of Wasfi Effendi to Kiserwan to restore order, but the patriarch forbids them entrance to the district.[15] Then, the patriarch wrote to the French authorities who pressured Khurshid Pasha to withdraw his military mission from the Maronite north.[16] No doubt, the Ottoman government would have welcomed any opportunity to intervene and to strengthen its hold over Mount Lebanon; it would not be inconceivable that the Ottoman authorities had a hand in those disturbances.[17] However, the patriarch decided to pacify the situation through his growing involvement in the conflict.

The patriarch's mediations could have been motivated by at least one other factor than his opposition to internal strife among the Maronites or his fear that it might lead to an Ottoman invasion of the north. Apparently, as the influence of Tanyus al-Shahin grew, the patriarch became fearful that a new authority with a broad base of support could be established and might challenge the Maronite establishment's sole hegemony over its co-religionists. Clearly, towards the end of the revolt, the patriarch opposed the tactics of Tanyus al-Shahin[18] and sought to regain control over the northern area; the Maronite stronghold of Kiserwan. In the final analysis, the peasant revolt of 1859 provided the Druze with an ideal opportunity to strike at the Maronites while the seat of Maronite power was in a state of flux.

While an upheaval occurred in the north, the Druze districts experienced a relative calm which they exploited in order to plan their revenge against the Maronites. In the winter of 1859-1860, the Druze chiefs met in secret with Khurshid Pasha in Beirut to map out their strategy and to receive supplies to strike against the Maronites.[19] No doubt, the Ottoman Empire was on the Druze side and, later, they proved their allegiance and loyalty to the Druze military campaign. Apparently, the Turks hoped that the conflict would destroy any new Maronite initiatives towards political independence. To that extent, the Ottoman Empire's officials may have been instigators as well as supporters of the conflict which they helped to design to increase Ottoman suzerainty over the Maronite nation.[20] The Druze, with heightened confidence, began to preach a "holy war" (*a jihad/struggle*) to the other Moslem sects and to some Bedouin tribesmen; but, as soon as these propaganda efforts began, the Christians learned of the Druze machinations.[21]

When the patriarch was informed of the plot against the Maronite nation, he began to take self defense measures for his flock. Bishop Tubiyya 'Awn organized the Young Men's League to raise funds and in the winter of 1860, the Maronites were able to purchase a large quantity of weapons.[22] Once again the bishops planned to excommunicate anyone who failed to participate in the struggle; and a general mobilization was sounded.[23] The Maronite clergy, furthermore, pushed for greater Christian unity in the face of the impending danger.[24] As spring grew near, both the Druze and the Maronites had completed their preliminary arrangements for war.[25] In the weeks preceding the initial clash, several armed Christians were attacked and killed on the open roads by roaming Druze bands.[26] In the mixed villages Druze oppression intensified and the Christian peasants, encouraged by the successful peasant revolt in Kiserwan, began to defy the Druze lords.[27] By May of 1860, the atmosphere in Lebanon had become highly explosive only awaiting a spark to set off a conflict.

The spark which ignited Lebanon in the May confrontation resulted from a series of clashes between the Maronites and the Druze. The critical point in the Maronite-Druze relationship came after an accidental occurrence involving two young men, a Druze and a Christian. From then on, the gun and the sword were the only means of communication between the two sects. The fighting spread from Bayt Miri to Hasbayya, Rashayya, Zahlah and Dayr al-Qamar resulting in a massacre of the Maronites unparalleled in its brutality and the zeal with which it was conducted.[28] The Ottoman forces either refused to help the Christians there or directly contributed to their ultimate destruction.[29] At Hasbayya, Uthman Bey promised to protect the Christians if they would surrender their arms but as soon as their weapons were collected, the arms fell into Druze hands and the defenseless Christians were slaughtered.[30] In Sidon, the Moslems attacked the Christians who sought refuge while the Ottoman troops pursued other fleeing Christians, killing many of them.[31] In a few instances, however, some Sunnite Moslems helped the Christians; and, Khurshid Pasha did attempt, in a limited way, to contain the struggle; but in the main, the Maronites had to depend upon their own resources for self-defense.

The Maronites fought bravely but they were no match for the Druze and the Ottoman troops. Even with the encouragement of the patriarch who had financed previous wars and this one in part,[32] the Maronites were destined to fail for they were cut off from reinforcements from the north. The Porte had clearly realized the nationalistic intentions of the Maronites and had moved to cut off supplies to

Kiserwan, to force the Maronites to leave their stronghold making them vulnerable to Ottoman attack, while leaving the north defenseless [33] and easy prey for another massacre. Hence, only a token force could be dispatched from the north; it failed to make a significant change in the situation. The success of the Druze-Ottoman alliance helped to incite an attack on the Christians of Syria.

In Syria, the conflict was intrinsically religious; and, therefore, it had only a superficial relationship to the struggle in Lebanon. Ever since Ibrahim Pasha had attempted to obtain greater freedom for the Syrian Christians and Sultan Abd al-Majid had issued the Khatt-i-Sharif (Noble Rescript, 1839) and Khatt-i-Humayun (Imperial Rescript, 1856) to placate the European Powers by eliminating some of the injustices done to the Eastern Christians,[34] the Moslem and Christian communities in Syria began to draw apart and to suspect the intentions of each other. For centuries, the Christians had been relegated to an inferior status in the Moslem lands and, therefore, these decrees were impractical since no effective preparation had been made for a drastic change in the social system. Some of the Christians took the edicts of the Tanzimat seriously and expressed their religious beliefs freely; built churches, marched in religious processions, and even entered new positions formerly forbidden to them.[35] However, not all the Christians were willing to accept the implied change in status. Several Christian religious leaders feared a loss of prestige and authority over their churches as a result of a changing social status.[36]. While the Ottoman decrees may have been intended in part to placate the European Powers,[37] the Porte also hoped that they would weaken the independent power of the local notables and clergy,[38] and replace them by a stronger Ottoman central authority. Indeed, the authors of the Tanzimat intended to have their edicts applied universally throughout the empire,[39] but they failed to achieve their objective, for the traditional forces in the Arab provinces retained their influence on local politics by joining the new administrative councils.[40]

When the Ottoman authorities were informed of the initiatives taken by the Christians they helped to foster the prevalent Moslem mood predisposed to putting the Christians back in their place. Consequently, the Moslems of Damascus had a free hand to launch a campaign to humiliate the Christians who constituted only about one sixth of the population of Damascus; 30,000 persons.[41] The campaign included insults, the drawing of crosses on the ground forcing Christians to step on them, threats of massacre were made, some Moslems entered churches claiming that they would soon become mosques, close relations with Christians were discouraged and, finally, some dogs were let loose through the streets wearing crosses tied around their necks.[42] The leaders of the campaign included members of the Moslem clergy as well as tradesmen, merchants, wanders, and members of other minority groups.[43] In some instances, those people had been directly affected by the advances the Christians had made and, hence, they believed that their economic or political interests were threatened.[44] Others believed that their religious prerogatives had been insulted by the manifestation of religious freedom among the Syrian Christians. For the most part, the majority of the Moslems in Damascus saw the change in status among the Christians as an objectionable occurrence trespassing upon cherished traditions in an arrogant manner.[45] Hence, sympathy for the anti-Christian initiatives was abundant. As for the notables of Damascus, they were the only class that appears to have taken an ambivalent course of action. Some of them supported the religious leadership in their attempt to intimidate the Christians;[46] while others among them tried to restrain the impending violence.[47] However, none of the notables were prepared to help or support the Christians.

Since the Christians were too small in number to constitute a strong independent socio-political force, their relationship with the European nations came under attack. To a certain degree the Moslems believed that the Syrian Christians were more loyal to the "Christian" European states and, consequently, they viewed them with extreme distrust.[48] In 1860, the Ottoman officials referred to the Christians of Syria as "The Key to the Franks" in order to incite the Moslems against them.[49] In view of the growing anti-Christian sentiment in mid-nineteenth century Syria, it seems highly possible that the Christians of Damascus did turn to the European Powers for protection and, to a great extent, the relationship between the Syrian Christians and the European Powers may have justified the accusation against them, charging them with disloyalty to both the local administration and to the Ottoman Empire. Yet, it should be remembered that the Christians were becoming an isolated community in an increasingly hostile atmosphere so that the common ties of language and culture were insufficient to guarantee their rights and safety, therefore, they began to rely on the European Powers to a far greater extent than in the past. In part, the Syrian disturbances may be regarded as political for throughout the conflict, the Jews of Damascus remained unaffected. Nor was the clashes to include any other religious minority; but, it equated all Christians as the enemies of Islam in Syria. Finally on July 9, 1860, Moslem fanaticism broke forth in Damascus in a reign of death and destruction upon the Christians of Syria.

With the contrivance of the Ottoman troops in Damascus, the Syrian Moslems attacked the Christian quarters in the city shouting: "Death to the Christians," "Kill them!," "Butcher them!," "Burn their houses!," and, within hours no Christian could call his life his own or his home a place of safety, as the Christian quarters was put to the torch.[50] The Ottoman authorities, clearly, could have prevented the outbreak of violence but they preferred to encourage it by withdrawing their protection of the Christians, or by helping the Moslems.[51] During the entire episode, the Druze of Lebanon lent only some sporadic encouragement to the Moslems of Syria. The Syrian Christians were caught totally defenseless; but, even in that moment of darkness a ray of light appeared in the person of Abd al-Qadir ibn Muhyad-Din al-Jazairi.

As an exiled Algerian freedom fighter, Abd al-Qadir and some of his men had made their way to Damascus; during the violence of 1860, he and his troops saved approximately 12,000 Christians by escorting them to various places of safety: his home and the citadel of the city where his troops guarded them while Abd al-Qadir refused to surrender any of them to the hostile mobs.[52] For ten days, his home was besieged and finally, on the tenth day, he rode into the crowd with some of his followers and challenged them saying:[53]

> Wretches is this the way you honor the Prophet? May his curse be upon you! Shame on you, shame! You will yet live to repent. You think you may do as you please with the Christians; but the day of retribution will come. The Franks will yet turn your mosques into churches. Not a Christian will I give up.They are my brothers. Stand back or I will give my men the order to fire.

Abd al-Qadir's show of force dispersed the cowardly crowd, and, shortly afterwards, he was honored for his courage and justice by the European Powers which had begun to actively intervene in the crisis.

The large scale massacre of Christians in Lebanon and Syria alarmed the Ottoman authorities to the danger of European intervention in the affairs of the Levant. By July of 1860, speeches in the British Parliament called for relief of the Christians and three British Warships Gannet, Mohawk, and Firefly were ordered to begin relief operations.[54] Britain's policy called for "collective intervention"[55] to relieve the hard pressed Christians of the East; and, it seemed to have been generated by a sincere humanitarian concern. Although the British had favored the Druze in 1845, they were not betraying them in 1860; rather, Great Britain was attempting to aid the Christians and to pressure the Porte to control the situation more justly.

As protectors of the Maronites, France sent immediate aid to the Lebanese Christians and extended its protection to the other Christians of the East. French influence had penetrated Lebanon since the time of Louis XIV and, no doubt, the Maronite establishment would have favored direct French military intervention with little hesitation, if any at all. Had France intervened alone it would have been possible for Lebanon to proclaim its independence as a French protectorate under the patriarch's leadership. But British-French rivalry was becoming increasingly manifest in Lebanon; and, thus, European intervention frustrated those conditions.

European involvement in Ottoman affairs had enabled Greece to proclaim its independence in 1826, but it could not free Lebanon from Ottoman rule in 1860. Greece was at the periphery of the Ottoman Empire and its independence could not have affected world politics to any great extent. Nor could a tiny independent Lebanese state threaten the Ottoman Empire; but, an independent Lebanon in the heart of the Turkish Empire might have resulted in the partial dismemberment of the Ottoman Empire at a time when both Great Britain and France wanted to preserve the Ottoman State. Thus, France did not object greatly to collective intervention, nevertheless, Lebanese hopes for independence were dashed by outside factors. Meanwhile, the Porte had been attempting to gain complete control of the situation and thus anticipated actual European intervention.

Before an Ottoman military mission could be sent to restore order, the Druze was encouraged to establish peace with the Maronites if the Maronites would accept full responsibility for the civil war of 1860.[56] The refusal of John (Yuhanna) al-Hajj, the Christian qaim maqam, to sign a truce[57] of that nature led to a scramble between Europe and the Ottoman Empire to restore order in Lebanon and Syria.

As a result of an international convention Great Britain, Austria, Prussia, Russia and the Ottoman Empire decided on intervention in the Lebanese province.[58] On July 17, 1860, an Ottoman military mission under the command of Fuad (Fu'ad) Pasha arrived in Lebanon.[59] He quickly moved to punish the guilty; Ahmed Pasha and Khurshid Pasha were sent to Istanbul, several Druze leaders were condemned to death or sentenced to life imprisonment or exile, and Fuad restored the property taken from the Christians.[60] Najib Pasha, the former agent of Muhammad Ali in Istanbul, was named governor of Damascus and order was soon established in that province.[61]

Meanwhile, France acted on its own initiative and dispatched a 12,000 man force to Lebanon under the command of General Charles de Beaufort d'Hautpoul. The French troops arrived on August 16, 1860; as they advanced towards Dayr al-Qamar, the Maronite troops following them attacked any armed Druze they encountered along the way.[62] Upon his arrival, the French general was met by the Maronite shaykhs who pledged themselves and the Maronite nation to France.[63] France, however, could not accept the pledge. Ottoman intervention under Fuad Pasha and the threat of European involvement would have precipitated a conflict between France and Great Britain and, possibly, the other powers. Consequently, France could not support the national aspirations of the Maronite clergy and people for a totally independent Lebanon allied to France. Instead, France opted for the reestablishment of a Shihabi Christian hakim to rule Lebanon.[64] However, the Porte and the European Powers had already decided on a new system of government to regain a semblance of order in Lebanon known as the mutasarrifiyah (the governor-generalship) of Mount Lebanon.

From the end of Shihabi rule to the establishment of the mutasarrifiyah, Lebanon underwent a period of stress at the hands of the Maronite clergy. In 1841, the Maronite establishment attempted to spread its political control into the mixed districts hoping to establish unity as a prerequisite for independence. Ottoman assistance to the Druze turned the second civil war into a true Maronite independence movement against both the Druze and the Porte. Finally, in 1860, the Druze and the Ottoman forces took the initiative to put an end to Maronite pretension towards independence The civil war of 1860 failed to free Lebanon from the Ottoman Empire; after two decades of struggle, the Maronite establishment was unable to achieve its objective.

1. Salibi, *The Modern History*, p. 71; Al-Khazin, *Lamahat Ta'rikhiyah*, p. 37.

2. Salibi, *The Modern History*, p. 71.

3. Holt, *Egypt and the Fertile Crescent*, p. 239; Salibi, *The Modern History*, p. 71.

4. Holt, *Egypt and the Fertile Crescent*, p. 239; Farah, *The Politics of Interventionism*, pp. 458-460; Tibawi, *A Modern History of Syria*, p. 100; Pere Henry Lammens, *La Syrie: Precis Historique*, Beyrouth: Imprimerie Catholique, 1921, p. 176; Salibi, *The Modern History*, p. 71; Pierre Dib, *History of the Maronite Church*, (Trans. by Rev. Seely Beggiani), Washington; The Maronite Seminary, n.d., p. 91.

5. Lammens, *La Syrie:* p. 176; Tibawi, *A Modern History of Syria*, p. 101; Salibi, *The Modern History*, p. 72.

6. Salibi, *The Modern History*, p. 72; Holt, *Egypt and the Fertile Crescent*, 239-240.

7. Salibi, *The Modern History*, pp. 76-77; Ismail, *Histoire du Liban*, p. 314.

8. Salibi, *The Modern History*, p. 78; Ismail, *Histoire du Liban*, p. 317.

9. Daghir, *Batarikat al-Mawarinah*, p. 97; Salibi, *The Modern History*, p. 83; Holt, *Egypt and the Fertile Crescent*, p. 240; Farah, *The Problem of Ottoman Administration*, p. 222.

10. Churchill, *The Druze and The Maronites*, p. 125; Salibi, *The Modern History*, pp. 85-86; Al-Aqiqi, *Lebanon in the Last Years of Feudalism*, p. 48; Dominique Chevallier, *"Aux origines des troubles agraires libanais en 1858,"* *Annales: Economies, Societes, Civilisation*, vol. 14, no. 1, (Janvier-Mars), 1959, pp. 35-64.

11. Al-Aqiqi, *Lebanon in The. Last Years of Feudalism*, pp. 20-23, 48, 53; Hitti, *Lebanon in History*, p. 436; Bolt, *Egypt and the Fertile Crescent,* p. 240; Salibi, *The Modern History*, p. 85; Churchill, *The Druze and The Maronites*, p. 125.

12. Daghir, *Batarikat al-Mawarinah*, p. 98; Churchill, *The Druze and The Maronites*, p. 122; Hitti, *Lebanon in History*, p. 436; Holt, *Egypt and The Fertile Crescent*, p. 240; Tibawi, *A Modern History of Syria*, p. 123; Tarabayn, *Azmat al-Hukum fi Lubnan*, pp. 105-106.

13. Hourani, *Syria and Lebanon*, p. 32; Al-Aqiqi, *Lebanon in the Last Years of Feudalism*, p. 23; Tarabayn, *Azmat al-Hukum fi Lubnan*, p. 105.

14. Holt, *Egypt and the Fertile Crescent*, p. 240; Al-Hattuni, *Nubdhah Ta'rikhiyah*, p. 343; Dominique Chevallier, *La Societe du Mont Liban a l'epoque de la Revolution Industrielle en Europe*, Paris: Geuthner, 1971; Toufic Touma, *Paysans et institutions feodales chez les druses et les maronites du Liban du XVIIe siecle a 1914*, 2 vol., Beirut: L'Universite Lebanaise, 1971-1972.

15. Al-Hattuni, *Nubdhah Ta'rikhiyah*, p. 349; Tarabayn, *Azmat al-Hukum fi Lubnan*, p. 108.

16. Al-Hattuni, *Nubdhah Ta'rikhiyah*, p. 350; Tarabayn, *Azmat al-Hukum fi Lubnan*, p. 110.

17. Daryan, *Nubdhah Ta'rikhiyah*, p. 261.

18. Al-Aqiqi, *Lebanon in the Last Years of Feudalism*, p. 22.

19. Churchill, *The Druze and The Maronites*, p. 138; Monterde, *Precis D'Histoire*, p. 129; Lammens, *La Syrie*, p. 181; Salibi, *The Modern History*, p. 89; Holt, *Egypt and the Fertile Crescent*, p. 241; *The Times*, (London), July 6, 1860, p. 11; Hitti, *Lebanon in History*, p. 437; Hourani, *Syria and Lebanon*, p. 32.

20. Anderson, *History of the Missions*, p. 436; N. N. Nimri, "The Warrior People of Djebel Druze: A Militant Minority in the Middle East," *Journal of Middle East Studies*, vol. 1, part 1, 1946-1947, p. 57.

21. Al-Hattuni, *Nubdhah Ta'rikhiyah*, p. 352; Francois Lenormant, *Histoire des Massacres de Syrie en 1860*, Paris: L., Hachette et Cie, 1861, p. 48.

22. Salibi, *The Modern History*, p. 89; Jouplain, La Question du Liban, p. 382; Tibawi, *A Modern History of Syria*, p. 124; Albert Hourani, "Lebanon From Feudalism to Modern State," *Middle East Studies*, vol. 2, no. 3, 1966, p. 258.

23. Ismail, *Histoire du Liban*, p. 337, Tibawi, *A Modern History of Syria*, p. 124.

24. Churchill, *The Druze and The Maronites*, p. 137.

25. Farah, *The Problem of Ottoman Administration*, p. 242.

26. Churchill, *The Druze and The Maronites*, p. 139; Hitti, *Lebanon in History*, p. 427; James L. Farley, *Massacres in Syria*, London: Bradbury & Evans, 1861, p. 123.

27. Jouplain, *La Question du Liban*, p. 587; Farah, *The Politics of Interventionism*, pp. 531-535; Meo, *Lebanon*, p. 30; Michael Hudson, *The Precarious Republic, Political Modernization in Lebanon*, New York: Random House, 1968, p. 36.

28. Al-Aqiqi, *Lebanon in the Last Years of Feudalism*, pp. 58-59; *The Missionary Herald*, 1860, p. 241; Farah, *The Politics of Interventionism*, p. 569; *Further Papers Relative to The Disturbances in Syria*, part IV, June 1860, pp. 40-42; Monterde, *Precis Histoire*, p. 130; Husain Abu Shaqra, *Al-Harakat fi Lubnan ila Ahd al-Mutasarrifiyah*, Beirut: Matb'at al-Ittihad, 1952, pp. 113-130; Farley, *Massacres in Syria*, p. 5, 27, 42; Hitti, *Lebanon in History*, pp. 437-438; Scheltema, *The Lebanon in Turmoil*, p. 67, 76, 88-89, 103; *The Times*, (London), July 6, 1860, p. 11; July 9, 1860, p. 9; July 21, 1860, p. 10; July 23, 1860, p.9; Al-Hattuni, *Nubdhah Ta'rikhiyah*, 354-355; *Hansard's Parliamentary Debates*, London: T. C. Hansard, 1860, vol. 159, House of Lords, July 10, 1860, p. 1649.

29. Hudson, *The Precarious Republic*, pp. 36-37; *Affaries Etrangeres, Documents Diplomatiques*, (Paris, 1860), July 6, 1860, p. 196; *Hansard's Parliamentary Debates*, vol. 159, House of Lords, July 10, 1860, p. 1651.

30. Farley, *Massacres in Syria*, p. 27; *Further Papers*, part IV, June 1860, p. 41; Hitti, *Lebanon in History*, p. 438; *The Times* (London), July 21, 1860, p. 10; *Hansard's Parliamentary Debates*, House of Lords, July 10, 1860, p. 1652.

31. Churchill, *The Druze and The Maronites*, p. 145; 156-157; Bliss, *The Religions of Modern Syria*, p. 177; Holt, *Egypt and the Fertile Crescent*, p. 241; Salibi, *The Modern History*, p. 96; Ismail, *Historie du Liban*, p. 341.

32. Daghir, *Batarikat al-Mawarinah*, pp. 99-100.

33. Al-Hattuni, *Nubdhah Ta'rikhiyah*, p. 356.

34. Hitti, *Lebanon in History*, p. 438; Philip K. Hitti, "The Impact Of The West On Syria And Lebanon In The Nineteenth Century," *Cahiers D'Histoire Mondiale*, vol. II, no. 3, 1955, pp. 626-627; R. H. Davidson, "Turkish Attitudes Concerning Equality in The Nineteenth Century," *The American Historical Review*, vol. LIX, no. 4, (July, 1954), p. 847; Antonius, *The Arab Awakening*, pp. 56-57.

35. Moshe Ma'oz, *Ottoman Reform in Syria and Palestine, 1840-1860*, and Oxford: Clarendon Press, 1968, p. 209; Colonel Charles Henry Churchill, *Life of Abdel Kadir*, London: Chapman and Hall, 1867, p. 309.

36. Davidson, *"Turkish Attitudes,"* AHR, vol. LIX, (1954), p. 854; Hitti, "The Impact of the West," *Cahiers D'Históire Mondiale*, vol. II, (1955), pp. 626-627.

37. Davidson, *"Turkish Attitudes,"* AHR, (1954), p. 583; Hitti, "The Impact of the West," *Cahiers D'Histoire Mondiale*, (1955), pp. 626-627; Churchill, *Life of Abdul Kadir*, pp. 309-311.

38. W. R. Polk and R. L. Chambers, *Beginnings of Modernization in the Middle East -The Nineteenth Century*, Chicago: Chicago University Press, 1968, pp. 32-33, 54.

39. S. J. Shaw, "The Origins of Representative Government in the Ottoman Empire; an Introduction to the Provincial Councils 1839-1876," *Near East Round Table*, New York, 1969, P. 57; Polk and Chambers, *Beginnings of Modernization*, p. 33.

40. Shaw, "The Origins of Representative," *Near East Round Table*, pp. 66-67; Polk and Chambers, *Beginnings of Modernization*, p. 60.

41. Farley, *The Massacres in Syria*, p. 75; Churchill, *Life of Abd al-Kadir*, pp. 310-311.

42. Lenormant, *Histoire des Massacres*, pp. 100-101; Farley, *The Massacres in Syria*, p. 75; Davidson, *"Turkish Attitudes,"* AHR, (1954), p. 855; Ma'oz, *Ottoman Reforms in Syria*, p. 188.

43. Polk and Chambers, *Beginnings of Modernization*, pp. 188-189, 342.

44. Polk and Chambers, *Beginnings of Modernization*, p. 333.

45. Polk and Chambers, *Beginnings of Modernization*, p. 191.

46. Polk and Chambers, *Beginnings of Modernization*, p. 190.

47. Polk and Chambers, *Beginnings of Modernization*, p. 197.

48. Lenormant, *Histoire des Massacres*, pp. 100-101; Ma'oz, *Ottoman Reform in Syria*, p. 209.

49. Churchill, *Life of Abdul Kadir*, p. 309; *The Times* (London), July 23, 1860, p. 9.

50. Churchill, *The Druze and The Maronites*, p. 212; Farley, *The Massacres in Syria*, p. 76; Al-Aqiqi, *Lebanon in The Last Years of Feudalism*, p. 67; Scheltema, *The Lebanon in Turmoil*, p. 131; Churchill, *Life of Abdul Kadir*, p. 314; Hitti, *Lebanon in History*, p. 438; *Further Papers*, part IV, 1860, p. 34; part II, p. 41; *Affaires Etrangeres, Documents Diplomatiques*, July 16,1860, p. 198; *Archives of The United States, Documents and Dispatches*, Alexandria, July 28, 1860.

51. Anderson, *History of The Missions*, pp. 349-350; Churchill, *Life of Abdul Kadir*, p. 313, 316; *Le Moniteur Universal*, August 4, 1860, p. 933; *Affaires Etrangeres, Documents Diplomatigues*, July 16, 1860, p. 198.

52. Churchill, *The Druze and The Maronites*, p. 216; Churchill, *Life of Abdul Kadir*, pp. 314-317; Al-Aqiqi, *Lebanon in The Last Years of Feudalism*, p. 68; Bliss, *The Religions of Modern Syria*, pp. 196-197; *Further Papers*, part IV, 1860, p. 49; Holt, *Egypt and the Fertile Crescent*, p. 241; *The Times*, (London), July 27, 1860, p. 6; Scheltema, *The Lebanon in Turmoil*, pp. 134-135; Hitti, *Lebanon in History*, p.438; *Archives of The United States, Documents and Dispatches*, Alexandria, July 28, 1860.

53. Churchill, *Life of Abdul Kadir*, p. 316; Churchill, *The Druze and The Maronites*, p. 217.

54. *The Times*, (London), July 12, 1860, p. 9; July 21, p. 5, p. 10; *Further Papers*, part II, 1860, p. 40; Churchill, *The Druze and The Maronites*, p. 158; *Hansard's Parliamentary Debates*, House of Lords, vol. 159, July 10, 1860, p. 1649, 1652; Antoine Abraham, "Lebanese Communal Relations," *Muslim World*, LXVII, no. 2, 1977, p. 101.

55. Jouplain, *La Question du Liban*, p, 587; *Affaires Etrangeres, Documents Diplomatiques*, July 19, 1860, p. 204.

56. Al-Hattuni, *Nubdhah Ta'rikhiyah*, p. 358.

57. Al-Hattuni, *Nubdhah Ta'irkhiyah*, p.358; Daghir, *Batarikat al-Mawarinah*, p. 100; Dib, *History of the Maronite Church*, pp. 92-93; Farah, *The Politics of Interventionism*, p. 586.

58. Hitti, *Lebanon in History*, p. 439.

59. Abu Shaqra, *Al-Harakat fi Lubnan*, p. 133; Farah, *The Politics of Interventionism*, pp. 603-636; Al-Aqiqi, *Lebanon in the Last Years of Feudalism*, p. 70; Scheltema, *The Lebanon in Turmoil*, p. 144; Holt, *Egypt and the Fertile Crescent*, p. 241.

60. Hitti, *Lebanon in History*, p. 439; Abu Shaqra, *Al-Harakat fi Lubnan*, p. 134, 143; Tibawi, *A Modern History of Syria*, p. 130; Ismail, *Histoire du Liban*, p. 365; Scheltema, *The Lebanon in Turmoil*, pp. 152-153; Churchill, *The Druze and The Maronites*, p. 230; *Le Moniture Universal*, July 29, 1860, p. 905.

61. Churchill, *The Druze and The Maronites*, p. 222.

62. Abu Shaqra, *Al-Harakat fi Lubnan*, p. 135.

63. Hitti, *Lebanon in History*, p. 439; Baptistin Poujoulat, *La Verite sur la Syrie*, Paris: Gaume Freres et Duprey, 1861, p. 21; Verney, Noel and George Dambmann, *Les Puissances etrangeres dan le Levant, en Syrie et en Palestine*, Paris: Guillaumin et Cie, 1900, p. 72; Aub Shaqra, *Al-Harakat fi Lubnan*, p. 132; Hourani, *Syria and Lebanon*, p. 32.

64. Abu Shaqra, *Al-Harakat fi Lubnan*, pp. 138-139; Daghir, *Batarikat al-Marwarinah*, p. 101; Al-Hattuni, *Nubdhah Ta'rikhiyah*, p. 363.

CHAPTER 7

THE MUTASARRIFIYAH OF JABAL LUBNAN:
THE ARAB WORLD'S FIRST REPRESENTATIVE GOVERNMENT

The guns fell silent, the swords were sheathed, and an imposed peace settled upon Mount Lebanon, in August of 1860. The civil war in the Lebanese mountains and the uprising in Damascus were ended by foreign intervention, and by more rigorous efforts on the part of the Ottoman Empire to prevent the loss of Mount Lebanon (Jabal Lubnan) to the European Powers-France, Great Britain, Austria, Prussia and Russia. (In 1867, Italy joined the group as an auxiliary power.) Thus, the Turkish Empire found itself with new partners in the Lebanese province. It had no choice but to co-operate with the imposing Europeans to end what had become a rapidly deteriorating situation in the heart of its Arab lands. Although they never trusted one another, the European Powers and the Ottoman authorities had to co-operate with each other to maintain control over Mount Lebanon and to prevent its independence. In doing so, they ushered in a new era of semi-autonomy known as the Mutasarrifiyah of Jabal Lubnan (*The Governor-Generalship of Mount Lebanon*).

The Ottoman Empire's main concern at this juncture of events was to obtain and maintain as much authority and power for itself in future Lebanese affairs. To that extent, before negotiations between it and the Powers would begin, Fuad Pasha, the Ottoman Foreign Minister, attempted to gain concessions from the leaders of Mount Lebanon to accept Ottoman rule as sufficient for peace and justice, for all the communities. An agreement was signed under duress in Beirut by the Christian and Druze qaim maqams, but Father John Hadj, the patriarchal deputy, refused to endorse this "treaty" of July 6, 1860; in fact, he lobbied against it and called for the independence of Mount Lebanon. When Fuad Pasha presented the coerced document to the Ottoman Empire's allies, it was rejected,[1] the Ottoman Empire, therefore, lost all hope of avoiding or excluding foreign intervention in Lebanese affairs. To placate the Turks, the European Powers agreed to exclude all Lebanese representation from the forthcoming meetings in Beirut.[2] No doubt, having been excluded from participating in their own future, the Lebanese communities considered any new arrangement as a temporary measure.

Prior to the departure of the French troops from Lebanon on June 5, 1861, Marquis Charles de Beaufort d'Hautpoul, commander of the French forces, completed his relief mission to stabilize the mountain district; and Fuad Pasha, representing the Ottoman forces, completed the preparations for an International Commission to discuss new arrangements for Mount Lebanon and the Lebanese province. The signatories of the Protocol of August 3, 1860 would represent their governments in Beirut: Fuad Pasha for the Ottoman Empire; M. Beclard for France; Lord Dufferin for Great Britain; E. P. Novikof for Russia; and one delegate each 3 for Austria and Prussia.[3] Fuad Pasha served as president of the commission.

Fuad's mission was problematic from the start. His main concern, of course, was to limit European encroachments on Ottoman territory. But he also found that the European Powers had no unified position on Lebanon's future. Thus, he had some leeway to play-off the European nations against each other to enhance his objective to reinforce the Ottoman hold on Lebanon. It was clear from the beginning that while Christian Europe intervened in the east to save the Arab Christians, their motivations were more complex and self-serving[4] to encourage commercial dealings, trade, and strategic concerns.

In regard to the future of the Lebanese province, the European Powers held differing views on its reorganization and leadership. The first of many meetings took place on October 5, 1861; the negotiations lasted for eight months[5] before Fuad Pasha could suggest an acceptable compromise. Austria and Prussia, more often than not, supported the French proposals which were designed to enhance French prestige with the Maronite Catholics, just short of support for independence.[6] To support any gesture of independence at that time would invite insurmountable problems for France with both Great Britain and the Ottoman Empire. France favored the idea of continued Maronite rule in an autonomous district.[7] The British supported the Druze and offered a plan to establish three qaim maqams; one Maronite, one Druze, and one Orthodox Christian, under a Moslem ruler and, later, they proposed another plan calling for a vice royalty similar to the Khedive of Egypt.[8] The Russians, at first, supported the Orthodox Christians and the first British proposal but, later, they switched sides favoring the French plan.

After exhaustive deliberations, Fuad Pasha and the International Commission agreed upon a compromise. An autonomous Mount Lebanon would be ruled by a Catholic Christian, but not a Maronite, under indirect Ottoman rule with a six power guarantee for the peace and safety of all the sects. The Maronites and the French preserved the autonomy of Mount Lebanon; Great Britain weakened French and Maronite influence and the Ottoman Empire retained the functionary of its choice as the legitimate ruler.[9]

On June 9, 1861, a new statute for Mount Lebanon was approved; called the Reglement et protocole relatifs a la reorganisation du Mont Liban-or more simply as a "constitutional" document, Reglement Organique du Liban; it was witnessed by the ambassadors of the European Powers. Nine days later, an Ottoman imperial decree (firman) read in the Pine Grove outside Beirut, before a large audience, gave life to a new dismembered Lebanon.

To facilitate control over Lebanon, the new administration set up by the Reglement Organique[10] separated the mountain region from the remainder of the province; hence, an autonomous sanjak[11] (sub-province/administrative district) was created truncating the former region, giving it a new special status. The mountain area was largely separated from Beirut, Tripoli, Sidon, al-Biqa/Biqa' and the Akkar region of the north along with other areas.[12] Those regions remained under direct Ottoman rule; but the mountain became, more or less, an isolated entity, and its inhabitants were separated from their co-religionists who remained under the ever watchful eyes of the Turks. Economically, Mount Lebanon became handicapped in several ways.[13] The inhabitants of the mountain came to the conclusion that this new arrangement would not benefit them; there was no interest in the reform or in the development of the mountain district from an economic or social perspective;[14] it actually disrupted economic activities already in progress.

The political administration of Mount Lebanon, however, proved to be quite successful during the era of the Mutasarrifiyah. According to the European Powers and the Porte, the Reglement Organique served as a "constitution" for the new "independent" sanjak. Originally promulgated in 1861, it was revised in 1864, amended in 1912 and, finally, terminated in October of 1915. It provided Mount Lebanon with almost half a century of peaceful political evolution and social co-operation.

The Reglement Organique, in its seventeen article code, planted the seeds for a unique mode of government in the Middle East, one that would be based, at least in part, on popular representation. It remained in effect for about fifty years with slight alterations. In 1861, the administration of Mount Lebanon established the region as an autonomous or semi-autonomous sanjak, but as a single unit this proved to be too difficult to be effectively administered and, consequently, the Protocol of September 6, 1864 revised the region creating and confirming seven separate districts (qada):[15] Shouf, Metan, Djezzin, Zahlah, Koura, Keserwan and Batroun. (Before 1864, Keserwan and Batroun were jointly administered.) Dayr al-Qamar became the administrative headquarters (mudiryah) and, later, several sub-districts (nahiyat) were added to further facilitate the administration.

The Mutasarrif (Governor-General/plenipotentiary) held administrative, public works, fiscal, and legal authority; and he had the rank of marshall (mushir) for policing powers.[16] He was appointed by the Porte, reported to Istanbul, and held the approval of all the foreign powers involved in the Protocol. He was an Ottoman citizen but could never be Lebanese because the Porte cited the independence minded Maronites, Druze and the Shi'ites (the Mutawalli) as "problematic". The mutasarrif did allow for some Lebanese participation in the government but, he was clearly the focal point; the centralized authority rested upon his decisions.[17] The mutasarrif held all executive power.

In order to enforce his decisions and to prevent full autonomy and possibly independence with foreign support, the mutasarrif created a religiously mixed police force, called the gendarmeire libanaise, recruiting seven men per one thousand inhabitants.[18] (Only a small Ottoman garrison could be temporarily stationed in the mountain.) Taxes and duties were collected for the administration; surplus funds were designated for the imperial treasury in Istanbul; and local mixed courts were to adjudicate cases.[19] The mutasarrif allowed for open meetings, mass petitions, and, on occasions, public gatherings under local leaders known as Shuykh al-Shab (the people's shaykhs). In 1912, at the request of the Lebanese leaders, the mutasarrif amended the 1864 Statute giving the commercial courts Lebanese jurisdiction; he also changed the local election procedures, and established new fiscal arrangements.[21]

And, finally, to introduce Lebanese participation into the administration, a Central Administrative Council (CAC/AC; majlis idarah) was created to assist the mutasrrif. At the behest of the Ottoman Foreign Minister, religious representation was to be introduced into the governing body-the Confessional System (a modification of the Ottoman millet system still in use at that time)[22]-to create a balance of power in the mountain thereby facilitating the mutasarrif's rule.

The CAC was a religiously balanced council designed to maintain a communal balance of power among the major sects. In 1861, the CAC was composed of twelve elected members from the six major sects: 2 Maronites, 2 Druze, 2 Greek Catholics, 2 Greek Orthodox, 2 Sunnite Moslems and 2 Shi'ite Moslems.[23] However, both the Maronites and the Druze complained that the representation was not proportional and should be adjusted to reflect the approximate ratios among the communities.[24] Thus, in 1864, the CAC was altered to reflect the approximate population of Mount Lebanon: 4 Maronites, 3 Druze, 2 Greek Orthodox, 1 Greek Catholic, 1 Sunnite Moslem and 1 Shi'ite Moslem.[25] Thus, a 7:5 ratio of Christians to Moslems for legislative representation was adopted and accepted by all groups based upon an unofficial count in 1865: 117,800-Maronites; 28,560-Druze; 29,500-Greek. Orthodox; 19,370-Greek Catholics; 7,611-Sunnite Moslems; 9,820-Shi'ite Moslems.[26]

The appointment of the first Mutasarrif was also problematic from the start. Even before the selection of the governor-general was agreed upon, the French continued to lobby for a Shihabi to fill the post. Amir Majid al-Shihab was the official candidate but his quest proved to be fruitless. The Porte had decided, with British support, that a European of "oriental background" would rule, to make him more acceptable to the Lebanese.[27]

Daud Pasha (Affendi), an Armenian of the Roman Catholic faith, former director of the telegraph bureau in Istanbul, author of a legal text on Anglo-Saxon law in the French language, and a diplomat who had served as an attaché at the Ottoman Embassy in Berlin and as counsel-general in Vienna, was appointed mutasarrif,[28] on June 6, 1861.

Although he was intelligent, resourceful and had some political savvy, Daud Pasha new little about Lebanon and its people,[29] but he had been already warned by Fuad Pasha before he arrived in Beirut at the end of June, 1861. He took office at Dayr al-Qamar but, later, relocated his residency to Ba'abda in the winter and Bayt al-Din in the summer. Almost immediately upon his arrival, Daud Pasha found himself facing stiff opposition from several quarters including: the Shihabi Party and other notables; the Maronite Church and Patriarch Bulus Masad; the former acting qaim maqam of Mount Lebanon, Yusuf Bek Karam (appointed in 1860 by Fuad Pasha to replace Bashir Ahmed Abu al-Lami') and the CAC, all of whom objected to Daud's non-Lebanese origins[30] as well as having their own personal, individual, grievances against a system that had deliberately overlooked the indigenous sources and centers of power. Through his involvement with these groups, and his shrewd management of affairs, Daud tried to placate his opposition. In the long run, he achieved limited success.

The new system of government signaled the end of the old feudal system that had existed for centuries; and, no doubt, the notables clearly saw the mutasarrifiyah as a threat to their power. The Shihabi Party retained its influence after the conflict of 1860 and with the aid of France had sought to regain its political prominence. With the co-operation of several other amirs and shaykhs they all sought inclusion into the new ruling body, the CAC. Daud acted quickly to calm their fears by appointing several of the notables to the district seats: Yusuf Bek Karam became the administrator (mudir) of Jazzin; Murad Abi Lami' and Abd Allah Abi al-Lami' were appointed to the northern district and the region of Zahle; Amir Majid al-Shihabi took control of al-Matn; Amir Hasan obtained possession of al-Kura; and the prominent Druze Amir Milhim Arslan became the administrator of al-Shuf.[31] Thus a form of "phantom" feudalism continued under the mutasarrifiyah, and still exists in a modified form at present.

Meanwhile, the Maronite Church and its Partriarch Bulus Masad (Mas'ad) took the lead in rejecting Daud's authority by objecting to his foreign origin. They wanted a local Maronite government,[32] and would accept the mutasarrif as a temporary administrator.[33] The patriarch feared that Daud would limit or restrict Maronite religious prerogatives and temporal authority.[34] Furthermore, the Maronites continued to object to the reduction of Lebanese territory imposed by the Reglement[35] which they saw as an attempt to separate their co-religionists from the Maronite heartland, and which had resulted in an economically unviable position creating difficulties in reaching the ports, particularly the port of Beirut. Thus the patriarch did all that he could at times to undermine the authority of the mutasarrif.[36] Although the mutasarrif was a Catholic, Daud's loyalty to the Porte did not win for him much support among the Maronite population.

The greatest challenge to Daud's rule came from a secular nationalist with powerful ambitions, a man from an honorable but not noble family, Yusuf Bek Karam. His life and political career remains an enigma, depending upon one's point of view. To the European Powers and the Porte, Yusuf was an unbridled opportunist; to the Maronite Church he was as opposite political pole, a secularist who challenged their authority; but, to the majority of the Lebanese people, Yusuf Bek Karam was a genuine folk hero!

Even before Daud Pasha began his rule as mutasarrif (1861-1868), Yusuf Bek Karam was already a well known personality. In 1839, Ibrahim Pasha was a guest of Yusuf for several days and, it was reported that the noted traveler Prince Jouniville had visited Karam and served as the best man at his daughter's wedding.[37] Karam was also well versed in western literature, particularly the careers of Peter the Great and Napoleon Bonaparte.[38] No doubt, Yusuf Bek Karam may have had some grandiose ambitions of his own.

In March of 1857, a group of Maronite priests issued a "document" indicating that Yusuf was in charge of their affairs, and that he represented them in secular matters.[39] Soon after, in 1860, Karam was appointed acting qaim maqam of Mount Lebanon for which he was paid 11,250 piastres[40] a month, making him financially independent. He also used the money to purchase arms and train young men and women in the use of fire-arms for self defense.

Despite his activities, Karam was not popular with all the Maronites of the north. He opposed Majid Shihab and the Shihabi Party for he hoped to be named the mutasarrif of Mount Lebanon.[41] And, as qaim maqam of the north, Karam continued to face a double challenge from folk hero Taniyus Shahin and from Bishop Tubiyah Awn ('Awn) of the Maronite Church. Although he was successful against both of his rivals, Yusuf Bek had limited backing.[42] The church supported his opposition to foreign rule, but it also disliked his growing, secular, independence from them. Daud, therefore, had room to act to weaken all rivals to his authority in the north. He offered Yusuf Bek Karam an important position, that of commander of the mountain's army, and appointed him qaim maqam of Jazzin which he accepted for a few days,[43] but, later, Karam refused both generous offers. It was reported at that time that Yusuf Bek said, "I do not serve any system that is against the national rights of my country."[44] This left only one option for him- continued conflict with Daud Pasha for control of the north,[45] and possibly all of Mount Lebanon.

Yusuf Bek Karam carefully prepared his propaganda campaign against the mutasarrif both inside and outside of Lebanon.[46] He made public statements to the Vatican and the European Powers defending his opposition to Daud Pasha. He objected to the non-Lebanese origin of the mutasarrif, accusing him of dictatorial behavior, the unfair restructuring of some of the Christian districts, as well as adjucating commercial cases in Beirut rather than in the mountain using the mixed courts, and, finally, of making the Lebanese fiscal policy dependent upon Istanbul's prerogative.[47]

The opportunity for a clash between Yusuf Bek Karam and Daud Pasha came in 1861, during a tax crisis.[48] After a few serious encounters between Yusuf's volunteers and Daud's local forces, Yusuf was summoned to Beirut by Fuad Pasha for negotiations where he was quickly apprehended and exiled to Istanbul.[49] Before his exile in 1862, Karam, once again, explained his position to the European Powers, but it was to no avail. The Austrian and Russian representatives were sympathetic but England and France withheld any support for Yusuf and the Turks remained indifferent to his pleas. Nevertheless, Yusuf Bek was well received in the Ottoman capital and he chose to go to Alexandria, Egypt to await the end of Daud's first term in office,[50] before returning to Lebanon.

On the sixth of September, 1864, the Reglement was revised and Daud Pasha was reappointed as mutasarrif for another five years. Thus, the exiled Maronite leader decided to return in secret to Lebanon to resume his struggle against the Porte and its representative. The renewal of Daud's tenure was seen by Karam as a major set-back to the possibility of an independent Mount

Lebanon. He arrived at the port of Tripoli on November 22, 1864 and quickly departed for Zgharta.[51] Karam's return buoyed his supporters; he secretly made an alliance with Amir Salman Harfush, a prominent Shi'ite leader.[52] Then Karam moved with a small band of volunteers to Ihdin and initiated hostilities in January of 1866 when his supporters in Kiserwan refused to pay their taxes and sought his assistance. A major revolt broke out and several clashes occurred. Despite arms and ammunition smuggled into Lebanon from France by Dominique and Abd Allah Khadra,[53] Karam's force of about 2,500 men was certainly no match for the anti-Karamist troops which included the local police and a large contingent of Ottoman soldiers. Karam appealed to all Lebanese in the mountain to fight for their "liberty and independence" without distinction,[54] but he won little support.

After approximately one year of continued skirmishes, Karam was defeated. Yusuf Bek did not win the support of France which was still committed to a divide and rule policy; and the Maronite Patriarch did not fully support him, for the church did not appreciate his secular tendencies.[55]

Karam was safeguarded by his supporters in the Batroun region where he initiated negotiations, through Patriarch Masad, with Daud Pasha. Rizq Allah Khadra[56] made contact with Karam, and safe conduct was established for Yusuf Bek to go to Algeria on January 31, 1867. He then traveled on to Paris and died in exile, in Naples, Italy, on April 7, 1888; at the approximate age of 63. He is still regarded by many as Lebanon's first modern secular national hero.[57]

With the demise of Yusuf Bek Karam conditions in the mountain became more stable with the exception of the Druze leadership. As the mutasarrif began to consolidate his rule in the mountain, the traditional Druze leadership began to agitate against the new order which they saw as an infringement on their autonomy and, soon after, they sought to revolt when taxes were raised.[58] Daud had his hands full with Karam's revolt; Thus he acted prudently to off-set any new confrontation with the Druze. Taxes were reduced, and additional funds, presumably from the taxes collected, were provided for a Druze educational endowment (*waqf*).

Daud had promised to build a school for the Druze; and, he had kept his word. Al-Daudiyah, the first modern school built for the Druze sect (1862), still bears the mutasarrif's name. It was constructed at 'Abayh with the assistance of a large Druze endowment[59] to which Daud continued to make several generous contributions, to placate his opposition. The head of the school was the mutasarrif and he was assisted by a Druze board of trustees.[60]

Soon after, several other schools were built which stressed foreign language training for the inhabitants of the mountain;[61] these schools included the one at Al-Aramun (1865) and another at Qarnot Shiwan/Shihwan (1870), destined to play a leading role in reviving the literary and intellectual traditions of both Lebanon and the Arab World.

Towards the end of his rule, Daud Pasha continued his attempt to pacify north Lebanon and to suppress several reoccurring vendettas.[62] Also, the mutasarrif began to take an active interest in developing the infrastructure of the region. To that extent, not only did he foster schools, but he wanted to make the mountain more economically viable by extending and creating new roads (eventually reaching 5,950 meters);[63] a French company constructed the Beirut-Damascus highway;[64] and to improve commerce, Daud petitioned the Porte to reattach the truncated parts of Lebanon to the mountain district- al-Biqa, and the port cities of Beirut, Sidon and Tripoli.

His effort on behalf of his Lebanese subjects made him look suspicious in the eyes of the Porte; Istanbul mistrusted him[65] and, soon after, Daud Pasha resigned his post (1868), one year before it expired. Five years later, in 1873, he died in Europe.

The mutasarrifs who followed in Daud's foot steps were ambitious men, loyal to the Empire that sent them, and friendly to the foreign powers that kept watch over them;[66] but they were not necessarily very able men or individuals who cared about their charge.

Daud's successor Nasri (Qusa/Cusa) Franko Pasha (1868-1873) was born in Istanbul in 1814; he studied foreign languages and entered the Ottoman Foreign Ministry rising to the post of chief secretary of foreign affairs. He served as Fuad Pasha's advisor and chief legal aide in 1860. Nasri Franko achieved the rank of vizir and was appointed mutasarrif by the Ottoman decrees of June 5 and 11, 1868.

Nasri Franko Pasha had the support of Maronite Patriarch Bulus Masad who had not been on good terms with his predecessor.[67] In return Franko gave the Maronite bishops greater independence without disfavoring the Moslem population.[68] He tried to reconcile all opposing factions but ran into some difficulties with the Armenian Catholics over control of the monasteries in the Kiserwan region.

Nevertheless, Nasri's reign was peaceful and productive, although he had opposed Daud Pasha's request to reattach al-Biqa, and the port cities to the mountain. This won him favor at court, but also some opposition from France. During his tenure in office, eleven schools were built, roads were repaired, enlarged and extended, several bridges were constructed, agriculture was fostered, and a tapestry factory was founded at Dayr al-Qamar.[69] However, Nasri Franko enforced strong censorship of the press and other publications which called for greater autonomy or independence in the mountain; and he implemented the Hanifite Code (a Sunnite Moslem legal rite) along side secular codes, thus winning favor with the Islamic legal establishment (the Shari'ah Courts).

Nasri Franko Pasha was appointed for two terms in office (ten years), but he died suddenly on February 2, 1873.

Rustum Pasha (1873-1883) succeeded Nasri Franko as mutasarrif. Born in 1810, in Florence, Italy, of noble ancestry, Rustum began his political career as an aide to the Ottoman Ambassador to Rome; he moved to Istanbul where he entered the foreign ministry after obtaining Ottoman citizenship. Rustum rose quickly through the ranks of power and was designated Ottoman Ambassador to St. Petersburg.[70]

In February of 1873, Rustum Pasha was appointed vizier and mutasarrif of Mount Lebanon. Upon his arrival in Lebanon, he ran afoul the Maronites by supporting the secular tendencies of the CAC.[71] His chief adversary among the Maronites was Bishop Butrus al-Bustani of Dayr al-Qamar who called for Lebanese independence.[72] A revolt was in the making when the bishop was forced to accept exile to Jerusalem, as a guest of the Latin Patriarch. Also, France had counseled the Maronites against any revolt; however, peaceful relations between Rustum and the Maronite Church were never attained.

During his term in office, Rustum Pasha continued the work of his predecessor building more schools, roads, bridges, and police stations. Major towns and villages were connected by new roads from all directions. While still overseeing this work, Rustum died in London (1885) two years after the expiration of his term.

Wasah Pasha (1883-1892) was next in line for the office of mutasarrif. Wasah was born in Albania in 1824 and was educated in Rome as a Latin Catholic. Schooled in languages and literature, he traveled to Istanbul and joined the Ottoman Foreign Service. While in service to the Porte, Wasah was assigned to Aleppo, Syria, where he learned Arabic and, soon afterwards, be became a compromise candidate for the post of mutasarrif.

Prior to Wasah's appointment, in June of 1883, a split had occurred in the CAC which aggravated the selection process for a new mutasarrif. The Maronite representatives split into two powerful factions; "the government party" which accepted autonomy but wanted it expanded, and "the church party" which sought the total independence of Lebanon.[73] Complicating matters further, the British had supported the re-election of Rustum[74] whom they hoped could control the CAC more strongly, while the French opposed Rustum's re-election,[75] claiming that he had arbitrarily arrested members of the opposition (the church party) including: Tanous al-Hakime (*Maronite*), Sheikh Bashir Sulayman (*Druze*), and Shaykh Muhammad Sa'id (*Shi'ite*). Thus, a compromise candidate was sought and Wasah Pasha was acceptable to all, because he had successfully opposed Yusuf Dibs, the Maronite bishop of Beirut who had created an independent secular party of his own.[76]

Wasah Pasha was succeeded by Na'um (Tatunji) Pasha (1892-1902). Born in the Ottoman capital, in 1846, he was a Latin Catholic of Armenian descent. Na'um attended the imperial school system which prepared him for a career in the Foreign Ministry. He served in the Ottoman Embassy in St. Petersburg and, later, in the Foreign Correspondence Office in Istanbul. Na'um rose to the rank of vizier and mutasarrif in August of 1892.

Na'um Pasha's term in office saw considerable peace and security; he resolved a festering problem in Kiserwan between the Maronite Christians and the Shi'ite Moslems without conflict and, thus, he showed himself to be pan-Lebanese.[77] He had the support of the Maronite Church,[78] and he allowed immigration to the United States. He extended roads and built bridges and reformed the fiscal and judicial systems.[79] And, Na'um supported the creation and expansion of the Beirut-Damascus-Hawran railway system (completed in

1895). Despite these activities, his rule was not completely popular; Na'um was accused of corruption and of supporting a tobacco monopoly owned by several members of the CAC.[80] Na'um Tatunji Pasha returned to Istanbul in 1902; he died in Paris, in 1911.

Muzaffar Pasha (1902-1907), of noble Polish descent and a Latin Catholic by faith, entered the service of the Porte in 1863. He fought in the Ottoman-Russian War of 1877 and quickly distinguished himself in the Sultan's service; soon after, be became the commander of the Imperial Stable.[81] He was appointed mutasarrif in October of 1902.

Muzaffar was reform minded; he established a nineteen point program for the mountain, added communication lines (telegraph service) and prevented gambling.[82] He won the support of the CAC and tried to make Juniyah a major port, in 1903. His program of reforms proved to be unsuccessful; they were never fully implemented. Muzaffar proved to be a popular ruler at least with the CAC for he supported their secular tendencies.

Yusuf (Franko) Pasha (1907-1912), a Greek Catholic, was born in Istanbul, lived in Lebanon and, later, joined the Ottoman Foreign Ministry as one of its private secretaries. He was elevated to the rank of vizier and appointed mutasarrif on July 9, 1907.

Yusuf Pasha began his term in office with the trust of all sectarian leaders and the CAC members, but he soon found himself involved in the Young Turk Revolt of 1908 which turned the Lebanese against him.[83] The Turkish Committee of Union and Progress (CUP) "invited" the mutasarrif to send representatives from the mountain to the newly proclaimed Ottoman Parliament. The CAC refused; they saw this initiative as nothing more that an attempt to "consolidate the autonomy of Lebanon" as part of Syria.[84] The CAC had wanted to upgrade itself into an independent legislature,[85] perhaps equal to the Ottoman Parliament or at least similar to it in its independence. Furthermore, for the mountain dwellers, the status of Lebanon was temporary: since they were not consulted on the formation of the mutasarrifiyah, they would not participate in the founding of the Ottoman Parliament, thus withholding legitimacy from it.

Yusuf Pasha had no choice but to threaten to dismiss the CAC, but he found the opposition in Lebanon united and powerful. The opponents[86] included: Kan'an al-Daghir, Habib Pasha Sa'ad, Amir Shakib Arslan, Nassib Junblat and Mustafa Arslan; the Lebanese north also remained unresponsive to the mutasarrif's request. The majority of the CAC members were in agreement to stay aloof of the Ottoman Parliament thereby reinforcing their own independence and the mountain's autonomy. Faced with so much opposition, Yusuf Pasha backed down, but to save face for the empire he loved, he passed several laws to restrain the free press in Lebanon and he forced Philip and Farid Khazin to stop their opposition party's paper, *The Cedars*.[87] Unhappily, the mutasarrif completed his term in office and then sought anonymity.

The last of the mutasarrif was Ohannes Koyoumjian (1912-1915), an Armenian Catholic, who served in the Foreign Ministry and as the Ottoman Embassy's counselor in Rome. He was appointed vizier and mutasarrif on

December 23, 1912 but his rule was cut short, in June of 1915, when World War I forced him to resign, ending the six power arrangement, consequently placing all Lebanon under direct Ottoman rule.

Upon his arrival in Lebanon, Ohannes Pasha called for a meeting with the Maronite Patriarch and some of the notables at Ba'bda to ask them to support the empire,[88] and, then, he announced the exile to Jerusalem of some of the Ottoman Empire's opponents. He faced a police revolt over salaries, and, later, Ohannes called upon the Porte to subsidize Lebanon's deficit and budget.[89] During his rule, three new seaports were made operational; and, he favored the use of Lebanese commercial courts to settle cases that involved only the Lebanese, thereby advancing Lebanese sovereignty.[90] Ohannes's term in office ended abruptly when Jamal Pasha took over and dissolved the CAC and declared the mutasarrifiyah null and void, as a consequence of the First World War.

Ohannes was the last of the Christian mutasarrifs. With the outbreak of World War I, the Reglement Organique was terminated on July 11, 1915; the Ottoman forces occupied the mountain district; and direct Turkish rule ensued. Three Moslem governors were appointed to administer Mount Lebanon: Ali Munif Bey (September 25, 1915 -May 15, 1916) who later became the governor of Beirut; Isma'il Haqqi Bey (May 15, 1916 -July 14, 1918); and, lastly, Mumtaz Bey (August 25, 1918 -September 30, 1918).

The mutasarrifiyah of Jabal Lubnan proved to be a period of peace and prosperity, after the exile of Yusuf Bek Karam. It was a period of infrastructural development, intellectual and literary awakening and, foremost, independent political activity. Despite the loyalty of the mutasarrifs to the Porte and, at times, their incompetence, a cultural revival took place alongside a degree of economic activity and prosperity. The mutasarrifiyah actually represented a period of communal cooperation and security among the sects in the mountains.

For almost half a century Mount Lebanon, and to a considerably lesser extent, the Lebanese province in general, saw constant evolution and development towards modernization. Lebanon, it has been said, led the way that the other Arab lands would soon follow in the twentieth century.

In comparison with the other states or provinces in the Near East, the mutasarrifiyah of Jabal Lubnan was clearly a period of development towards modernization[91] in the form of industrialization and commerce, public works, and an Arabic literary revival. No doubt, the intellectual and literary awakening affected the entire Arab World through the revival and establishment of an Arab Press, foreign and domestic schools, and scientific and literary societies. This work began with Butrus al-Bustani and others:[92] As'ad and Fares al-Shidyaq, Tannus al-Haddad, Mikha'il Mishaqah, Nasif al-Yaziji, Yusuf al-Asir, Jurji Zaydan, Ya'qub Sarruf, Faris Nimr, Salim and Bishara Taqla, Ibrahim al-Ahdab, and Ilyas Fawwaz.

But the greatest achievement of the mutasarrifiyah came in the political sphere. In the mountain district, Ottoman Turkish rule was seen, at best, as foreign and unacceptable; only the Sunni Moslems of Lebanon held some affinity towards the Turks, as Moslems of the same sect. For the other minorities, the mutasarrifiyah was a temporary or transitional stage that afforded them continued autonomy. But, some Lebanese notables, without doubt, also saw Ottoman rule in a negative light as a source of Lebanon's problems and its loss of dignity.[93]

As a transitional phase in the history of Lebanon, the mutasarrifiyah produced a remarkable amount of political change and development. First of all, it continued the autonomy and proto nationalism of the past that the Mani and Shihabi amirs and the Maronite clergy had fought so hard to establish. For almost fifty years, the mountain district had "relatively autonomous and peaceful development" providing a degree of "self confidence" so that it could run "its own affairs."[94] Thus, Lebanese autonomy, at least in Mount Lebanon, was strongly consolidated.

The CAC also proved to be the nucleus for the political modernization of Lebanon. Proportional representation allowed the sects to be represented and, therefore, no group would be neglected. This, in fact, was a modification of the Ottoman millet system which injected religious representation into the political system. It allowed for members of all the sects to work together as a legislature or national assembly, in a policy of consensus and co-operation, to govern the affairs of their own country.[95] Furthermore, the CAC opened the political leadership to the burgeoning middle class-the lawyers, journalists, entrepreneurs and other educated people of all sects.[96] Clearly, however, not all the CAC members were, or saw themselves as, "national" leaders; many only sought to advance their own fortunes and prestige.[97] But, this is not unusual for any country. The CAC on the whole was very successful because it acted as a counterbalance to the executive power of the mutasarrifs and, hence, Lebanese interests and developments could not be disregarded. The CAC became the forerunner of the Lebanese Parliament.

Within the CAC a rudimentary form of government and democracy took root. The authority of the Lebanese clergy and notables (ayan) were severely restricted, although religious involvement in support of candidates still existed, and a phantom feudalism remains in the choice of political candidates. However, the CAC members were, for the most part, elected in representative fashion. The people elected the village shaykhs who in turn elected the members of their sect to the CAC. Every two years, one third of the CAC stood for re-election. The CAC was the first truly representative legislature in the Arab World.

1. Rev. Pierre Dib, *History of The Maronite Church*, trans. by Rev. Seely Beggiani, Beirut, Lebanon: Imprimerie Catholique, 1971, pp. 92-93.

2. Chekri Ganem, *Comite Libanais De Paris, Memoire Sur La Question Du Liban*, Paris, 1912, p. 5.

3. John P. Spagnolo, *France and Ottoman Lebanon, 1861-1914*, London: Ithaca Press, 1977, p. 36.

4. Amin Al-Rihani, *Al-Nakabat*, Beirut: Matba'at Sadr Rihani, 1948, p. 143; Lahd Khatir, *Ahd al-Mutasarrifin fi Lubnan*, Beirut: Matba'at al-Katulikitah, 1967, p. 10.

5. K. S. Salibi, *The Modern History of Lebanon*, New York: Greenwood Press, 1965, p. 109.

6. J. P. Spagnolo, "Mount Lebanon, France, and Daud Pasha," *IJMES*, vol. 2, no. 2, April, 1971, pp. 150, 165.

7. N. A. Ziadeh, *Ab'ad al-Ta'rikh al-Lubnani al-Hadith*, Cairo; 1972, pp. 118-120. (Both the Porte and the British were against the continuation of a Shibabi amir in power.)

8. H. Levantin, "Quarante Ans D'Autonomie Au Liban," *Etudes*, vol. 92, Annee 39, July-Sept. Paris, 1902, pp. 32-33; Salibi, *The Modern History*, p. 110.

9. M. Jouplain, *La Question Du Liban*, Paris, 1908, pp.468-469.

10. The text of the Regelemant in Arabic and French may be found in Asad Rustum, *Lubnan fi Ahd al-Mutasarrifiya*, Beirut: Dar al-Nihar, 1973, pp. 35-39; and in Gabriel Noradounghian (ed.), *Recueil d'actes internationaux de l'Empire Ottoman*, Paris, 1897-1902, vol. 3, pp. 144-150, 223-228. For the English version of the text see: *British and Foreign State Papers, 1860-1861*, vol. li, London, 1886, pp. 288-292; and Thomas E. Halland, *The European Concert in The Eastern Question*, Oxford, 1885, pp. 212-218.

11. Robin Fedden, *The Phoenix Land, Syria and Lebanon*, New York, 1965, p. 250; Jouplain, *La Question*, p. 467; J. C. Hurewitz, "Lebanese Democracy in Its International Setting," *MEJ*, vol. 17, (1963), p. 493.

12. Levantin, *"Quarante Ans,"* p. 35; Alphonse Jottre, *Le Mandat de la France sur La Syrie et le Grand-Liban*, Lyon, 1924, p. 19; Meir Zamir, *The Formation of Modern Lebanon*, New York; Cornell University Press, 1985, p. 13.

13. Elizabeth P. Mac Cullum, *The Nationalist Crusade in Syria,* New York, 1928, pp. 59-60; Ganem, *Comite Libanais,* p. 6.

14. Yusuf Murad, *Fi Sabil Lubnan,* New York, n.p., n.d., p.6.

15. Adel Ismail, *Lebanon, History of a People,* Beirut, 1972, p. 174; V. Cuinet, *Syrie, Liban, èt Palestine,* Paris, 1896, p. 205. Hurewitz, *"Lebanese Democracy,"* p. 493; Joffre, *Le Mandat,* p. 22; J. J. Malone, *The Arab Lands of Western Asia,* New Jersey; Prentice-Hall, 1973, p. 11; Levantin, *"Quarante Ans,"* pp. 37-38; Salibi, *The Modern History,* p. 110.

16. S. H. Longrigg, *Syria and Lebanon Under French Mandate,* London: Oxford University Press, 1958, p. 22.

17. Ganem, *Comite Lebanais,* p. 11.

18. Cuniet, *Syrie, p.* 206; Levantin, *"Quarante Ans,"* pp. 159.

19. Levantin, *"Quarante Ans,"* pp. 49, 157; Salibi, *The Modern History,* p. 111; Ganem, *Comite Lebanais,* pp. 12-13; Georges T. Labaki, *La Fiscalite Et Le Financement DC L'Habitat Au Liban,* Paris: Librairie Generale De Droit Et De Jurisprudence, 1987, Pp. 94-95.

20. A. Hourani, "Lebanon from Feudalism to Modern State," *Middle East Studies,* vol. 2, April 1966, no. 3, p. 259.

21. Longrigg, *Syria and Lebanon,* p. 23.

22. The *millet* system accords political representation to religious groups.

23. M. F. Ghuraiyib, *Al-Ta'ifiah wa al-Iqta'iyah fi Lubnan,* Beirut: Samiya Press, 1964, p. 34; Joffre, *Le Mandat, p.* 22; Jouplain, *La Question,* p. 46; Yusuf Murad, *Fi Sabil Lubnan,* New York: n.p., n.d., pp. 16-20.

24. Spagnolo, *France and Ottoman,* pp. 42-43.

25. Ismail, *Lebanon,* p. 174; Zamir, *The Formation,* p. 11; L. M. T. Meo, *Lebanon, Improbable Nation,* Indiana: Greenwood Press, p. 34; John P. Spagnolo, "Constitutional Change in Mt. Lebanon:1861-1864," *MES,* vol. 7, no. 1, (Jan. 1971), p. 43; Fahim I. Qubain, *Crisis in Lebanon,* Washington: The Middle East Institute, 1961, p. 13; August Adib Pasha, *Le Liban Apres La Guerre,* 1918, p. 117.

26. Spagnolo, *"Constitutional Change,"* p. 46.

27. Spagnolo, *"Constitutional Change,"* p. 34; Jouplain, *La Question,* P. 490.

28. P. K. Hitti, *Lebanon in History,* New York: St. Martin's Press, 1957, p. 443; Salibi, *The Modern History,* p. 111; Khatir, *Ahd al-Mutasarrifin,* pp. 26-27; Yusuf al-Sawda, *Fi Sabil Lubnan,* Alex., Egypt: 1919, pp. 352-353; Ahmad Tarabayn, *Lubnan Mundhu Ahd al-Mutasarrifiyah ila Bidayat al-Intidab, 1861-1920,* Cairo: 1968, pp. 15-16; M. Gustave D'Alaux, "Le Liban Et Davoud Pasha," *Revue Des Deux Mondes,* XXXV Annee, Seconde Periode, vol. 58, July 1865, p. 145.

29. Tarabayn, *Lubnan Mundhu,* p.15.

30. Al-Sawda, *Fi Sabil,* p. 353; Spagnolo, *France and Ottoman,* p. 54; Spagnolo, *"Mount Lebanon,"* pp. 150-151; Khatir, *Ahd al-Mutasarrifin,* p. 27; Ziadeh, *Ab'ad al-Ta'rikh,* p. 123; Tarabayn, *Lubnan Mundhu,* pp. 20-21; Spagnolo, *"Constitutional Change,"* pp. 37-38; Jouplain, *La Question,* p. 485; Zamir, *The Formation,* p. 10; Al-Masudi, *Al-Dawlah al-Uthmaniah fi Lubnan wa Suriyah, 1877-1916,* n.p., n.d, p 74.

31. Spagnolo, *France and Ottoman,* p. 62; S. Khalaf, "Primordial Ties and Politics in Lebanon," *Middle East Studies,* vol. 4, no.3, April 1968, P. 249; Salibi, *The Modern History,* p. 111.

32. Jouplain, *La Question,* p. 485.

33. Spagnolo, *"Constitutional Change,"* p. 37; Spagnolo, *France and Ottoman,* p. 70.

34. Spagnolo, *"Mount Lebanon,"* p. 151; Spagnolo, *France and Ottoman,* p. 70.

35. Zamir, *The Formation,* p. 13.

36. Engin Akarli, *The Long Peace, Ottoman Lebanon, 1861-1920,* Berkeley: University of California Press, 1993, p. 152.

37. Nasim Nawfal, *Kitab Batal Lubnan,* Alex., Egypt: 1896, p. 234.

38. Nawfal, *Kitab Batal,* p. 227.

39. Nawfal, *Kitab Batal,* pp. 228-229.

40. Nawfal, *Kitab Batal,* p. 240.

41. Ziadeh, *Ab'ad al-Ta'rikh*, p. 124; Jouplain, *La Question*, p. 490; Tarabayn, *Lubnan Mundhu*, p. 10.

42. Tarabayn, *Lubnan Mundhu*, pp. 11-12.

43. Salibi, *The Modern History*, p. 113; Akarli, *The Long Peace*, p. 37.

44. Khatir, *Ahd al-Mutasarrifin*, p. 28.

45. Al-Masudi, *Al-Dawlah al-Uthmaniah*, p. 74.

46. Ziadeh, *Ab'ad al-Ta'rikh*, p. 124.

47. Hitti, *Lebanon in History*, p. 444

48. M. Gustave D'Alaux, *"Le Leban et Davoud Pasha,"* *Revue Des Deux Mondes*, XXXVI Annee, Seconde Periode, vol. LXII, May 1, 1866, p. 34.

49. Tarabayn, *Lubnan Mundu*, pp; 41-43.

50. Tarabayn, *Lubnan Mundhu*, pp. 43-56; Salibi, *The Modern History*, p. 113.

51. Tarabayn, *Lubnan Mundhu*, p. 110.

52. Jacques Nantet, *Histoire Du Liban*, Paris: Les Editions de Minuit, 1963, p. 209; Spagnolo, *"Mount Lebanon,"* pp. 154-155.

53. Spagnolo, *"Mount Lebanon,"* p. 155; Spagnolo, *France and Ottoman*, pp. 105-107; Tarabayn *Lubnan Mundhu* 161-162.

54. Najib Dahdah, *Evolution Historique Du Liban*, 3rd. ed., Beirut, 1967, p. 209.

55. Spagnolo, *"Mount Lebanon,"* p. 157; Tarabayn, *Lubnan Mundhu*, pp. 119-121; Al-Sawda, *Fi Sabil Lubnan*, p. 356.

56. Spagnolo, *"Mount Lebanon,"* p. 160.

57. Hitti, *Lebanon in History*, p. 444.

58. Hitti, *Lebanon in History*, p: 444.

59. Hitti, *Lebanon in History*, pp. 444-445; Ziadeh, *Ab'ad al-Ta'rikh*, pp. 193-194.

60. Ziadeh, *Ab'ad al-Ta'rikh*, p. 1

61. Ziadeh, *Ab'ad al-Ta'rikh*, p. 194.

62. Salibi, *The Modern History*, p. 113; D'Alaux, *"Le Liban et Davoud Pasha,"* vol. LXII, p. 12.

63. Al-Sawda, *Fi Sabil Lubnan*, p. 367; Rufus Anderson, *History of the Missions of the American Board of Commissioners For Foreign. Missions to the Oriental Churches*, vol. 2, Boston: Congregational Publishing Society, 1872, pp. 369, 380.

64. Hitti, *Lebanon in History*, p. 445.

65. Ismail, *Lebanon*, p. 176.

66. Hitti, *Lebanon in History*, pp. 445-447; Akarli, *The Long Peace,* pp. 194-199; Yusuf al-Hakim, *Beirut wa Lubnan fi Ahd al-Uthmani*, Beirut, 1964, pp. 21-23; Salibi, *The Modern History*, p. 114; Ismail, *Lebanon*, p. 176; V. Cuinet, *Syrie, Liban et Palestine,* p. 207; Al-Masudi, *Al-Dawlah al-Uthmaniah*, pp. 76-79; Louis de Baudicour, *La France au Liban*, Paris, 1879, pp. 269-279.

67. Khatir, *Ahd al-Mutasarrifin*, p. 36.

68. Spagnolo, *France and Ottoman*, p. 126; Nantet, *Histoire Du Liban*, pp. 211-212.

69. Khatir, *Ahd al-Mutasarrifin*, pp. 43-44.

70. Khatir, *Ahd al-Mutasarrifin*, pp. 47-63.

71. Spagnolo, *France and Ottoman*, pp. 142-147.

72. Al-Sawda, *Fi Sabil Lubnan*, pp. 368-369; Tarabayn, *Lubnan Mundhu*, pp. 318-326; Khatir, *Ahd Al-Mutasarrifin*, p. 64; Akarli, *The Long Peace*, p. 43; Laurence Oliphant, *The Land of Gilead with Excursions in the Lebanon*, Edenburgh: W. Blackwood and Sons, 1880, pp. 355, 471; Great Britain, Foreign Office, Turkey 1883, no. 1:*Correspondence Respecting the Affairs of Lebanon and the Appointment of a Governor-General:* Presented to Both Houses of Parliament by Command of Her Majesty, 1883, vol. 82, pp. 741-742; John W. Jandora, *"Butrus al-Bustani, Arab Consciousness, And Arabic Revival,"* The Muslim World, vol. LXXIV, no. 2, April, 1984, pp.71-84.

73. Akarli, *The Long Peace*, p. 52.

74. Great Britain, F.O., Turkey, no. 1, 1883, *Correspondence*, pp. 740, 746-747.

75. Great Britain, F.O., Turkey, no. 1, 1883, *Correspondence,* pp. 739, 743-746.

76. Akarli, *The Long Peace,* p. 55.

77. Khatir, *Ahd al-Mutasarrifin,* pp. 151-160.

78. Akarli, *The Long Peace,* pp. 59-61.

79. Al-Sawda, *Fi Sabil Lubnan,* pp. 371-372; Nantet, *Histoire Du Liban,* p. 214.

80. Al-Sayyar (Newspaper), *KitabFada'ih Lubnan,* Alexandria, 1901, pp. 9-55.

81. Akarli, *The Long Peace,* p. 197.

82. Khatir, *Ahd al-Mutasarrifin,* pp. 162-163; Al-Sawda, *Fi Sabil Lubnan,* p. 372; Spagnolo, *France and Ottoman,* pp. 222-223; Maurad, *Fi Sabil Lubnan,* pp. 72-73.

83. Khatir, *Ahd al-Mutasarrifin,* pp. 177-186; Hitti, *Lebanon,* P. 447.

84. Spagnolo, *France and Ottoman,* pp. 267.

85. Zamir, *The Formation,* pp. 19-23.

86. Spagnolo, *France and Ottoman,* pp. 249-250.

87. Al-Sawda, *Fi Sabil Lubnan,* pp. 374-375; Khatir, *Ahd al-Mutasarrifin,* p. 186.

88. Antun Yamin, *Lubnan fi al-Harb, 1914-1919,* Beirut, 1919, p. 19

89. Khatir, *Ahd al-Mutasarrfin,* pp. 376-377.

90. Al-Sawda, *Fi Sabil Lubnan,* pp. 376-377.

91. Ziadeh, *Ab'ad al-Ta'rikh,* p. 123; Salibi, *The Modern History,* p. 141.

92. A. L. Tibawi, "The American Missionaries in Beirut and Butrus al-Bustani," *St. Anthony Papers,* no. 16, *Middle Eastern Affairs,* no. 3, pp. 139-179; Ibrahim Nasif al-Yaziji, *Al-Arab wa al-Turk,* Pub. in No. America, 1910; Salibi, *The Modern History,* pp.. 143-145; 153-154; Ziadeh, *Ab'ad al-Ta'rikh,* p. 192.

93. Yaziji, *Al-Arab wa al-Turk,* pp. 7-14.

94. Akarli, *The Long Peace,* p. 78.

95. Akarli, *The Long Peace,* p. 189.

96. Spagnolo, *France and Ottoman,* p. 288.

97. Murad, *Fi Sabil Lubnan,* pp. Introduction, 61-73.

98. Abdo I. •Baaklini, *Legislative and Political Development: Lebanon, 1842-1972,* North Carolina: Duke University Press, 1976, .p. 50.

CHAPTER 8

UNDER FRENCH RULE: THE INTERWAR
YEARS AND THE ORIGINS OF POLITICAL MODERNIZATION

The outbreak of World War One ended the six power arrangement that had governed Mount Lebanon for almost fifty years; the Mutasarrifiyah of Jabal Lubnan came to a precipitous end after the Ottoman Empire entered the war in October of 1914. The European Powers that had created the Reglement Organic for the Lebanese mountain district found themselves on the opposite sides of the battlefield-England, France and Russia as the "Allied" camp and the Ottoman Empire, Austria, Hungary and Germany as the "Central Powers."

The Arab lands of the Turkish Empire were almost immediately suspect of disloyalty in the eyes of the Porte. Therefore, it is not surprising that the Ottoman Empire took stringent efforts to closely control its territories, and to forestall any rebellious activity that might be construed as pro-Allied or as anti-Ottoman. No doubt, in time, all the Arab lands would participate in what would be called the Arab Revolt against an oppressive and overpowering overlord. From the Porte's perspective, the war enabled the Sultan to rid himself, to a significant extent, of the meddling affairs, rivalries, and internal interference of France and England in his empire, particularly in the Lebanon.

Within the Lebanese province, news of the war was received with varying degrees of trepidation; the future of Lebanon would have to await the outcome of the battles, it would hang in the balance for a while. Nevertheless, almost all the sectarian groups, to a considerable extent, hoped that the outcome of the war would retain autonomy for the mountain district or bring the Lebanese province to full independence. Unfortunately, that proved to be only wishful thinking.

When the Ottoman Empire entered the war on October 29, 1914, the ruling triumvirate in Istanbul (Jamal, Enver and Talat) sent Jamal Pasha to Damascus, Syria, as governor general of that province and as commander-in-chief of the Fourth Army Corp stationed there, to conduct all necessary military operations. Immediately upon his arrival, Jamal Pasha replaced Zaki Pasha al-Halabi as the head of the Fourth Army.[1] Before his departure, al-Halabi warned Jamal of the overt and covert opposition the Turks faced in the form of revolts and secret societies. Perhaps for that reason, Jamal Pasha would rule Lebanon with an "iron fist."

Before leaving for Beirut, Jamal Pasha sent a contingent of troops to defend Lebanon and to forestall the growing opposition to Turkish rule. The group was led by Rida Bek Say'in who was cautiously welcomed, feted and dined.[2] But, Rida was no fool; despite the niceties, he suspected the Lebanese notables, particularly the Maronites and the Sunnites, of harboring hidden loyalties to France and Sharif Husayn's Arab Revolt. Thus, he warned the Lebanese political and religious leaders against "dealing with or showing sympathy for" the enemies of the empire.[3] Rida Bek quickly conveyed his suspicions to his commander-in-chief.

Jamal Pasha, upon his arrival in Lebanon, called for a meeting at B'abda with the Maronite Patriarch, Moslem and Christian notables, and members of the Central Administrative Council (CAC/AC) to invoke their faithfulness to the Ottoman Empire.[4] He then outlined his plan for Lebanon:[5] All previous protocols were dissolved; the new government for the mountain would be located in 'Alay; the CAC was abolished and, later, on May 26, 1915 a new administrative council was appointed to try to enhance Lebanese loyalty; and, of course, the autonomous status of Mount Lebanon was abolished (as of October, 1915), making Lebanon an ordinary province. In addition, Jamal Pasha imposed a system of conscription on the Sunnite Moslems, debased the currency and dismissed the leadership of the various millets; he controlled the ports and requisitioned private property; he controlled the importation of all medical supplies, and ended all existing capitulations; Jamal converted monasteries into fortifications and, finally, the Turkish Pasha confiscated provisions and beasts of burden for his troops.[6] These measures resulted in enormous hardships for all the Lebanese.

It has been estimated that during the First World War, Lebanon lost close to 100,000 persons from famine, the lack of medical care, and the absence of medications. All shipping to and from Lebanese ports was halted; Mount Lebanon found itself isolated from the main cities, remittances from abroad were ended, and people died of hunger and disease.[7] Men were conscripted by force,[8] houses were searched and property was confiscated. A system of exchange (badal) enabled some families to exchange grain for the military service of family members, but this further impoverished the countryside.[9] (Relief operations were not begun until 1916 by the American Near East Relief Committee headed by Bayard Dodge.)

It was, however, Jamal's response to the independence movement in Lebanon that focused the anger of all the sects and communities against the Turks. Martial Law had been imposed on Lebanon by Jamal Pasha who set up his courts of inquiry in 'Alay. These courts were empowered to investigate anyone suspected of treasonable anti-Ottoman activity.

The courts were kept busy.[10] First of all, they had to punish all those who avoided military service. Then, those who supported the foreign powers or the Arab Revolt could be imprisoned, exiled or, if there was some actual evidence against them, they could be put to death. (The head of the Maronite Bishops of Beirut, Butrus Shibli, was exiled to Anatolia where he died, and the Maronite Patriarch was similarly threatened.) Membership in any organization, society or club that espoused independence or autonomy or the Allies brought swift punishment. Any local or foreign communication that could be deemed suspicious was enough to bring a person before the court; even associating with blacklisted persons was seen as political "heresy" and subject to an inquest. The situation was intolerable; however, it was the rampant and flagrant executions of

Christian and Moslem patriots that enraged the Lebanese. The long list of martyrs and heroes began in 1915.

Documents captured by the Turks in the French Consulate in Beirut yielded a rich source of names for the court in 'Alay. The first person executed for treason was Father Yusuf al-Hayik, on the twenty-second of March, 1915, in Damascus.[11] On July 27, 1915, the Maronite Patriarch visited Jamal Pasha at his headquarters in Ayn Sawfar to protest his policies and the execution, but the visit proved to be fruitless.[12] Arrests continued and trials resumed yielding cases against as many as 58 Christian and Moslem "conspirators." On April 5, 1916, Yusuf al-Hani, a prominent Beirut political leader, met his fate on the gallows.[13] Between 1915 and 1916 leaders were convicted of treason for supporting the French or Sharif Husayn's Arab cause, or both. Fourteen Moselms and Christians were hung in Beirut on May 6, 1916 and seven more in Damascus on July 11, 1916. Among the prominent martyrs were:[14] Philip and Farid Khazin, Shaykh Ahmad Tobbara, Fr. Yusuf al-Hayik, Muhammad and Mahmud Mahmasani, Umar Hamad, and Abd al-Wahhab al-Inglisi. Those hung in Lebanon have been commemorated at Martyr's Square (sahat al-shuhada/Burj Tower), in Beirut. It was reported that these men met their fate bravely, even heroically, exhorting the crowd to fight for Lebanese independence and the Arab Cause.[15]

Obviously, the Turks had sufficient reason to suspect the Lebanese. At least two Arab secret societies were clamoring for independence: The Youth Society (Al-Fatat) and The Covenant (Al-Ahd) were well known to Jamal Pasha.[16] The Khazin brothers called for freedom and independence in their journal: The Cedars (Al-Arz) and, later, in 1910 a brief was circulated entitled: Perpetuelle independance, legislative et judiciaire du Liban calling for Lebanese freedom and modernization.[17]

Outside Lebanon, those exiled and others who emigrated or escaped to the West formed societies to propagate Lebanese independence and their views on the future of their homeland. These organizations included:[18] L'Alliance Libanaise-Buenos Aires (1916), and the Comitte Lebano Centro Renascenca Lebaneza a San Paulo (1913); in Egypt, Joseph Saouda published a brochure entitled: Lubnan fi-t-Ta'rikh (Lebanon in History) translated into French as L'independence du Liban a travers l'histoire meanwhile, Antoun Gemayal established a committee called L'Alliance Lebanaise (Al-Ittihad) to unite the émigrés. This group evolved into the Alliance Libanaise D'Egypt founded in Cairo; it called for autonomy and the recreation of Lebanon's historic frontiers.[19] In New York, Ibrahim Salim Najjar founded the Lebanese League for Progress (An Nahdat al-Lubnaniyat) in 1911. This organization issued a similar program for independence and the unification of Lebanese territory along the pre-mutasarrifiyah borders.[20] But, the most extensive Lebanese activity for independence was centered in Paris where the peace talks would eventually take place.

In Paris, in 1908, M. Jouplain *(Paul Njaym)* published a book entitled: *La Question du Liban, Etude d'Histoire Diplomatigue et de Droit International* calling for the independence of Lebanon and the restoration of its frontiers.[21] That study helped to launch the Comite Libanais De Paris (1911-1912) which published its *"memorandum"* on Lebanese independence and called for the rectification of Lebanon's borders to their pre-mutasarrifiyah boundaries.[22] The president of the committee was Chekri Ganeum and its secretary was K. T. Khair Allah (Khairallah). These men, among others, led the battle for Lebanese independence and territorial integrity.

Meanwhile, in the Lebanese province, the end of Ottoman rule produced a vacuum of power. No doubt, nearly all Lebanese were happy to see the departure of the Turks. But, soon after, ominous clouds would congeal over the future direction Lebanon would take to fulfill its historic quest for freedom and independence. Various groups in Lebanon realized that Lebanon would not be left alone by the foreign powers to chart its own course. Most of the Lebanese did not want to become the new subjects of yet another "empire," if possible. Thus, they sought influence among the Arab nationalists and the European Powers; each sect or group trying to find its own client as an ally in mapping out its future vision of Lebanon. The problem of Lebanon, from that time on, is that there are too many views of what Lebanon should be like, as well as, whether or not Lebanon should exist as an independent entity. To a significant extent, one could conclude that every group or community or sect has produced a version of its own "foreign policy." This problem strongly manifested itself politically in the years after World War One, especially during the Paris peace conference.

Nevertheless, in Lebanon, as the Ottoman forces withdrew, everyone awaited the allied presence. A French naval force was first to arrive off the coast of Beirut, followed by a contingent of British infantry. Amir Faysal's troops entered Beirut to establish the first Arab nationalist government which lasted about one week. Faysal was quickly encouraged to move to Damascus.

In the Lebanese capital, the Ottoman appointed governor, a pro-Lebanese Shi'ite Moslem, Ismail Haqqi Bay (May 15, 1916-July 14, 1918), turned over the government to the mayor of Beirut, Umar al-Da'uq who supported Faysal's government in the Syrian capital.[23] At Ba'abda, the seat of the last Turkish mutasarif, Mumtaz Bey (August 25 to September 30, 1918), the departing Turkish leader appointed Habib Fayyad to head the government in the mountain.[24] Thus, Lebanon slipped out of Turkish hands.

An Arab provisional government was declared in Beirut and the Sharifian flag of Amir Faysal flew high in the port city, shortly after a token Arab force led by Shukri al-Ayyubi arrived there. But this situation, a temporary independence was not to stand. The European Powers had already decided the fate of Lebanon.

While the European Powers, primarily England and France, prepared to implement their war time agreements regarding the former Ottoman possessions, the United States was not a party to their plans. The American interest in the Near East resulted from its own war aims, known as the Fourteen Points issued by President Woodrow Wilson. That document called for "national self-determination" for all subject peoples. Therefore, the United States sent a commission of inquiry to ascertain the wishes of the people of Lebanon and Syria.

The King-Crane Commission, led by Henry C. King of Oberlin College and businessman Charles R. Crane, and their staff, visited Palestine, Syria and Turkey and issued their report in the fall of 1919, but it was disregarded. England and France had already agreed on an arrangement between themselves. The inhabitants of the region favored an American trusteeship under the League of Nations, if independence was not forthcoming. The United States, however, did not join the League of Nations and Wilson's incapacity terminated the commission's initiative.

The commission's report, however, remains of some significance for it sheds a bit of light on Lebanese communal relations.[25] The Maronites and Greek Catholics favored independence and the establishment of Greater Lebanon (Lubnan al-Kabir) to restore Lebanon's historic boundaries. The Greek Orthodox were divided between a pro-Syrian policy and support for total independence in a Maronite state backed by France. (The Orthodox had lost their foreign support (Russia) as a consequence of the 1917 Bolshevik Revolution.) The Druze leadership wanted continued autonomy and was, more or less, pro-British and anti-French. The Shi'ites feared domination from an aggressive Sunnite Moslem Syrian state. (The Druze and the Shi'ite were considered heterodox sects at that time.) And, finally, the Sunnite Moslems split between a pro-Syrian faction and a pro-independence party under a British or American (non-French, non-Catholic) trusteeship.

Meanwhile, Amir Faysal, fully aware of British and French machinations, hoped to gain some support within Lebanon. To that extent, Faysal petitioned the Lebanese for their support. From Damascus, Faysal's Deputy Amir Sa'id al-Hassan al-Jaza'iri sent telegrams to village leaders, the Maronite Patriarch, the Druze notables, and the mayor of Beirut to support Faysal's government.[26] His energetic efforts were to no avail, but he won considerable support from the Syrian Congress which rejected the separation of Lebanon and Palestine from the Syrian heartland.[27] They called for the immediate creation of Greater Syria (*Suriya al-Kubra*).

The fear of being incorporated into a Sunnite Moslem Syrian state eventually led some Druze and Shi'ites to support the Maronite Patriarch's call for an independent Lebanon, under a French Mandate. Under the mandate, Lebanon was to include its lost territories as Greater Lebanon; however it would lose the predominance of the Maronite population. With the support of some Druze and Shi'ites, the Patriarch began to assume increasing authority as a representative of the Maronites and, to a lesser extent, some members of the heterodox Moslem communities. The governor of the mountain district, Habib Fayyad, would soon be deposed by a temporary Provisional Government under Malik Shihab and Adil Arslan who would press for a Greater Lebanon policy among the Druze and for the total independence of Lebanon. (With the patriarch's help, Fayyad was politically isolated and then deposed by Shukri Pasha al-Ayyubi. He was replaced by Habib Pasha al-Sa'd, a pro-Greater Lebanon Maronite).[28]

With the support of the Administrative Council, the patriarch assumed the leading role as defender of Lebanese independence and the establishment of Greater Lebanon, on behalf of the majority of the population of the Lebanese province. But, he still faced very strong opposition from the Sunnite establishment; many of its leaders continued to favor Sharifian rule and the establishment of Greater Syria. This final confrontation would be resolved in the French capital where the future of both Lebanon and Syria would be decided.

The CAC of the mountain decided to take matters into its own hands and send a delegation to Paris. In October of 1918, Habib Pasha al-Sa'd reappointed the former councilors to the CAC.[29] When it reconvened, it represented all the sects: Maronites, Druze, Greek Orthodox, Greek Catholics, Sunnite and Shi'ite Moslems. The members included:[30] Da'ud 'Ammun (*Dayr al-Qamar*), Sulayman Kan'an (*Jazzin*), Sa'ad Allah al-Huwayyik (*Batrun*), Mahmud Junblat (*Jazzin*), Fuad Abd al-Malik (Shuf), Muhammad Sabra (*Matn*), Ilias Shuwayri (*Matn*), Niqula Ghusn (*Kura*), Husayn al-Hajjar (*Matn*), Muhammad Muhsin (Kiserwan/Kisrawan), and Yusuf Baridi (*Zahle*).

Although the council represented all Lebanese communities, it had some problems, and some opposition within Lebanon. The CAC which remained in session for about twenty months called for the establishment of Greater Lebanon and continued autonomy under a French Mandate.[31] But, some Sunnite Moslems preferred Sharifian rule and sent their own delegation to Damascus; it was quickly apprehended by the French forces.[32] They then decided to send a second delegation to Paris to call for a unified Syrian state that included Lebanon, however nothing came of this delegation's efforts in the European capital.[33]

Among the Maronites, there was some controversy as well. Some Maronites felt that creating Greater Lebanon would reduce the numerical superiority that they had enjoyed in the mountain. They wanted a federation with the rest of Lebanon, with continued self-rule in Jabal Lubnan. Some Druze leaders concurred with them, apparently fearful of Sunnite domination in an independent, unified, Lebanon. To some extent their fears were justified; the Druze were always a minority among the Lebanese. The Maronites who numbered about eighty percent of the mountain's population would be reduced to slightly over fifty percent of a Greater Lebanon.[34]

In all, three delegations would be sent to Paris from Lebanon to exhort Lebanese independence from Syria, to reconstitute Lebanon's historic borders, and to seek French protection and assistance in modernizing their country.

The first delegation representing the CAC arrived in Versailles, and quickly departed for Paris (January, 1919) with its program for Lebanese independence. It consisted of six members of the CAC:[35] Da'ud 'Ammun (Maronite), Mahmud Junblat (Druze), Abd Allah Khouri Sa'adeh (Greek Orthodox), Ibrahim Abu Khatir and Abd al-Halim Hajjar. (Mahmud Junblat was replaced by Najib Abd al-Malik.) Others joined the group in Paris including a young nationalist named Emile Edde (*Iddi*).

The delegation met with the Council of Ten at Quai d'Orsay which included Prime Minister Lloyd George, President Woodrow Wilson, Prime Minister Georges Clemenceau and the Italian and Japanese representatives. At the first meeting Shukri Ghanem and Da'ud 'Ammun presented their case for Greater Lebanon along its former borders and the territories once ruled by Lebanese amirs. But the French drew the borders coterminous with an ancient map of Phoenicia, and that apparently satisfied the Lebanese delegation's wishes. (This idea was later propagated and popularized in Lebanon by Charles Qurm (Corm), a Lebanese author and intellectual who stressed the Phoenician origins of the Lebanese people.)

On May 20, 1919, the CAC declared Lebanese independence and its support for Greater Lebanon,[36] along the proposed "Phoenician" borders. This declaration prompted a second mission to Paris, this one led by Maronite Patriarch Ilias Butrus Huwayyik,[37] Shukrallah Khoury, Ignatius Mubarak, Butrus Faghali, Cyril Mughabghah, Theoduthius Ma'luf, and Leon Huwayyik. (All of them clergymen except for Leon Huwayyik.)

Approximately five months later, on October 27, 1919, the patriarch gave an energetic and detailed speech and memo to the conference leadership calling for the unity and independence of Lebanon within its historic boundaries and "natural" frontiers,[38] in the name of the CAC and, later, the patriarch departed for his homeland. In response to the cleric's speech and memo, Georges Clemenceau issued an "understanding" to the patriarch on November 10, 1919 detailing the autonomy of the Lebanese province along its enlarged (Phoenician) borders;[39] and in keeping with French traditions, he supported the independence of Lebanon from all "political parties and groups," except France!

The last delegation, led by Bishop Abd Allah Khuri, representing the CAC was dispatched to Paris in February of 1920 and it spoke with a unified voice on the independence of Lebanon along its historic frontiers, while only accepting French "assistance and collaboration."[40] (This was the last mission that represented all the sects: Alfred Musa Sursuq (Orthodox), Ahmad Bey al-Asa'd (Shi'ite), Amir Tawfiq Arslan (Druze), Shaykh Yusuf Gemayel amd Emile Edde (Maronites.)

Despite the unified effort of the CAC, there was still some opposition to the Mandate authorities. On July 10, 1920, in a final effort to gain Syrian assistance and backing for a Greater Syria, seven members of the CAC attempted to go to Damascus to request Syrian intervention. The French forces quickly arrested them and exiled them to Paris. The seven influential members were: Sa'ad Allah Huwayyik, Sulayman Kan'an, Fuad Abd al-Malik, Khalil 'Aql, Mahmud Junblat, Ilias Shuwayri and Muhammad Muhsin.[41] In Paris, their efforts were unsuccessful.

The Mandate for Lebanon was a done deal; during the war, the British and French had proposed and signed the Sykes-Picot Agreement (May 16, 1916). The secret agreement established the primacy of the two European-Powers in the former possessions of the Ottoman Empire. The text, negotiated by Sir Mark Sykes and Mr. Georges Picot on behalf of their governments, led to the convening of the San Remo Conference (April, 1920) which confirmed Britain and France as the only "rightful" heirs to Ottoman Near East. (Syrian resistance was crushed on July 24, 1920 at the battle of Maysalun, thus ending any serious armed resistance to French plans.) In August of 1920, Turkey signed the Treaty of Sevres renouncing the Ottoman Empire's former rights to the Arab lands; this was reconfirmed in the Treaty of Lausanne (July, 1923).

On July 24, 1922, the Mandate[42] was signed in London officially placing Lebanon and Syria in the care of France, under the auspices of the League of Nations, and the supervision of the Permanent Mandates Commission.

The Mandate system, it has been said, owes its origins to an initiative by General Jan Christian Smuts of South Africa, and President Woodrow Wilson's Fourteen Points.[43] The United States, although only an indirect party to the agreement, sought to secure the self-determination of the people of Lebanon and Syria, and continually supported their quest for independence throughout the Mandate period.[44]

The Class-A Mandate signified an advanced area to be guided towards independence, but no specific time or procedure was given to establish or achieve that goal. The European Powers considered the Mandate system a "noble" act on behalf of the British and French. The Lebanese considered the Mandate to be just another temporary arrangement, short of full independence, but useful in modernizing the state. The Mandate abolished all previous capitulations, established both Arabic and French as the official languages, public instruction was to be given in Arabic, and control over missionary activity was to be regulated by the mandatory power. In all, the twenty articles in the text of the Mandate would govern Lebanon's domestic and foreign policy in accordance with French imperialistic and international designs but, also, it did provide for Lebanese independence from Syria, and granted freedom of religion and conscience to all. And, thus a degree of autonomy and democracy was preserved.

The Mandate was, no doubt, comprehensive in its details and designs to modernize the infrastructure of a future independent state. But the French government intended to remain in Lebanon and Syria indefinitely, hoping to incorporate them as colonies of the French Empire, and especially to prevent Great Britain from gaining influence in any abandoned French territories. But, true to the Mandate's inspiration for modernization, an extremely ambitious policy and program, with strong French overtones, was imprinted upon both countries. Virtually every area of modern life was touched upon; but no training for independent self-rule was manifested. The Mandate's reforms, however, were extensive[45] and beneficial to the future of both Lebanon and Syria. Modern twentieth century administrations and states would rise from the debris of the former Ottoman provinces.

In the interim period between the Paris Peace Conference and the arrival of the first High Commissioner, several administrators set the stage in motion for

French rule: Colonel de Piepape (Chief Administrator of the War-time French Zone); Francois Georges-Picot (former French consul in Beirut); and Robert Coulondre (French Deputy).[46] These men were later replaced during the Mandate by French governors appointed by the High Commissioner: they were Captain Georges Trabaud (1920-1923), A. Privat-Aubonard (1923-1924), General Vandenberg (1924-1925), and Leon Cayla (1925-1926).[47] Despite their best efforts to rule in the name of the Permanent Mandates Commission, real power resided in the hands of the French High Commissioners.

The French High Commissioners were men of great ambition, and capable administrators who despite their best efforts to contain, control, or impede any form of Lebanese nationalism actually encouraged it, through their attitudes and activities. Those Commissioners General Henri Gouraud (1919-1923), General Maxime Waygand (1923-1924), General Maurice Sarrail (1925), Henri de Jouvenel (1925-1926), Henri Ponsat (1926-1933), Count Damien de Martel (1933-1938), General Gabriel Puaux (1938-1940), General Henri Dentz (1940-recalled 1943), and Delegate-General Georges Catroux and Jean Helleu , had the best interests of France at heart, but they were also doing what they thought was best for Lebanon.

However, these men failed to understand the dynamics of the situation they faced; thus, they ruled Lebanon as if it was a backwater colony in the French Empire. They acted in a paternalistic manner with a highly sophisticated Lebanese leadership that clearly resented that attitude. Furthermore, there were no set rules of engagement to put limits on the application of the High Commissioner's power. In fact, only the High Commissioner's personality and character governed his day to day activities and attitudes towards the Lebanese officials. The entire period may be characterized as one in which control was directed through colonial administrators witnessing a decline in Lebanese autonomy.[48]

The first three High Commissioners were military men who ruled Lebanon as a colony in military style, as if it remained a military encampment of sorts.[49] No doubt, their loyalties were first and foremost to France; they helped, nevertheless, to advance Lebanese independence.

General Henri Gouraud assumed authority in Beirut on April 31, 1920, and carried out his duties as exemplified in a speech before a host of Lebanese dignitaries proclaiming the establishment of Greater Lebanon on either August 31, 1920 or September 1, 1920 along its historic boundaries.[50] The Maronites, above all, welcomed Gouraud's initiative while the others acquiesced to the reality of French rule. A small minority among the Shi'ites in al-Biqa' led by Mulhim Qasim and, later, several Druze from al-Shuf under Sultan al-Atrash revolted against French authority.[51] Although both attempts represented Lebanese nationalism, they proved to be inconsequential and, consequently, premature and unsuccessful.

The CAC was quickly dissolved and a new Representative Council (RC) took its place on March 8, 1922 with 30 elected delegates representing a new distribution of sectarian power along the same confessional lines: 10 Maronites, 4 Greek Orthodox, 2 Druze, 6 Sunnites, 5 Shi'ites, and 3 minority.[52] The allocation of delegates to the RC was based upon an imperfect or approximate census[53] or count that showed the population to be composed of 330,000 Christians; 275,000 Moslems; 43,000 Druze, and 3,500 Jews. The president of the RC was Habib Pasha al-Sa'd; the council sat for three years, until 1925, and then it was reelected.[54] It served to adopt Lebanon's first constitution (1925).

While the issue of Greater Lebanon was at least temporarily resolved, the focus of the French High Commissioner centered upon what kind of government would be established in Lebanon. The French wanted a modern secular state that they could deal with, but they soon found themselves enmeshed in the problem of the Confessional System. Thus, they combined the old and the new to create the "Lebanese Formula." Religious representation would be carried over into a new structure for the future. Gradually, a tradition evolved whereby the president would be chosen from the Maronite Christians, the prime minister would be selected from the Sunnite Moslems, the chairman of the chamber of deputies (the parliament which had evolved from the CAC and the RC) would be designated from the Shi'ite community and the Chief-of-Staff or Minister of Defense would be drawn from the Druze sect. All this to continue a policy of sectarian co-operation, prevent the neglect, marginalization, or victimization of any sect at the hands of the others, and because of a basic lack of trust that prevails among the communities.

This arrangement, however, had additional precedents. In the 1920s and early 1930s, the Lebanese press, in some of its editorials, and several featured articles in some journals, debated the distribution of power along religious grounds.[55] In Islam there is no separation between church and state, thus a problem arose. If the Lebanese presidency were assigned to a Moslem sect, the president would be obligated, as a matter of faith and conscience, to try to initiate an Islamic administration that would be under only Islamic Law. The Christians could find themselves outside the ideology of the state, perhaps even seen as disloyal to it; and the law could discriminate against them. Eventually they may be removed from all meaningful political posts. Also, ideological and theological problems occurred over which Moslem sect would predominate, while the others would feel legally persecuted under a legal system that was not of their own sect or under their own leadership.

Consequently, a convenient ploy was proposed and employed to put the presidency in the hands of the Christians, so that a more of less secular state could emerge under secular law. (Only personal, family, law was relegated to each sect's religious prerogatives.) The 1932 census showing the Maronites as the largest single community became the ideal rationale for a Christian presidency, thereby safeguarding the population from possible religious persecution. (The census of January 31, 1932 showed the population to consist of: 178,100 Sunnite Moslems; 155,038 Shi'ite Moslems; 53,334 Druze; 227,800 Maronites; 46,709 Greek Catholics; 77,312 Greek Orthodox; 31,992 Armenians; 3,558 Jews and 4,256 Protestants.) A Maronite Catholic presidency would certainly suit France's future plans for Lebanon; and it certainly sat well with the Maronites. A crisis in government was thereby averted; no future census would ever be taken, or even called for within Lebanon. The Lebanese Christian presidency sent a message to the neighboring states saying that Lebanon was Arab but also different from the other Moslem states.

The provisional Lebanese Constitution does not designate the religion of the president, nor did the official constitution of 1926 or any of its various revisions indicate a sect of choice for the presidency.[56] Thus, the Lebanese Constitution acted as the benchmark for the evolution of national democratic thought and a democratic form of government along the lines of the French Constitution.[57] (The Lebanese Constitution was a remarkable document but it was suspended twice, once in 1932 when a Sunnite Moslem from Tripoli, Muhammad al-Jisr (a former President of the Senate and a Parliamentary deputy (1926-1932), ran for President, and again in 1939 over the independence of Lebanon.)

The Lebanese Constitution was the brainchild of Michel Chiha, a Greek Orthodox banker and intellectual from Beirut, who served as the secretary of the drafting committee. He insisted that the constitution represent all Lebanese citizens as equals before the law, with freedom of worship, speech, press, assembly, and education so that they all could achieve public office and political prestige.[58] Chiha pleaded and argued for a secular constitution with a genuinely democratic form of government with provisions for a modern parliamentary system. Henri de Jouvenel, the first civilian High Commissioner lent his support to the drafting committee.

A two chamber (*bi-cameral*) parliament was inaugurated but, later, the Senate Chamber was eliminated in October of 1927, leaving only one chamber composed of the RC members which in fact became the Lebanese Parliament or Chamber of Deputies consisting of thirty representatives.[59] Thus a constitutional republic was born.

The Lebanese Constitution was originally drawn up in Paris by a French committee that consulted with the Lebanese legislators;[60] it was then promulgated in Beirut. The document did not satisfy all the Lebanese but, in reality, it was the best they could get and a step in the right direction. All the Heads of State under the Mandate supported the constitution with some reservations: Charles Dabbas (Greek Orthodox, May 26, 1926-May 10, 1934); Habib Pasha al-Sa'd (Maronite, January 30, 1934-January 30, 1936); Emile Edde (Iddi) (Maronite, January 20, 1936-September 21, 1939 and September 21, 1939-April 9, 1941); Alfred Naccache (Maronite, April 9, 1941-December 1, 1943); Ayoub Tabet (Protestant, March 19-July 21, 1943); Petro Trad (Greek Orthodox, July 21-September 21, 1943. Almost all of them objected to the non-Lebanese origin of the document, and that it was presented to them in an almost final draft. The French, however, saw themselves as only in an advisory capacity implying that the RC was the constitution's true author.[61] In either case, dissatisfaction with the constitution revolved around two critical issues.

The first issue which infuriated the Maronite Christians concerned the appointment of French advisors to government offices thereby exercising control over the Lebanese decision makers.[62] (Later on, the offensive articles that authorized those officials were removed or eliminated.) The second issue surfaced when some Sunnite Moslem leaders saw a plot in the constitution's reference to the inability of the state to be ceded or to alienate any part of its territory to another entity or state meaning Syria.[63] Later, the Greek Orthodox and Druze communities also objected to the overwhelming French presence under the constitution. These objections led to the rise of special conferences, opposition leaders and modern parties.

Maronite opposition to the Mandate coalesced around the office of the Patriarch Antun (*Antoine/Anthony*) 'Aridha (1932-1955) who saw the constitution as prolonging the Mandate, rather than a step towards independence.[64] For the patriarch and the Maronite community, the Mandate was just another temporary arrangement, but now it had taken a degree of permanence. By 1936, the patriarch had won the support of several influential Moslem leaders when he called for full independence and sided with strikers against a tobacco monopoly.[65] In his book entitled: *Lebanon and France*, the patriarch demanded the establishment and preservation of Lebanese independence and an end to France's "perpetual tutelage."[66]

The Lebanese political elite also held divergent views on the French Mandate. Two political poles emerged and led to the rise of political parties centered around two influential candidates for the presidency: Emile Edde and Bishara al-Khuri. Emile Edde held traditional Maronite Christian perspectives that Lebanon was an indigenous Christian Arab homeland, free and independent of Syria.[67] He formed the National Bloc party. Edde's opposition was led by Shaykh Bishara al-Khuri whose Constitutional Bloc party tried to reach an accord with Lebanon's Arab Nationalists and Moslem parties. For Khuri, Moslem-Christian co-operation would protect Lebanese and Christian interests; he called for an effective partnership among the Lebanese.[68] The continuous rivalry and ambitions of those two men provoked an alternate method[69] to achieve and protect Lebanese national independence. A pan-Christian, but primarily Maronite, political party with an armed militia appeared in 1936; led by Shaykh Pierre Gemayel (Jumayyil), the Phalangist (*al-Kata'ib*) Party took a strong stance in support of secular Christian-Moslem equality in an independent Arab Christian state. That action led to the rise of another paramilitary organization called the Najjada (Moslem Scouts/Succor) to preserve and protect Moslem power in Lebanon, within an Arab Nationalist framework. The leader of Najjada was the famous Druze intellectual and scholar Shaykh Kemal Junblat.[70] Junblat, however, did not speak for the whole Druze community; His opposition among his own sect was based upon clan loyalties and identities, his foreign origins, and his personality. His nemesis was the renowned and ambitious diplomat and writer on behalf of Arab Nationalism and Islamic revivalism against all western encroachments on Lebanon and the Moslem lands, Amir Shakib Arslan of the Shuf region.[71] Hence, the Druze clans were divided as were the Greek Orthodox community. Without a foreign sponsor or support, the Orthodox split into two factions, the pro-Arab group in the Kura district of north Lebanon, and the pro-independence faction in the capital. This schism could also be found among the Sunnite leadership. The Sunnite Moslems split along similar lines between the Tripoli leadership under Shaykh Abd al-Hamid Karami and Dr. Abd al-Latif Bissar who proposed the attachment of Beirut, Sidon, and Tripoli to Syria, for both economic and political reasons, at the first Conference of The Coast (November, 1933);[72] while the Beirut leaders of the Sunnite community under Riad al-Sulh pointed out that the Lebanese Sunnites would eventually lose power and prestige in Syria, "becoming a very small cog in a very large Syrian wheel."[73] A second Conference of The Coast held in the home of Salim Salam on March 10, 1936, three years later, reaffirmed the previous notions;[74] but the second conference was also supported by members of the Syrian Nationalist Party, founded by Antun Sa'ada, which continued to interfere in Lebanese affairs,[75] consequently resulting in a localized clash between the Phalangist and the Najjada. A final Conference of The Coast took place in October of 1936; it was divided along its former lines. (At this important juncture, there was no true Lebanese consensus. At these meetings and after them, the Sunnite factions remained divided between Abd al-Hamid Karami in Tripoli and Muhammad al-Jisr in the capital; the Druze were factious between the Arslans and the Junblats; the Shi'ites remained cautiously split among pro-Syrians in the Biqa' and pro-Lebanese nationalists in south Lebanon.) These events took place in the same year that the Franco-Lebanese Treaty was signed implying the independence of Lebanon.

The Franco-Lebanese Treaty was modeled on the Anglo-Iraqi Treaty; and it was demanded by all Lebanese nationalists when the Franco-Syrian Treaty (September 9, 1936) was successfully completed and signed.[76] The Franco-Lebanese Treaty was negotiated in Beirut and signed on November 13, 1936 granting independence and recognizing Lebanese sovereignty.[77] The treaty was welcomed by the Maronites and their supporters for it confirmed the total independence of Lebanon from Syria; but it seemed to be a blow to the pro-Syrian faction;[78] it resulted in some further clashes that proved to be insignificant. More importantly, neither the Franco-Syrian nor the Franco-Lebanese treaties were ratified by the French Chamber of Deputies resulting in a hostile turn of events. The Lebanese nationalists felt a slap in the face or loss of dignity by the French chamber's lack of activity on their behalf. Opposition to the French Mandate found supporters among all sects and communities; as opposition intensified, conditions in Europe would play into the hands of the Lebanese nationalists.

As aversion to the French Mandate increased, High Commissioner Gabriel Puaux acted quickly to proclaim martial law, suspending the constitution, limiting presidential powers, and dissolving the Chamber of Deputies, in September of 1939.[79] These actions infuriated the Lebanese but, in fact, they did not last long. In the summer of 1940, the Nazi war machine occupied France and that would ultimately change conditions in the Levant. Puaux recognized the Vichy government in France and, in December of 1940, he was replaced by

General Henri Dentz; and, shortly afterwards, President Edde was replaced by Alfred Naqqash (November 1941-March 1943), assisted by Ahmad Da'uq.[80]

General Charles De Gaulle, leader of the Free French forces, became alarmed by this turn of events and with the assistance of British forces liberated the Levant in June of 1941, expelling the pro-Axis government there. Syria and Lebanon thus came under the British Middle East Command, and aid was channeled to Lebanon through the Anglo American Middle East Supply Company operating out of Egypt. This event also signaled the intensification of Anglo French rivalry in Lebanon and Syria, between 1940-1948. De Gaulle wanted to reestablish French primacy in the Near East, and thwart any British efforts to fill any gaps made by the departure of the Vichy Administration, or the rise of Lebanese independence. No doubt, the British tried to exploit the situation in their favor, by supporting Lebanese independence.[81]

The United States supported Lebanese independence and encouraged Great Britain and France to issue a statement to that effect. To that end, Great Britain declared its intent when Mr. Oliver Lyttelton, the British Minister of State in the Middle East, confirmed the position that Britain had no interest in Lebanon and Syria in August of 1941,[82] thus freeing France to act. On November 26, 1941, General De Gaulle appointed General Georges Catroux as Delegate General of Lebanon. He immediately proclaimed, in the name of the Free French, the independence of Lebanon.[83] The British Ambassador to Cairo, Sir Miles Lampson, supported the proclamation,[84] by stating that England had no interest in French prerogatives in the Levant. But, France did not believe the British; it acted out of its own concerns to placate the Lebanese nationalists. General De Gaulle issued a proclamation of Lebanese independence which sounded the death or end of the Mandate system on November 26, 1941, but the French tried to hold out a bit longer. Nothing much changed within Lebanon; however, the Lebanese leaders took the French declarations very seriously.

In September of 1943, the reestablished Chamber of Deputies, with a reintroduced Constitution, elected two pro-independence Arab nationalists to lead Lebanon. Bishara al-Khuri became the President and Riyad al-Sulh was his Prime Minister. The two leaders immediately demanded the dignity of independence that was promised earlier but never implemented. When no response came from the Delegate General, President Khuri called upon al-Sulh to form a new cabinet representing the six major sects to revise the constitution repealing all articles concerning the Mandate and French control over Lebanon.[85] This action defied the French authorities and brought matters to a head.

On November 8, 1943, the chamber deleted all words referring to the Mandate and modified the document with the unanimous vote of its forty-eight members. The following day the reforms were introduced to the public in the Lebanese press and demonstrations began in the streets of the capital.

The French had no choice but to act swiftly through the Delegate General's Office. The constitution was suspended and the president, prime minister, and most of the cabinet were arrested and sent into prison in the Castle of Rashayya (wadi al-Taym district). Two ministers, Habib Abu Shahla and Majid Arslan, escaped arrest and continued the revolt as the legal government (acting president and prime minister) from Bshamun (Bishamun),[86] in the Shuf district. When the parliament was dissolved the Lebanese took to the streets and called for a general strike. Both the Phalangist and the Najjada joined forces to rally the people against the foreign forces (French Marines and Senegalese auxiliary troops),[87] while Maronite Patriarch Aridha led some of the demonstrations. In Beirut, a new government was imposed on Lebanon with the appointment of Emile Edde as president; but it collapsed quickly when he received no support,[88] and Great Britain and the United States supported the exiled and imprisoned nationalists, calling on France to change its views and acquiesce to the reality of the situation. After eleven days of unrelenting crisis, on November 22, 1943, President Khuri, Prime Minister al-Sulh, and the cabinet were released from prison.

While in prison, in the dark and dank cell they occupied, the president and prime minister sought to strengthen Lebanese independence by a compromise pact to deal with the thorny problem of Lebanese ties with Syria and with France, and, more importantly, with the Arab World and Europe. The result of their conversations was the unwritten covenant called the National Pact (al-mithaq al-watani) which protects Lebanese national identity for both the Moslems and Christians; it was an attempt to unify the sects or communities against outside interference. The National Pact was deemed by its founders as a pledge to "build a new nation" but, in effect, it only "immobilized" confessional feelings and loyalties rather than encouraging mutual consent and national thought to create a truly new "social contract."[89] In effect, each side nullified the other, to produce a balance of power that, in many ways, did reduce tensions between the Christians and Moslems.

The details of the National Pact included a form of strict neutrality in foreign affairs involving the Arab-Moslem World and Christian Europe;[90] the Moslem leaders would be loyal to Lebanon with its Christian Head-of-State, and the Christians would respect, support and adopt Lebanon's Arabism; Lebanese sovereignty would be accepted by all. Thus, Lebanon would reject foreign protection and have an Arab face and identity with a special Christian character. The Pact was unanimously accepted and supported by all factions at that time. It was a gentleman's agreement meant to ease sectarian tensions and strengthen allegiance to the state.

By the end of 1944, the Lebanese government assumed all the powers of state and on January 19, 1946 Hamid Frangie demanded the withdrawal of all foreign forces from Lebanese soil,[91] to end the presence of the troupes speciales. Those troops who chose to remain became the nucleus of the new Lebanese Army under Colonel Fuad Shihab.[92] The evacuation of Lebanon was completed by December of 1946. Lebanon achieved full independence!

During the Mandate period, Lebanon and its people underwent a great deal of stress and strain. The birth of an independent Lebanon was by no means an easy task. And, the Lebanese themselves contributed to the difficulties and confusion as much as the French and the international community.

One of the main problems was to determine the borders of Lebanon and this was finally settled when the French drew the borders co-terminus with ancient Phoenicia. Thus, to some, the Phoenician origins of the Lebanese would be recognized but to others it would become an issue. Lebanon has been overrun and conquered by a host of invaders; however, at no time was the population carried off into exile, or evicted, or dispersed among others or massacred out of existence. To a great extent, it is true that the Lebanese of today are the descendants of the ancient Phoenicians, just as the Copts of Egypt are deemed the descendants of Pharonic civilization. But, the Lebanese people also intermarried with Crusaders from the West and Arabs from the East. Thus, today, Lebanon's people are the bearers of several great civilizations and contributors to many more.

As far as the pro-Syrian Sunnites of Lebanon are concerned the Idea of a Greater Syria incorporating Lebanon, Jordan and Palestine reflects the great heritage of the Syrian (Umayyad) Empire which ruled parts of Lebanon for about one hundred years, far less than many other conquerors of Lebanon. But, the Syrian nationalists have remained strong in the area, and have acted as a counterbalance to pro-western French feelings. However, the quest for unity with Syria was never unanimous among the Sunnites. Almost all the Lebanese sects were represented in the call for independence throughout the Mandate period, especially the heterodox Moslem groups. For all the Lebanese communities, the Mandate over their homeland was another temporary acquiescence, to be eliminated as soon as possible. Nevertheless, it is true that the Maronites were not as hostile to French rule or culture as were some Orthodox Christians and some of the Sunnite Moslems. This was so because the Maronites believed that the fastest road to modernization was cooperation with the French and the assimilation of some western and French culture and ideas, particularly in the field of science, education and the arts. Despite this sincere admiration of French civilization, most of the Maronites remained champions of Arab civilization and Lebanese culture; they remained in the forefront of the battle for Lebanese independence.

The ethnic and religious (*sectarian*) diversity manifested in Lebanese politics, culture and civilization has led some people within Lebanon and in the western world to question the existence of Lebanon as a political entity, meaning a unified nation-state. For the most part, these scholars refer to Lebanon as an "artificial state."[93] This raises the issue of what constitutes a non-artificial state, or an authentic one? Apparently, these scholars believe that an authentic state must meet certain criteria: a long ancient history, a single dominant religion, and one ethnic identification, perhaps calling to mind Arabia or Japan. These criteria would certainly invalidate Lebanon's right to exist. (In their view even the United States would have no right to exist, for they see it as a "political orphanage", the unwanted, throw away, people from around the world, with no common ties or origins, forming a political state or entity.)

Perhaps the incorporation of Lebanon into Syria was meant to "authenticate" the identity of the residents of Lebanon, eliminating any independent Lebanese identity.

Lebanon, like the United States and many other nation-states world wide, is more than a disconnected assortment of transplanted or indigenous people. The diversity within a nation does not nullify its national existence but, rather, acts to strengthen a people and make them into a nation with a composite culture and a common ideological belief system. It is the belief system in this case that created loyalty, not the accident of one's birth. In Lebanon, a nation composed of several religions minorities and cultures, the mechanisms that led to independence was the belief system of the people in cooperating for the security and prosperity of all, on the basis of consensus. The Confessional System, the Lebanese Formula, and the National Pact were devised to enhance consensus and cooperation among Lebanon's diverse communal groups and sects to bring them together despite their fears and numerical weakness. For a long time, Confessional politics, the Lebanese Formula, and the National Pact worked well as the Lebanese belief-system, but not without some tension and opposition from some groups and individuals who no longer believe in them.

1. George Haddad, *Fifty Years of Modern Syria and Lebanon*, Beirut: Dar al-Hayat, 1950, p. 46.

2. Antun Yamin, *Lubnan fi al-Harb, 1914-1919*, Beirut, 1919, pp. 17-18.

3. Yamin, *Lubnan fi al-Harb*, pp. 17-18.

4. Yamin, *Lubnan fi al-Harb*, p. 19.

5. Najib Dahdah, *Evolution Historique Du Liban*, 3rd. ed., Beirut, 1967, p. 226; Khatir, *Ahd al-Mutasarrifin*, p. 198; S. H. Longrigg, *Syria and Lebanon Under French Mandate*, London, 1958, p. 48; Hitti, *Lebanon in History*, p. 483.

6. Longrigg, *Syria and Lebanon*, p. 48; Haddad, *Fifty Years of Modern Syria and Lebanon*, p. 47; Hitti, *Lebanon in History*, p. 483.

7. Longrigg, *Syria and Lebanon*, pp. 48-49; Hitti, *Lebanon in History*, pp. 484-485; Al-Hakim, *Beirut wa Lubnan*, pp. 249-250; Yamin, *Lubnan fi al-Harb*, pp. 122-136.

8. Yamin, *Lubnan fi al-Harb*, p. 93

9. Yamin, *Lubnan fi al-Harb*, pp. 136-137.

10. Hitti, *Lebanon in History*, pp. 483-484; Donald J. Cioeta, "Ottoman Censorship in Lebanon and Syria, 1876-1908," in *IJMAS*, vol. 10, no. 2, May 1979, pp. 167-186.

11. Al-Hakim, *Beirut wa Lubnan*, pp. 234-235; Longrigg, *Syria and Lebanon*, p. 51; Yamin, *Lubnan fi al-Harb*, p. 63; Khatir, *Ahd al-Mutasarrifin*, p. 198.

12. Yamin, *Lubnan fi al-Harb*, p. 107.

13. Haddad, *Fifty Years of Modern Syria and Lebanon*, p. 48.

14. Rene Ristelhuber, "Liban, Cher Liban 1908! (Souvenirs)," *Revue D'Histoire Diplomatique*, Soixante-Quatorzieme Annee, Janvier-Mars, 1960, p. 18; Dahdah, *Evolution Historique Du Liban*, p. 226; Alfred Coury, *Le Martyre Du Liban*, Marseille, 1919, pp. 10-16.

15. Yamin, *Lubnan fi al-Harb*, pp. 64-87; James L. Gelvin, *Divided Loyalties: Nationalism and Mass Politics in Syria at the Close of Empire*, Los Angeles: University of California Press, 1998, pp. 175-178.

16. Longrigg, *Syria and Lebanon*, p. 50; Nicholas Z. Ajay Jr., "Intrigue and Suppression in Lebanon during World War I," in *IJMES*, vol. 5, no. 2, April 1974, pp. 140-160.

17. K. T. Khairallah, *Le Probleme du Levant, Les Regions Arabes Liberees*, Paris, 1919, p. 65.

18. Khairallah, *Le Probleme du Levant*, pp. 65-75.

19. See: Iskender 'Amoun, President de l'Alliance Lebanaise D'Egypt, *Memoire sur La Question Libanaise*, Cairo, January 1, 1913.

20. N. A. Mokarzel, "Les Voeux Du Liban," in *L'Asie Francaise*, Annee 18, no. 175, Fevrier-Juillet, 1919, pp. 189-190.

21. Khairallah, *Le Probleme du Levant*, p. 64; M. Jouplain, *La Question Du Liban*, Paris, 1908, pp. 570, 574, 577.

22. Chekri Ganem, *Comite Libanais De Paris, Memoire Sur La Question Du Liban*, Paris, 1912, pp. 5-17.

23. Zamir, *The Formation of Modern Lebanon*, p. 51; Khatir, *Ahd al-Mutasarrifin*, p. 206; Zeine N. Zeine, *The Struggle for Arab Independence*, Beirut, 1960, p. 37; Yamin, *Lubnan fi al-Harb*, p. 146; Salibi, *The Modern History of Lebanon,*_p. 160.

24. James J. Simon, "The Role of the Administrative Council of Mount Lebanon in The Creation of Greater Lebanon, 1918-1920," in the *Journal of Third World Studies*, vol. XIII, no. 2, Fall 1996, pp. 123-124; Salibi, *The Modern History*, pp. 160-161; Khatir, *Ahd al-Mutasarrifin*, p. 209.

25. Meo, *Lebanon, Improbable Nation*, pp. 47-49; Zamir, *The Formation of Modern Lebanon*, pp. 67, 84.

26. Simon, *"The Role of the Administrative Council of Mount Lebanon,"* p. 121; Zeine N. Zeine, *The Struggle for Arab Independence*, Beirut: Khayat Pub., 1960, pp. 35-37.

27. Haddad, *Fifty Years of Modern Syria*, P. 61; Daniel Pipes, *The History of an Ambition*, New York: Oxford University Press, 1990, pp. 36-37.

28. Simon, *"The Role of the Administrative Council of Mount Lebanon,"* p.123.

29. Simon, *"The Role of the Administrative Council of Mount Lebanon,"* p. 124

30. Simon, *"The Role of the Administrative Council of Mount Lebanon,"* p.124.

31. Akarli, *The Long Peace,* p. 176; Simon, *"The Role of the Administrative Council of Mount Lebanon,"* pp. 127-128.

32. Zamir, *The Formation of Modern Lebanon,* p. 90.

33. Simon, *"The Role of the Administrative Council of Mount Lebanon,"* pp. 125-126.

34. Zamir, *The Formation of Modern Lebanon,* p. 98. Meir Zamir, *Lebanon's Quest, the Road to Statehood 1926-1939,* London: I. B. Tauris & Co., 1997, p. 247.

35. Longrigg, *Syria and Lebanon,* pp. 88-89; Nantet, *Histoire* 190 Du Liban, p. 245; Simon, *"The Role of the Administrative Council of Mount Lebanon,"* p. 129.

36. Simon, *"The Role of the Administrative Council of Mount Lebanon,"* pp. 141-142.

37. Nantet, *Histoire Du Liban,* p. 246; Longrigg, *Syria and Lebanon,* p. 88

38. Longrigg, *Syria and Lebanon,* p. 88; Ismail, *Lebanon, History of a People,* Beirut, 1972, p. 198.

39; Ismail, *Lebanon,* p. 198; P. Rondot, "Lebanese Institutions and Arab Nationalism," *Journal of Contemporary History,* vol. 3, no. 3, July 1968, p. 40; Muhammad Jamil Bayhum, *Suriyah wa Lubnan, 1918-1922,* Beirut, 1968, pp. 90-91.

40. Longrig, *Syria and Lebanon,* p. 88; Zamir, *The Formation of Modern Lebanon,* p. 78; Simon, *"The Role of the Administrative Council of Mount Lebanon,"* p. 146.

41. Simon, *"The Role of the Administrative Council of Mount Lebanon,"* p. 146.

42. For the English Text of the Mandate see: Helen Miller Davis, *Constitutions, Electoral Laws, Treaties of State in the Near and Middle East,* N.C.: Duke University Press, 1953, pp. 283-290; Jack E. Vincent, *International Relations,* vol. 2, Lanham: University Press of America, 1983, pp. 13-14.

43. Hitti, *Lebanon in History,* p. 487.

44. Walter L. Brown, (ed.), *The Political History of Lebanon, 1920-1950*, vol. I, *Documents on Politics and Political Parties Under French Mandate, 1920-1936*, N.C.: Documentary Publications, 1976; and vol. II, *Documents on French Mandate and World War II, 1936-1943*, N.C. Documentary Publications, 1977. United States Treaty Series # 695, *Convention Between The United States And France-Rights in Syria and The Lebanon* (art. 20), Signed in Paris, April 4, 1924-Washington, 1924, pp. 1-9; and *The United States-French Accord* (appended art. 1-7), pp. 10-11.

45. Haut Commissariat de la Republique Francaise en Syrie et au Liban, *Ce Que Tout Francais Doit Savoir de la Syrie et du Liban*, Paris, 1922, pp. 14-36; *La Syrie et le Liban En 1922*, Paris, 1922, pp. 65-371; Monsieur Henri Ponsot, Haut Commissaire de la Republique Francaise a son excellence Monsieur Aristide Briand, Ministere Des Affairs Etrangieres, *Rapport sur La Situation De La Syria Et Du Liban*, (1924-1931) and (1934-1936), Paris, 1925-1932, 1935-1937; France: Haut Commissariat en Syrie Et Au Liban, *Le Mandat Devant Les Faits*, Paris, 1921; J. L. Gheerbrandt, "Syria and Lebanon," *The Asiatic Review*, New Series, vol. 23, no.75, July, 1927, pp. 396-399; Rene de Feriet, *L'Application D'Un Mandat*, Deuxieme Edition, Beyrouth, 1926, pp. 93-102; *Dix Ans Du Mandat -L'Oeuvre Francaise en Syrie et au Liban*, Paris, 1931, pp. 12-63; *Quinze Ans De Mandat, L'Oeuvre Francaise En Syrie Et Au Liban*, Beirut, 1936; pp. 14-69; Raymond O'Zoux, *Les Etats Du Levant Sous Mandat Francais*, Paris, 1931, pp. 66-68, 128-193; *La Syrie et Le Liban sous l'Occupation et le Mandat Francais*, 1919-1927, Nancy, 1929, pp. 15-332; Abdallah Sfeir Pasha, "Le Mandat Francaises En Syrie Et Au Liban," *La Revue Hebdomadaire*, Tome 8, (Aug., 1922, Annee 31) and Tome 9, pp. 89-98, 223-235; Labiki, *La Fiscalite Et Le Financement De L'Habitat Au Liban*, pp. 97-101.

46. Salibi, *The Modern History*, p. 162.

47. Salibi, *The Modern History*, p. 164; Baaklini, *Legislative and Political Development*, p. 71.

48. Hitti, *Lebanon in History*, pp. 488-489.

49. Eugenie Abouchdid, *Thirty Years of Lebanon and Syria, 1917-1947*, Beirut, 1948, pp. 45-46; Edmund Burke III, "A Comparative View of French Native Policy in Morocco and Syria, 1912-1925," *Middle East Studies*, vol. 9, no. 2, May, 1973, pp. 175-181.

50 Bayhum, *Suriyah wa Lubnan*, p. 92; Charles Burckhard, *Le Mandat Francais En Syrie Et Au Liban*, Nimes, 1925, pp. 86-97; Nicola A. Ziadeh, *Syria andLebanon*, London: Ernest Benn Ltd., 1957, pp. 49-51; Malone, *The Arab Lands of West Asia*, pp. 13-14; Salibi, *The Modern History*, p. 164; Simon, "The

Role of The Administrative Council of Mount Lebanon," p. 150; Anis Sayigh, *Lubnan al-Ta'ifi*, Beirut, 1965, p. 143; Meo, *Lebanon, Improbable Nation*, p. 47.

51. Sayigh, *Lubnan al-Ta'ifi*, pp. 144-145; Ismail, *Lebanon, History of a People*, p. 205.

52. Akarli, *The Long Peace*, p. 179; Salibi, *The Modern History*, p. 165; Burckhard, *Le Mandat Francais*, p. 100; Jean Donon, "L'Organisation De La Federation Des Etats De Syrie Et Du Grand Liban Sous Le Mandat Francais," *Revue Des Sciences Politiques*, vol. 47, Paris, 1924, p. 356; Rene de Feriet, *L'Application D'Un Mandat*, Deuxieme Edition, Beyrouth, 1926, pp. 19, 74; Haddad, Fifty Years of Modern Syria and Lebanon, p. 71. The only accurate census was taken in 1932, it showed: 178,100 Sunnites; 155,038 Shi'ites; 53,334 Druze; 227,800 Maronites; 46,709 Greek Catholics; 77,312 Greek Orthodox; 31,992 Armenians; 3,558 Jews; 4,256 Protestants. (Data taken from John Morgan Jones, *La Fin Du Mandat Francais En Syrie Et Au Liban*, Paris, 1938, p. 3.)

53. Longrigg, *Syria and Lebanon*, p. 127.

54. Baaklini, *Legislative and Political Development*, p. 62.

55. A. J. Abraham, *Lebanon: A State of Siege (1975-1984)*, IN.: Wyndham Hall Press, 1984, PP. 10-12; A. J. Abraham, *The Lebanon War*, Conn.: Praeger, 1996, p. XVI.

56. See: Davis, *Constitutions, Electoral Laws*, pp. 291-305; Baaklini, *Legislative and Political Development*, pp. 62-71.

57. Seifeddine Maamoun, *Le Pouvoir Executif en Droit Constitutionel Libanais et Syrien*, Lyon, 1930, p. 91.

58. Beirut College for Women, *Cultural Resources in Lebanon*, Beirut, 1969, pp. 75-76; Salibi, *The Modern History of Lebanon*, p. 167; Zamir, *The Formation of Modern Lebanon*, p. 125.

59. Ismail, *Lebanon, History of a People*, pp. 206-207; Nantet, *Histoire Du Liban*, p. 258; Haddad, *Fifty Years of Modern Syria and Lebanon*, p. 78.-60. Ziadeh, *Syria and Lebanon*, p. 51; Beirut College For Women, *Cultural Resources in Lebanon*, p. 78; Haddad, *Fifty Years of Modern Syria and Lebanon*, p. 78.

61. Louis Jalabert, *Syrie Et Liban, Reussite Francaise?* Paris, 1934, p. 31.

62. Salibi, *The Modern History,* pp. 167-168.

63. Elizabeth P. Mac Callum, *The Nationalist Crusade in Syria,* p. 191.

64. Longrigg, *Syria and Lebanon,* p. 206; Ziadeh, *Syria and Lebanon,* pp. 58-59.

65. Longrigg, *Syria and Lebanon,* p. 206; Zamir, *Lebanon's Quest,* pp. 166, 171.

66. Dahdah, *Evolution Historique,* p. 251.

67. Malone, *The Arab Lands,* pp. 17-19; Zamir, *The Formation of Modern Lebanon,* pp. 126-127; Salibi, *The Modern History,* pp. 171-173.

68. Salibi, *The Modern History,* pp. 172-173; Zamir, *The Formation of Modern Lebanon,* p. 126; Malone, *The Arab Lands,* p. 17.

69. Longrigg, *Syria and Lebanon,* p. 226; Nantet, *Histoire Du Liban,* pp. 226-228; Salibi, *The Modern History,* p. 181; Zamir, *Lebanon's Quest,* pp. 116-117.

70. Majid Khadduri, *Arab Contemporaries, the Role of Personalities in Politics,* Baltimore: The Johns Hopkins University Press, 1973, pp. 144-153; Longrigg, *Syria and Lebanon,* p. 226.

71. William L. Cleveland, *Islam against the West, Shakib Arslan and the Campaign for Islamic Nationalism,* Austin: University of Texas Press, 1985, pp. 4, 14-16; Zamir, *The Formation of Modern Lebanon,* p. 134.

72. Rondot, *"Lebanese Institutions and Arab Nationalism, "* pp. 45-46.

73. Zamir, *The Formation of Modern Lebanon,* p. 129-130; Abraham, *Lebanon: A State of Siege,* p. 12.

74. Salibi, *The Modern History,* p. 180; Sayigh, *Lubnan al-Ta'ifi,* p. 145; Zamir, *Lebanon's Quest,* pp. 108, 190-192.

75. Salibi, *The Modern History,* p. 180; Longrigg, *Syria and Lebanon,* p. 225.

76. Ismail, *Lebanon,* p. 210; Jean Godard, *L'Oeuvre Politique, Economigue, Et Sociale De La France Combattante En Syrie Et Au Liban,* Beyrouth, 1943, p. 20; Abouchdid, *Thirty Years of Lebanon and Syria,* pp. 52-54; Ziadeh, *Syria and Lebanon,* pp. 54-56; Salibi, *The Modern History,* p. 181; A. H.Hourani, Syria and *Lebanon, A Political Essay,* London: Oxford University Press, 1946, p. 200.

77. Ismail, *Lebanon,* p. 210; Hourani, *Syria and Lebanon,* p. 200.

78. Abouchdid, *Thirty Years of Lebanon and Syria*, p. 58; Hourani, *Syria and Lebanon*, p. 204; Sayigh, *Lubnan al-Ta'ifi*, p. 147; Handi Badawi al-Tahiri, *Siyasat al-Hukuin fi Lubnan*, Cairo; 1966, p. 120.

79. Salibi, *The Modern History*, pp. 183-184; Hitti, *Lebanon in History*, pp. 493-494; Nedko S. Etinoff, *Thirty Years in Lebanon and The Middle East*, Beirut, 1969, p. 21; Ziadeh, *Syria and Lebanon*, pp. 62-63.

80. Malone, *The Arab Lands*, pp. 17-18; Salibi, *The Modern History*, pp. 184-185.

81. Selim Deringil, *The Anglo-French Clash in Lebanon and Syria, 1940-1945*, New York: St. Martin's Press, 1987.

82. Hourani, *Syria and Lebanon*, pp. 244-245; Malone, *The Arab Lands*, pp. 17-18.

83. Hitti, *Lebanon in History*, p. 494; Salibi, *The Modern History*, pp. 185-186; Hourani, *Syria and Lebanon*, pp. 243-244; Text of Statement: Abouchdid, *Thirty Years of Lebanon and Syria*, p. 83.

84. Godard, *L'Oeuvre Politique*, pp. 32-34.

85. Haddad, *Fifty Years of Modern Syria and Lebanon*, p. 93; Jean-Pierre Alem, Le *Liban*, Paris, 1963, p. 69; Ismail, *Lebanon*, pp. 219-220; Sami al-Sulh, *Ahtakim ila al-Ta'rikh*, Beirut, 1970, p. 63; W. Spencer, *Political Evolution in The Middle East*, New York, 1962, p. 179.

86. Ziadeh, *Syria and Lebanon*, p. 77; Ismail, *Lebanon*, p. 221; Haddad, *Fifty Years of Modern Syria and Lebanon*, p. 94; Salibi, *The Modern History*, p. 190; Munir Taqi al-Din, *Wiladat Istiqlal*, Beirut: Dar al-'alm Llmalaiyn, 1953, pp. 105-135.

87. Etinoff, *Thirty Years*, p. 47; Salibi, *The Modern History*, p. 189; John P. Entelis, "Party Transformation in Lebanon: al-Kata'ib as a Case Study," *MES*, vol. 9, no. 3, Oct. 73, p. 326.

88. Ismail, *Lebanon*, p. 221.

89. Basim al-Jisir, *Ri'asah wa Siyasah wa Lubnan al-Jadid*, Beirut: Dar Maktabat al-Hayat, 1964; p. 40; 5. Khalaf, "Primordial Ties and Politics in Lebanon," *MES*, vol. 4, no. 3, April, 1986, pp. 260-261.

90. See text of the Pact in Al-Tahiri, *Siyasat al-Hukum fi Lubnan*, pp. 121-138; Fahim I. Qubain, *Crisis in Lebanon*, Maryland: The French-Bray Printing Co., D.C., 1961, pp. 17-18; Ephraim A. Frankel, "The Maronite Patriarch: An Historical View of a Religious Za'im in The 1958 Lebanese Crisis:' *The Muslim World*, vol. LXVI, no. 3, July, 1976, pp. 220-221; Beirut College for Women, *Cultural Resources*, p. 78; Albert Hourani, "Lebanon From Feudalism to Modern State," *MES*, vol. 2, no. 3, April, 1966, p. 261; P. Rondot, "Lebanese Institutions and Arab Nationalism," in the *Journal of Contemporary History*, vol. 3, no. 3, July, 1968, p. 50; Eli Kedourje, *Islam in The Modern World, and Other Studies*, New York: Holt, Rinehart and Winston, 1980, pp. 90-91.

91. Edmond Rabbath, "Constitution et independence au Liban: Un cas de genese conjointe," *Orient*, no. 47/48, (1968), p. 70; J. C. Hurewitz, "Lebanese Democracy in Its International Setting," *MEJ*, vol. 17, (1963), p. 499.

92. Salibi, *The Modern History*, p. 191.

93. Latif Abul-Husn, *The Lebanese Conflict, Looking Inward*, Boulder: Lynne-Rienner Publishers, 1998, pp. 78-79.

CHAPTER 9

INDEPENDENT LEBANON: CONFESSIONAL DEMOCRACY
AND POLITICAL TENSIONS

Lebanon's road to independence was certainly rocky; after independence, Lebanon found itself in uncertain and un-chartered territory, trying to balance itself between the old political realities and the newly inherited ones. This factor alone was responsible for the numerous tensions exhibited in the Lebanese system of Confessional Democracy. Furthermore, Lebanon appeared to be alone as the Arab World's only functional democracy of any kind.

Throughout almost thirty years of political independence, Lebanon was caught between periods of security and insecurity, a recurring aspect of the Lebanese polity. However, the state proved to be remarkably stable until the mid-seventies. The Lebanese political leaders weathered several storms, kept Lebanon on a course of economic, political and social progress, and thus represented a column of progress for the entire region.

Modern Lebanon had a lot of "baggage" that it had brought into the new political system. A "phantom feudalism"[1] persisted in the quest of the notable families (the ayan) to secure posts in the modern government for themselves and their offspring; in that, they were assisted by the local political leaders or political bosses or relatives (the Za'ims) who serve the leaders constituency,[2] and by middlemen, mediators, go betweens, or intermediaries who have the right means (connections/wasitah/wastah) in numerous circumstances.[3] If conditions warranted, the political elites could also rely upon the local strongmen (the qabadaiy/qabadaiyat) who often acted as "thugs" in the leaders' interest.

While these conditions or similar ones are not absent from other political systems or in other states, in Lebanon they became stronger in time because the Confessional System fostered factionalism, regionalism, sectarianism and parochial (city-mountain) ties in Lebanese politics.

The Confessional System was an outgrowth of the old Turkish millet system in which all communities had and needed religious identities to function and be properly represented. This idea was incorporated into the Lebanese Formula to allow all major sects a voice in the government through their sectarian leaders, so that no group or sect could dominate all the key positions or posts by virtue of education, competence, talent, threat or manipulation. In this respect, it worked well for a while; and it served to put the Christian Maronites and the Sunnite Moslems in the strongest and most powerful positions but not in total control of the state. The system was justified by an outdated census (1932) which showed the Maronites and the Sunnites as the most numerous groups. The other minorities acquiesced in this, but with some strong opposition at times, to thwart foreign interference or to try to achieve independence.

The system acted to protect Christian freedoms as well as those of the smaller Moslem sects and to stabilize the political scene and, in fact, to freeze it forever. The system reflected the fears of its supporters and opponents; it had several built-in problems.[4] It prevented the evolution of a true democracy in Lebanon so that a secular democracy was easily inhibited by the interfering religious elites and the local leadership. In order to develop a secular state, a secular thinking society is needed and Lebanon did not evolve that way. Thus, sectarian fears not only remained after independence but they intensified. (Even the nation's foreign policy was regulated to conform to the National Pact which was designed to balance Western Christian and Arab Moslem influences on the state.)

In the cities, like Beirut, sectarian rivalries were somewhat less noticeable than in the countryside which harbored and fostered its own sectarian ideologies and, thus, developed with different interests and views.[5] Clearly, Lebanon was not a totally integrated society but, rather, one that was mostly desegregated, more so in the cities than in the rural areas. Those conditions led the Lebanese politicians to speak differently to the sophisticated city dwellers and the more sectarian and religiously oriented villagers. A credibility gap has occurred; and this fostered confessional loyalties as well. The state, consequently, came under increased pressure from indigenous and foreign groups and parties.

Within the Lebanese state, there were several groups and parties that opposed the establishment, holding on to their own vision of what Lebanon should be like; they ran the entire political spectrum from "right" to "left." (Although the terms "right" and "left" do not precisely fit the ideologies of these groups, for lack of more accurate terms, they will be used to describe the full range of politics in Lebanon.)

The extreme "right" included the Syrian National Party/ Parti Populaire Syrien (*Al-Hizb al-Suri al-Qawmi al-Ijtima'i*) which called for Syrian unity that included Lebanon and Palestine; The Phalangist Party or Kataeb/Kata'ib which was originally a secularly oriented Maronite Party called for Lebanese independence and Christian prominence in the state. (It was founded by Pierre Gemayel with some strong Christian tendencies.) The Sunnite Helpers (*Najjada*) Party sought the opposite of the Kataeb, but often worked with them as well for independence, until it was eventually disbanded.

Opposing these groups were the radical "left" who objected to the sectarian nature of the Lebanese state. They were, more or less, secular in their thinking, but what they really wanted was to get into the political arena that had frozen them out, isolated them, for not having a sectarian base of support. These groups included the Communist Party or Christian Communists who mildly adhere to Marxist-Leninism, and the Moslem Marxists who reject the atheism of Communist ideology, but accept the Marxist economic ideology of the exploited masses (the Lebanese workers) by the nation's rich entrepreneurs and landlords.

The socialist parties and Arab Nationalist parties (the Arab Nationalist Movement-the ANM) fall somewhere in between the "right" and the "left." The most prominent socialist party is the Progressive Socialist Party (*Al-Hizb al-Taqaddumi al-Ishtiraki*) of Druze leader Kamal Junblat that primarily represents the Druze community; its ideology consists of a dose of European style secularism and modified socialism.[6] The party is extremely traditional and seeks to improve or enhance the status of the Druze community in Lebanese politics. All Arab Nationalist parties emphasize the unity of the Arabic speaking peoples as a single political entity or propagate the greatness of the Arab past. Among the most prominent groups are the Nassarist groups, and the Syrian Baath Party/Arab Socialist Renaissance Party (Al-Hizb al-Ba'th al-Arabi al-Ishtiraki).[7]

Of all the opposition groups, the most serious challenge to Lebanon's patchwork politics came from the numerous militant Islamic groups.[8] These organizations totally reject the legitimacy of the Lebanese state, regardless of whether it is an Arab state or not. These groups include: The Party of God (*Hizb Allah/Hizbollah*); The Islamic Group (*Al-Jama'a al-Islamiyya*); The Islamic Unification Movement (*Harakat al-Tawhid al-Islami*); the Islamic Amal (*Harakat Amal al-Islamiyya*); and the Islamic Jihad Organization (*Munazzamat al-Jihad al-Islami.*) All of these groups, the old and the newly created, adhere to the idea that Lebanon is part of the outside world to which they are irrevocably hostile, and with which no compromise can be made until Lebanon becomes Islamic in administration and under only Islamic law,[9] for it is Islamic law that determines the legitimacy of the state. (Unlike Christianity which is a pure commitment to God and Christ, Judaism is a national-legal religion and Islam is a political-legal religion.)

These and other fundamentalist groups in the "Islamic Tendency" hinder the evolution of a secular Lebanese loyalty or nationalism by obstructing it, avoiding it, diminishing it, or trying to do away with it altogether. This makes the problem of ruling Lebanon extremely difficult, for the Head of State and his government must prance around these groups and parties. Nevertheless, Lebanon remained remarkably stable until the recent conflict with only one other notable exception in 1958.

Lebanon quickly modernized its economy and social system,[10] so that it was never considered to be poverty stricken Third World nation receiving American largess. (Except in a few extraordinary instances, United States economic assistance was granted when needed.)

Lebanese nationalism is also hindered by the numerous foreign and parochial schools that vie for students alongside the national educational system. In addition, Lebanon's open intellectual atmosphere allowed for various foreign and domestic points of view to manifest themselves in the media which often criticized everything the government did. While freedom of thought and information is essential for any kind of democracy, Lebanon's system of democracy is too fragile to sustain too many attacks against its own existence, especially when they are made to advance foreign interests. The Arab World fought many of its verbal battles in Lebanon's liberal and open media while recruiting the like minded in the tiny republic to serve their interests against those of the Lebanese state.

During the period of Lebanese independence, with the notable exception of the civil war years (1975-1982), Lebanon had sought to develop its economy and social services to reach the majority of its citizens, and to avoid the neglect, marginalization, victimization, or exploitation of its citizenry, or anyone else in the work force.[11] Although statistical data remains difficult to obtain, it is quite clear that the Lebanese economy grew unevenly, and that the Maronites and Sunnites faired better than the Shi'ites and the Druze. This was obviously the result of human resource development: higher levels of education and lower birth rates among the Maronites and the Sunnites.[12]

Based upon the sketchy data available prior to the 1975 confrontation,[13] the Christian districts paid approximately 75 percent of all "legitimate" taxes collected while the Moslem districts paid about 25 percent. When the Beirut government reallocated or redistributed funds, the Moslem districts received 50-60 percent, while the Christian districts obtained 40-50 percent. In fact, in the last few decades before the 1975 conflict erupted, the Lebanese government returned approximately 60 percent of all "collected" taxes, about 30 million Lebanese pounds, to the poorer Shi'ite districts for use by the Council of The South to develop the infrastructure there, including education, housing, roads, electrification projects, water resources, medical-clinical facilities and so forth. The funds, it was said, were "squandered away" or "absorbed" by the leadership of the Shi'ite Council of The South, nicknamed or by-named the "pockets council."[14]

With "high rates of growth, little or no inflation, low unemployment...the pre 1975 private sector was a source of growth;" but, nevertheless, poverty still existed in Lebanon, however, it was far less in both percentage of the population and in intensity than in any of the surrounding Arab states, or in the non-western world.[15]

In fact, the poor in Lebanon had a higher standard of living than the middle class in many Arab and Middle Eastern states, and in Eastern Europe as well, as measured by the appliances and amenities in their homes. (Furthermore, the expansion of the tiny Beirut slum was largely the result of the on-again, off-again Arab-Israeli conflict in South Lebanon. The primarily agrarian Shi'ite southerners sought refuge in the largely commercial capital escaping from the Israeli policy of "hot pursuit," which devastated large areas of southern Lebanon. Some families were also evicted from their homes in the south by the Israeli backed South Lebanon Army for cooperating with the Shi'ite resistance. Unfortunately, the southerners were only able to obtain menial employment in the capital and this added to slum conditions.)

The above conditions, when exacerbated by foreign interest groups and other interested parties and individuals, produce a great deal of pressure on Lebanon's foreign policy. In fact, Lebanon has two simultaneous foreign policies: the foreign policy of the local communities and their sectarian leaders who pursue their own international version of what Lebanon's future should be, and the official foreign policy of the Beirut government. This situation invites foreign interference; and often the Beirut authorities can not speak for the whole nation. The fact that it is extremely difficult to be "just Lebanese," rather than a Lebanese Maronite, Sunnite, Shi'ite or Druze etc., confuses loyalties and priorities, and is often difficult to describe to outsiders, even if the foreigners have lived in other pluralistic societies and states. For in Lebanon, perhaps more than elsewhere, dual loyalties have survived and flourished as independent identities, as micro or proto nations and states, and political forces. Therefore, each community or sect has its own "hidden agenda:" They act as if they are domestic dependent micro-nations or micro-states within a larger independent political-national entity or state called Lebanon.

Within Lebanese politics, these conditions also manifest themselves in the problem of how to balance multi-culturalism, particularly in religion, with being a "secular" Lebanese first. Therefore, it is obvious that every Lebanese president since independence has had to adjust his style in office to meet and negotiate with a number of groups and individuals to accommodate the demands of the conflicting loyalties that he faces.

With these factors, situations, and conditions in mind, we can begin to chart the course of Lebanese independence. The study of Lebanese independence may best focus upon the role and tenure in office of the presidents, since they are the most authoritative and powerful figures in the bureaucracy. The system evolved that way to protect the rights of the Christians, particularly the Maronite sect, as well as the minority Moslem religious communities. The Lebanese Constitution does not specify the religion of the president of the republic. The president is, however, the symbol of the state, and a Christian presidency sends a message to the Moslem World that Lebanon is Arab, but different from its neighbors. Some Moslem groups have accepted this, others have not. All of this remains an "unofficial" position which keeps the level of tension high in Lebanon, particularly in times of crisis.

The Lebanese president has extraordinary powers; the chief executive can issue important or urgent legislation by decree; he can dissolve the parliament; and he could, until recently, appoint or name the prime minister; and, if he obtains a vote of no confidence from the cabinet, he may dismiss them. In theory, however, both the Lebanese president and the cabinet are responsible to the parliament. In reality, it is different, for a strong president can exert great influence over both the cabinet and the parliament; and, the office of the president remains the focal point around which Lebanese national politics revolves.[16]

The election of Bishara al-Khuri (1943-1952) as Lebanon's first president after independence proved to be an excellent choice; he had both the qualities of astuteness and political savvy. Educated in law in both Paris and Beirut, al-Khuri's political career began as a minister of the interior and, later, as a prime minister under the French authorities. He was a champion of Lebanese independence and founder of the Constitutional Bloc (al-Destour) against his foremost rival Emile Edde (Idde). Khouri believed in a balanced Moslem-Christian co-existence and in a Lebanon with an Arab face and heart,[17] thus achieving a strong degree of Moslem support. Khuri also utilized the Lebanese

Cabinet to bring the traditional leaders into the government, and to play them off against one another to increase his own power in office.[18] Khouri always relied upon the Moslem political leadership, particularly his Prime Minister Riyad (Riad) al-Sulh, to secure Moslem co-operation to uphold the Constitution and the National Pact. He fostered an "open" public administration to include many Sunnite and Shi'ite leaders in his regime.[19]

Apparently believing that he had popular and strong support, al-Khuri sought a second term in office, having a bill passed in parliament to secure his reelection (May 27, 1948),[20] but that turned the electorate against him. From that point on, Khouri's opposition grew to the point where he was openly criticized for nepotism, graft, favoritism, laxity in government and executive justice, and outright corruption.[21] By 1952, a vociferous and prolonged public outcry produced strikes and several demonstrations in the major cities and quickly spread to towns and even the villages;[22] the prime minister resigned[23] and no one would take his place; calls for Khouri's resignation filled the air as Cabinet ministers defected. The army refused to act on the president's behalf when he called on it to squelch the demonstrations,[24] thus, under duress Bishara al-Khuri was forced to resign on September 18, 1952.

Although seen as extremely ambitious, and accused of excessive political clientage, the most dangerous charge Khuri faced was parliamentary "fraud" to secure his second term in office. In defense of his presidency, Khuri wrote a detailed memoirs *Haqa'iq Lubnaniyya (Lebanese Truths/Realities),* 1961, while in retirement, but his public career was never resurrected. To his great credit, he is still remembered as the president who defended Lebanese independence, the constitutional system, and made the political transition to independence and sovereignty succeed.

On September 23, 1952, five days after Bishara al-Khuri resigned, the Lebanese Parliament elected Camille Chamoun (*Kamil Sham'un*), a Maronite lawyer who had been finance and interior minister in earlier cabinets, as the next president. Camille Chamoun had been a prominent member of the Constitutional Bloc; and along with Kamal Junblat, and other Sunnite and Shi'ite leaders, he was an opponent of al-Khuri. Chamoun had assumed the leadership role against the former incumbent.

Camille Chamoun had distinguished himself in his early career when he became Lebanon's first ambassador to Britain (minister to the Court of St. James, 1944) and as leader or head of the Lebanese delegation to the United Nations (1946). While in England and the United States, Camille Chamoun developed an interest and fondness for political, economic and social liberalism, specifically in the media. Eventually, after his presidential career ended, he would form Lebanon's National Liberal Party (*Hizb al-Wataniyy al-Ahrar/ al-Ahrar*) to continue to propagate his views. He was always anti-French and pro-British, and a powerful supporter of independent action, particularly as president (1952-1958). Consequently, he ran afoul his Cabinet Ministers and, quite often, his Prime Minister and other influential political and religious elites. Chamoun's troubles began when he sought a second term in office and when the National Pact's strict neutrality was violated or breached.

The president believed that he had a good chance to be reelected. His administration was exceedingly popular at first:[25] he favored freedom of the press; he reorganized and improved government departments and even tried to introduce electoral reform by reapportioning the Chamber of Deputies (the Parliament) and the electoral districts; and Chamoun supported and granted women the right to vote.

The president's liberal economic policies fostered new employment through a "trickle-down" process, and during Chamoun's term in office unemployment reached an all time low. He supported a Bank Secrecy Law; he abolished rent codes to stimulate the growing construction industry, and Chamoun favored both tradesmen and the nacient unions.[26]

Chamoun chose veteran politician Sami al-Sulh to assist him from a field of equally capable candidates such as Rashid Karami (Tripoli) and Abd Allah al-Yafi and Sa'ib Salam (from the capital). His cabinet included one of the main supporters of the opposition against Khuri, Kamal Junblat, who had called for the trial of the ex-president. No doubt, Camille Chamoun began his presidency as both a popular and charismatic leader. But, soon, that would change. Chamoun's independence and aggressiveness alienated his former allies; he began to disregard their advice, and to meet with them less frequently than he should.

One of the leaders of the opposition was the assertive and aggressive Kamal Junblat who sought to have Chamoun implement a more thoroughgoing social security system. Since the mid-1940's, Lebanon had established social legislation to avoid the circumstances prevalent in non-western cultures. Employment of children under the age of thirteen was prohibited, employment of women was regulated to avoid exploitation, an eight hour work day was standardized, maternity leave, sick leave, and injury compensation existed and compensation for dismissal or lay-off was in place for the parliament to act upon. But, Junblat wanted more including health insurance and educational assistance for the poor. Chamoun did not support the Progressive Socialist Party program; the two men drew apart.

In addition, Chamoun alienated the Maronite Patriarch through his secular tendencies. The patriarch, Peter Paul Meouchi (Ma'ushi), had been a strong supporter of President Khuri and, therefore, Chamoun disapproved of Meouchi's election to the patriarchate.[27] In the past, the patriarch had cautioned Chamoun not to join any alliance against the interests of the National Pact, to keep Lebanon neutral in its dealings between the sects and communities, and to respect Lebanon's distinctive lifestyle.[28] Chamoun felt the patriarch was interfering in the presidential prerogative to court Moslem support and favor in Lebanon and to support Arab Nationalism in general. Patriarch Meouchi had made his feeling known, on several occasions.

It was, however, President Chamoun's foreign policy that alienated the masses and, ultimately, led to his political downfall. The president's foreign minister was Lebanon's renowned philosopher-politician Dr. Charles Malik who had served as Lebanon's Ambassador to Washington and United Nations delegate and president of the United Nations General Assembly. Both men had a meeting of the minds on the future course for Lebanon, and that was clearly modernization and a pro-western (pro-American) foreign policy.

No doubt, the president and his foreign minister were anti-Communist, pro-Arab, and strong supporters of the Arab cause in Palestine.[29] At times, however, in private, the two leaders very mildly criticized some minor Arab and Islamic cultural practices as out of date, unproductive and contrary to modernization. Presumably, this made them anti-Arab to some people.

Chamoun's problems began in 1955 with a visit by the president and prime minister to Turkey, at a time when Turkey and Syria had deployed their forces along their common border. To some in Lebanon, this was seen as an irresponsible, anti-Arab, political act,[30] in not supporting Syria in its border dispute. Of even greater significance, the rise of General Gamal Abd al-Nassar and the creation of the United Arab Republic (*UAR*) made a powerful impression on Lebanon's Sunnite Moslem population. Nassar's call for a united Arab World, from the Atlantic to the Arab-Persian Gulf, inflamed Arab passions and found willing supporters in Lebanon. Nassar had caught the imagination of the Arab youth, a new wave of Arab Nationalism swept over the Middle East and North Africa. When the 1956 Arab-Israeli war broke out, Lebanon did not break relations with England and France and this further alienated the president from the Lebanese people and even his strongest supporters.

Chamoun's opposition used the media to attack his position which he tried to defend by claiming that breaking relations with England and Prance would be a temporary and meaningless gesture. But Chamoun could not silence the opposition. He believed that Lebanon's excessive attachment to Nassarism was dangerous to the state's independence. Many Lebanese Sunnites had openly called for the inclusion of Lebanon in the UAR.[31] Thus, Camille Chamoun acted in what he believed was the interest of Lebanon. Calling the Moslem support for Nassarism a breach of the National Pact, and Lebanon's neutrality, Chamoun took advantage of the Eisenhower Doctrine (1957).[32] That was, clearly, another unacceptable violation of the National Pact.

The crisis reached a head when an anti-Chamoun pro UAR editor was murdered on May 8, 1958. Nasib al-Matni, editor of *The Telegraph* (al-Tilighraf), was shot dead either by anti-UAR Syrian agents,[33] or by one of Chamoun's allies who feared that Lebanon was surely drifting into the UAR.

The situation continued to deteriorate when the anti-Chamoun coalition called for strikes and circulated anti government leaflets in Tripoli.[34] Demonstrations exploded all over Lebanon, riots and strikes proliferated with outside support and internal opposition that wanted Chamoun out of power.

Several months earlier, on March 28, 1958, a Moslem led mob in Tyre trampled a Lebanese flag in the streets of the city,[35] calling for union with the UAR; and, on the ninth of May armed rebellion began in Tripoli.[36] By the twelfth of May a full scale insurrection broke out in the capital.[37] A National

Front had been formed by Saib Salam[38] with a broad base of support: Rashid Karami (Tripoli), Abd Allah al-Yafi, Kamal Junblat (Shuf), members of the Constitutional Bloc, and the Maronite Patriarch. Even the normally quiet Armenian community joined the demonstrations. Husayn al-Oueyni, Nassim Majdalani, Sabri Hamadi and Kamal al-Assad joined the opposition which had the support of the Bathists, the Najjada, and the Lebanese Communist Party.

Chamoun could only rely upon the Phalangists, the anti-UAR Syrian Nationalists,[39] and the National Bloc. And, the Shi'ite community, ever fearful of any Sunnite dominated state, threw their support behind the president. Finally, the very powerful Druze Arslan clan supported the government and called for negotiations.

Chamoun, in a desperate effort to stop the civil war unfolding in the capital called for the Arab League to mediate the conflict, but they considered the problem an internal one. At the United Nations, the Lebanese government blamed the UAR for instigating the crisis and supplying arms to the rebels from Syria, in the Belgian Consul-General's car.[40] But the best the United Nations could do was to send a fact finding group to Lebanon and to establish the United Nations Observer Group in Lebanon (*UNOGIL*). Thus, Chamoun turned to the United States for military aid; 10-15,000 U. S. Marines were dispatched to Lebanon to seek a compromise solution. American mediation, with the assistance of special envoy Robert Murphy, ended outside interference, and sought a compromise candidate by non-aligned Lebanese politicians who had formed a Third Force to respond to internal issues and reform. Chamoun stepped down when his term in office ended on September 22, 1958.

To many members of the Third Force (the National Front members) acceptance of the Eisenhower Doctrine was a betrayal of the Arab struggle in Palestine, for it indirectly made Lebanon an ally of the West implying a connection with Israel.[41] In addition, they believed that Chamoun and al-Sulh were dishonest in their intentions, really trying to turn Lebanon against the Arabs and Arab Nationalism (*Nassarism*) to make Lebanon another Israel in their midst.[42] To them, Chamoun was taking Lebanon backwards to the time when it was influenced by foreign countries (meaning France).[43] Thus, to the majority of Lebanon's Sunnite Moslems, the 1958 civil war was not caused by pro-Nassarist sentiment or Egyptian-Syrian interference as Chamoun claimed.[44] To some extent, this is true for the anti-Chamoun forces included members of all sects who felt that the president had violated the provisions of the National Pact. But Chamoun believed that outside interference from Egypt and Syria encouraged some Arab Nationalists to attempt a take over of the state, disregarding the National Pact and Lebanese nationalism.[45] Chamoun retained some support among several minority groups opposed to any federation with the UAR. To a considerable extent, the 1958 conflict may have been a clash between Lebanese and Arab Nationalisms.

The United States, through its growing Involvement in the crisis, helped to re-establish the balance of power in Lebanon, thus pro Arab sentiment and pro western feelings cancelled each other out. A "no victor, no vanquished" scenario was achieved. The real winner, however, in the revolt was the wily leader of the PSP, Kamal Junblat, who brought his reform package to the forefront of the peace process, as a prerequisite for an end to the hostilities. To implement the social reform program, a highly capable leader who could hold the confidence of all parties and sects was needed.

On July 31, 1958, the Lebanese Parliament chose General Fu'ad Chehab (*Shihab*), Commander of the Lebanese Army, who had been politically non-committal during the civil war and had kept the army neutral during the fighting, as the next president of Lebanon (1958-1964). Chehab came from a prominent Lebanese family that had once ruled Mount Lebanon. He was respected by both sides in the conflagration, and this was unusual in Lebanon for both the military and the politicians held a degree of disdain for one another.

Chehab quickly formed a new cabinet with Rashid Karami of Tripoli at its head, and it included participants from both sides of the 1958 conflict.[46] Kamal Junblat supported Chehab who favored the PSP reform program; the Lebanese nationalists were represented by the Phalangist Party. However, Chehab retained a link to the Deuxieme Bureau (the Army Intelligence Branch) to discourage his opponents.[47] Above all, the president supported the National Pact, an independent Lebanon, and he sought a wider base among all sects in his administration. Also Chehab was a military man accustomed to delegating authority to men who could carry out his orders. (To that extent, Chehab's style in office was similar to President Eisenhower's.) Chehab ran a technocratic cabinet whose members achieved moderate social reform in a stable atmosphere.

Chehab was a modernist who favored France and its life-style. In 1959, he commissioned a French research firm to study Lebanese socio-economic conditions and to report on ways and means to improve them. The Institute International De Recherches Et De Formation En Vue Du Developpement (*IRFID/IRFED*) reported that some regions were "neglected" and others suffered (minor) "disparities" in development that called for increased assistance.[48] Although good intentioned, Chehab's efforts to help the under rated Shi'ite districts was often opposed by the local leadership there[49] that often resented the interference of the Beirut government. The program of reform, called Chehabism,[50] included improving the military, state planning, administrative reforms, an increased number of Moslems in the government and bureaucracy, new public works projects, an expansion of education facilities, a new Central Bank, a social security law was signed on September 26, 1963 and an end of service compensation law was enacted. (Under Chehab's administration, illiteracy had dropped to about 10 per cent of the male population.)

Despite his efforts to create a healthy and prosperous state, Fu'ad Chehab faced some very strong opposition when he sought another term in office, in 1963. The opposition forces coalesced about the figures of Camille Chamoun, Saib Salam, Raymond Edde (Iddi), the influential publisher of Al-Nahar, Ghassan al-Tuwayni, and the Maronite Patriarch who found Chehab too secular for his tastes. By 1964, the opposition held enough seats in parliament to discourage any attempt at re-election by the incumbent.

Chehab's opposition, however, had no common policy and, at times, were antagonistic to one another, thus they sought a compromise candidate. Charles Helou (*Hilu*), an intellectual, journalist, and diplomat was well suited for the task. He was an astute politician with years of experience in balancing the conflicting sectarian and communal issues and personalities in Lebanon. However, his enemies saw these traits as weaknesses rather than strengths.

Charles Helou was one of the founders of the Phalangist Party and, later, an active member of the Constitutional Bloc; he served in several administrations, and he was an envoy to the Vatican. Hilou was strongly pro-French and a modernist and, consequently, it is not surprising to find him supporting Chehabism (al-Nahj al-Shihabi/The Shihabi Method). Hilou and his supporters were referred to as the Nahjis (the methodists).[51]

Helou was elected president (1964-1970) and followed a more or less neutral policy in Lebanese affairs not to alienate the Arab Nationalists who remained pro Nassarists, nor the Lebanese Nationalists who wanted to distance themselves from Nassarism. Consequently, Helou proved to be moderately successful in his policy.

Charles Helou continued the expansion of Lebanon's infrastructure: water works, electrification and health care to reach the outlying districts. Unfortunately, he was not very successful due to the local Shi'ite opposition in the south and east. Despite his energetic efforts in those areas, he lost heart due to the charges against him. He was seen as interfering in the autonomy of those regions

Towards the end of his reign, the Helou administration found itself embroiled in the Arab-Israeli conflict, a conflict in which Lebanon was the least likely Arab state to influence any outcome. Nevertheless, involvement in the struggle would split the Lebanese population between the Lebanese Nationalists and the Arab Nationalists.

All Lebanese leaders and the entire population in general supported the rights of the Palestinian people (the refugees) in their struggle against Israel; this was never in question; the key issue in Lebanon was freedom of action for the Palestinians- their right to armed conflict on Lebanese soil. Helou like many other Maronite leaders wanted to avoid antagonizing Israel, or finding themselves in a war with Israel that would end in the occupation of Lebanon. The Deuxieme Bureau kept an eye on the Palestinians, and many Sunnite Moslems resented that. A small number of Lebanese Sunnites called for giving the Palestinians Lebanese citizenship, but neither the Palestinians nor any of the other sects agreed to it, or wanted to be engulfed in an overwhelming Sunnite population.

In 1964, the Palestine Liberation Organization was formed with the express purpose of armed struggle to bring the Israelis to the negotiation table. Lebanon was seen by them as a border "confrontation state" and, thus, President Helou tried to outline limits for the Palestinian struggle there; while the Deuxieme Bureau was to control all the PLO camps.[52]

Matters came to a head on December 28, 1965 when a Palestinian commando, Jalal Ka'wash, died in custody.[53] The Deuxieme Bureau said that he had died of natural causes, but most likely he had died from torture. This event led to a call for an investigation of the activities of the Deuxieme Bureau by Kamal Junblat and several other anti-Shihabists. In the following year, the Palestinian Intra Bank, which had been created with the advice and assistance of the Lebanese banking establishment, went bankrupt; yet the PLO blamed the Lebanese government and the Nahjis for its failure and saw it as a move against the PLO presence. When the 1967 Arab-Israeli war broke out, Lebanon retained its non-aggressive posture. General Emile Bustani put the Lebanese Army on alert, but did not open a new front. Only diplomatic action was taken; and, the American and British Ambassadors were asked to leave Lebanon.

In the aftermath of the 1967 war, PLO-Jordanian relations deteriorated; in Lebanon, the PLO began stronger raids into Israel from South Lebanon. By the end of 1968, the PLO camps were the main strongholds of the PLO's offensive; within a year, as a consequence of the Cairo Agreement (1969) negotiated between the Lebanese Army and the PLO leadership, the Lebanese Army and police would vacate all PLO camps. The subsequent Malkart Agreement (1973) confirmed the Cairo Agreement, thus the PLO would police its own forces in Lebanon and co-ordinate its activities with the Lebanese Armed Forces. Neither side could honor the agreements, although they did try, in a limited way.

By the end of 1969, the PLO camps were "fortified arsenals" for the Palestinians and seen as a great danger by the predominantly Christian (Maronite) population, the Lebanese Nationalists, and the southern Shi'ites. The Sunnite Moslems for the most part, some radical Christian leaders and the Lebanese Communist Party supported the PLO resistance. When Khalil al-Jamal, a Lebanese commando, was killed in an assault on Israel, he received a hero's funeral in Tyre, and demonstrations followed calling for the full freedom for the PLO in Lebanon. This action was supported by the Lebanese Prime Minister Abd Allah al-Yafi. The government had to acquiesce. Consequently, Helou was deemed a weak and indecisive leader by the status quo politicians.

Finally conditions in Lebanon produced a crisis for the government. In 1970, a clash occurred between the Jordanian government and the PLO which resulted in the transfer of several thousand heavily armed PLO commandos to Lebanon. These groups, armed and financed independently, came loosely under the PLO umbrella. In time, they came to dominate Lebanese politics to the extent that several Christian right-wing leaders viewed them as an "army of occupation" whose uncontrolled, sprawling, presence endangered Lebanese independence. They chose to take action against what they saw as a loss of sovereignty to the conflicting PLO groups.

As early as August 30, 1967, the three major Maronite Christian leaders formed a broad based alliance seeking constructive dialogue with the PLO regarding its operations from Lebanese territory.[54] The Triple Alliance (Al-Hilf al-Thulathi/The Triple Oath or Pledge) brought Camille Chamoun (NLP), Pierre Jumayel (Phalangists), and Raymond Edde (National Bloc) together to head an anti-Helou coalition for the 1970 presidential election. They were supported by the Maronite Patriarch who saw the PLO as a new threat to Lebanese sovereignty; the anti-Shihabists opposed Helou because they felt that Lebanon's reforms had gone far enough to make Lebanon's villages, towns, and cities prosperous and more advanced than many parts of southern Europe; while the powerful Druze leader, Kamal Junblat, objected to Helou's support for the Nahjis who had avoided his counsel. Thus, Jumblat's PSP joined the group; the radical left wing groups (the Christian Communists and the Moslem Marxists) resented the Confessional System that left them out in the cold; they and many others of all sects despised the activities of the Deuxieme Bureau. Furthermore, many Lebanese had come to believe that Lebanon was losing its capitalistic edge and was drifting into socialism, similar to the states of northern Europe, as a result of Shihabism.

The search for a new, stronger, president began amid clashes between the Palestinian groups, and between the Lebanese Army and some Palestinian groups, and during a revival of Israeli raids: the Lebanese PLO clash at Dayr Mimas; the clash at the Ayn Hilwa camp; the invasion of the Palestine Liberation Army (PLA) from Syria occupying Lebanese territory; and, finally, the infamous Israeli raid on the Beirut Airport which plunged President Helou into a confrontation state with Israel. These and other incidents weakened the Beirut government and made Lebanon look powerless and helpless in the eyes of the world. The central government was discredited. A strong president was Lebanon's last hope to stop its drift into open conflict and chaos.

All hopes were pinned on the new president, Sulayman (*Suleiman*) Franjieh (*Franjiyyah*), a parliamentarian and diplomat from Zagharta, in north Lebanon; he was quickly elected to the presidency (1970-1976). In his early career, Franjieh was involved in a political incident, a violent altercation that led him to Syria where he befriended its future president, Hafiz al-Assad. He, later, returned to Lebanon with a reputation for strong leadership. Franjieh was supported in the 1970 presidential race by a right wing alliance called the Center Group, backed by the Triple Alliance. He won the election against Elias Sarkis, governor of the Central Bank, by one vote that of Kamal Junblat who withdrew his support from Franjieh two years later. Franjieh assumed the office of Head of State on August 17, 1970.

Sulayman Franjieh was a powerful defender of Lebanese nationalism and of Lebanon's status quo in the Arab-Israeli wars; he sought to control the un-policed PLO presence in Lebanon, and to limit PLO commandos to the un-populated regions of South Lebanon. Unable to control the military power of the PLO, Franjieh allowed the right wing parties to arm and train militias for self defense. In all this, he had the support of Syria; and this alienated many of his former supporters. With Syrian backing, the president issued the Constitutional Document (1976) aimed at controlling the PLO, to prevent an Israeli pretext to invade Lebanon, and at the same time, Franjieh sought to increase the Shi'ite Moslems in the government. The document placated no one.

Sulayman Franjieh's most implacable enemy was, in fact, the man whose vote put him in power: Kamal Junblat. In the period leading up to the first major clash of the Lebanese civil war in April of 1975, Junblat did everything in his power to lead the opposition to the Beirut government by depicting it as weak, sterile, and out of touch with Arab Nationalism and the growing Islamic Tendency in Lebanon which sought to create an Islamic state there. All urban unrest and labor problems were blamed on the Confessional System[55] including: the Ghandour Chocolate Factory strike (1972); the pro-PLO student demonstrations in the colleges (1973) and the Tobacco strike (1973); the Phalangist-Popular Front For The Liberation of Palestine clash at Dekwana (1974); and the strike at the joint Kuwaiti-Lebanese Protein Company (1975), a fishing enterprise in Sidon which would employ any fishermen who lost their jobs because of the company; and finally, the murder of Ma'ruf Sad, a prominent Nassarist and leftist leader in Sidon[56] all these events were projected as anti-government demonstrations. And, furthermore, Franjieh lost the support of key Moslem leaders such as Rashid Karame, Sa'ib Salam, and members of the Tripartite coalition, as well as the extremely powerful Raymond Edde.

The remainder of Franjieh's term in office was plagued with problems between his Lebanese opposition and the Palestinian resistance on Lebanese soil.

Lebanon's weakness since independence has been the unresolved problem caused by conflicting nationalisms: Arab Nationalism and Lebanese Nationalism. Arab Nationalism, in its Syrian form, espouses the extension of Syrian hegemony throughout the Near East,[57] and that includes Palestine and Lebanon. Inclusion into any kind of Moslem state is the great fear of the Christians. They have continuously believed that the Moslems of Lebanon are susceptible to schemes to achieve that, and thereby extinguish the Christian character and civilization of Lebanon. However, not all Moslems seek the incorporation of Lebanon into any other Arab state. Some members of the Arab National Movement (the MM) wanted an independent Arab-Moslem Lebanon in which the secularism of that state would be replaced by Islamic Law and values.[58] Only in this way can some Moslem Lebanese feel free from subjugation to a "Christian" government.[59] Real or imagined, many Moslems living in non-Moslem states, feel persecuted for they do not have the advantages or the empowerment that they would have in a Moslem state, and they can not express all their cultural beliefs openly or end those that are not Islamic. This puts them at a disadvantage in regard to other minorities, for secularism establishes absolute equality for all. Thus in Lebanon, to the Moslem fundamentalists, the outward and open display of Christianity is seen as offensive to many Moslems.

Minority Moslem groups, like the Druze in Lebanon, do not favor either of the above options, for they would become a persecuted minority; but they would certainly prefer a more balanced system to the current confessional politics of

Lebanon, which was not agreed to by them.[60] In the imbalance created, some Moslem minority groups complain about under representation in the fixed ratio confessional system, and see themselves as "subjects" of a Christian state rather than fully participating citizens.[61]

The Maronite Christians of Lebanon unanimously support Lebanese nationalism (Lebanonism) above and before Arab Nationalism. In this they are no different than the citizens of any other Arab state. However, perhaps because Lebanese Nationalism has a Christian component, some Moslems object to it in favor of Arab Nationalism. Lebanese Nationalism is in no way anti-Arab or anti-Moslem, but unfortunately, there may be some confusion or misinformation among some people who think so.

Led by the Phalangist Party in particular, the Maronite Christians uphold the idea of an independent sovereign Lebanon in which Christian-Moslem equality must persist, and that Lebanon must not be engulfed or absorbed by the problems of the Arab World.[62] They see Lebanon as belonging to the Arab World in the same way "Italy belongs to the Latin World or Denmark to the Scandinavian World,"[63] involved with but not overwhelmed by the region or its problems, an interested party that is fully independent. In this way, Arab Nationalism, devoid of any Islamic Fundamentalism, would not conflict with secular Lebanese Nationalism. (In this regard, the Phalangists follow the lead of the Maronite intellectual Habib al-Bustani whose views of Arab Nationalism were based upon cultural, linguistic and moral/ethical issues rather than political union.)

For many others, the National Pact did not resolve the problem of Lebanon's foreign relations it only magnified them because it was based on "two negative relations,"[64] rather than a positive policy. It was a starting point that went nowhere, because the sectarian fears prevailed. Despite all the advantages Lebanon has, despite its reforms and modernization, without national unity, Lebanon's peace will always remain precarious. This has been the case since Ottoman times.[65]

Although the worn out theories of religious hostilities, economic deprivation, and foreign intervention persist in explaining Lebanon's conflicts since independence, behind them, the underlying problem in Lebanon is drawn from an identity crisis. Lebanon is a Mediterranean nation-state, it straddles Europe and the Arab World; it is Christian and it is Moslem, and only its people can resolve their own identity problem. To reduce the fears the Christians experience and to fulfill the aspirations of the Moslems, it would help those communities if they held several meetings to chart out their future, relations, free from fear and any hidden agendas.

1. R. Hrair Dekmejian, *Patterns of Political Leadership: Lebanon, Israel, Egypt,* New York: State University of New York Press, 1975, pp. 16-18.

2. Leonard Binder, *Politics in Lebanon,* New York: John Wiley and Sons, 1966, pp. 85-105; Dekmejian, *Patterns of Political Leadership,* pp. 11-22; Nadim Shehadi and Dana Haffar Mills, *Lebanon: a History of Conflict and Consensus,* London: I. B. Tauris, and Co., 1992, pp. 181-200.

3. Frederick Charles Huxley, *Wasita in A Lebanese Context: Social Exchange among Villagers and Outsiders,* Anthropological Papers: Museum of Anthropology, No. 64, Michigan: University of Michigan, 1978.

4. Enver M. Khoury, *The Crisis In The Lebanese System, Confessionalism and Chaos,* Washington: American Enterprise Institute for Public Policy Research, 1976; Hilal Khashan, *Inside The Lebanese Confessional Mind,* Lanham: University Press of America, 1992; Binder, *Politics in Lebanon,* pp. 167-186; Halim Barakat, *Lebanon In Strife, Student Preludes to the Civil War,* Austin: University of Texas Press, 1977; Michael W. Suleiman, *Political Parties in Lebanon,* Ithaca: Cornell University Press, 1967; Sofia Saadeh, "Greater Lebanon: the Formation of a Caste System?" in Youssef M. Choueiri (ed.), *State And Society in Syria and Lebanon,* New York: St. Martin's Press, 1993, pp. 62-73.

5. Leila Tarazi Fawaz, *Migrants and Merchants in Nineteenth Century Beirut,* Mass.: Harvard University Press, 1983; Leila Fawaz, "The City And The Mountain: Beirut's Political Radius In The Nineteenth Century As Revealed In The Crisis of 1860," *IJMES,* vol. 16, Nov. 1984, no. 4, pp. 489-495; Roger Owen (ed.), *Essays on the Crisis in Lebanon,* London: Ithaca Press, 1976; Carolyn L. Gates, *The Merchant Republic of Lebanon, Rise of an Open Economy,* Center For Lebanese Studies and I. B. Tauris and Co. , 1998, p. 15; Charles Issawi, "British Trade and the Rise of Beirut, 1830-1860," *IJMES,* vol. 8, no. 1, Jan. 1977, pp. 103-116.

6. Kamal Junblatt, "Why Am I A Socialist?," in Amour Abdel-Malek (ed.), *Contemporary Arab Political Thought,* London: Zed Press, 1983, pp. 182-184; Kamal Junblat, *Fi Majra al-Siyasah al-Lubnaniyah,* Beirut: Dar al-Tali'ah, 1958; Kamal Junblat, *I Speak For Lebanon,* London: Zed Press, 1982, pp. 40-64, 94; Nazih Richani, *Dilemmas of Democracy and Political Parties in Sectarian Societies: The Case of The Progressive Socialist Party of Lebanon, 1949-1996,* New York: St. Martin's Press, 1998.

7. Robert Olson, *The Ba'th And Syria, 1947-1982,* New Jersey: The Kingston Press, 1982, pp. 3-20, 148-154; Antoun Saadah, "Syria, Mother of Nations," in Anour Abdel-Malek (ed.), *Contemporary Arab Political Thought,* pp. 92-95.

8. Marius Deeb, *Militant Islamic Movements in Lebanon: Origins, Social Basis,and Ideology,* Occasional Papers Series, Center for Contemporary Arab Studies, Georgetown University, 1986.

9. A. J. Abraham and George Haddad, *The Warriors of God: Jihad (Holy War) and The Fundamentalists of Islam,* IN.: Wyndham Hall Press, 1989, pp. 16-17; Muhammad Husayn Fadl Allah, *Al-Islam wa Muntaq al-Quwah,* Beirut: Dar al-Maarif lil Matbuat, 1978.

10. See; Elie Adib Salem, *Modernization without Revolution, Lebanon's Experience,* Bloomington: Indiana University Press, 1973; Michael Adams (ed.), *The Middle East,* New York: Facts on File Publications, 1988, pp. 78-81, 425.

11. Adams, *Facts on File,* pp. 78-80.

12. A. J. Abraham, *Lebanon: A State of Siege (1975-1984), IN.*: Wyndham Hall Press, 1984, p. 26; J. Chamie., "Religious Groups in Lebanon: A Descriptive Investigation," *IJMES,* vol. 11, no. 2, April, 1980, pp. 175-187.

13. Pierre Gemayel, "A Call From Christian Lebanon," in *Al-Amal,* Beirut: Aug. 20, 1954, p. 11; B. J. Odeh, *Lebanon: Dynamics of Conflict,* London: Zed Press, 1985, p. 102, 108; Agustus Richard Norton, *Amal And The Shi'a, Struggle for the Soul of Lebanon,* Austin: University of Texas Press, 1987, p. 45.

14. Norton, *Amal and the Shi'a,* p. 45.

15. K. S. Salibi, "The Personality of Lebanon in Relation to the Modern World," in Binder, *Politics in Lebanon,* pp. 263-270. On the pre-1975 Lebanese economy see: Andre Chaib, "Economic life in Lebanon And Its Future," in Edward E. Azar and Robert F. Haddad, *Seminar On The Reconstruction Of The Lebanese Economy: Plans for Recovery- abstract,* Center for International Development and Conflict Management, 1985, p. 18.

16. George Lenczowski (ed.), *Political Elites in the Middle East,* Washington D.C.: American Enterprise Institute for Public Policy Research, 1975, p. 214; Dekmejiah, *Patterns of Political Leadership,* pp. 29-30.

17. Malone, *The Arab Lands of Western Asia,* p. 17; Sami al-Sulh, *Ahtakim ila al-Tarikh,* Beirut: Dar al-Nahar lil Nashr, 1970, P. 61; Dekmejian, Patterns of Political Leadership, pp. 34-41.

18. Michael C. Hudson, *The Precarious Republic, Political Modernization in Lebanon,* New York: Random House, 1968, pp. 264-273.

19. Salibi, *The Modern History of Lebanon,* p. 192-193.

20. Eyal Zisser *Lebanon :The Challenge of Independence,* London: I.B. Tauris, 2000, pp 139-143: Hudson, *The Precarious Republic,* p. 267.

21. P. K. Hitti, *A Short History of Lebanon,* New York: n.p., 1965, p. 226; Fahim I. Qubain, *Crisis in Lebanon,* Washington, D.C.: The Middle East Institute, 1961, p. 22; Hitti, *Lebanon in History,.*p. 506.

22. Hitti, *Lebanon in History,* p. 506; Hamid Badawi al-Tahiri, *Siyasat al-Hukum fi Lubnan,* Cairo: Al-Dar al-Qawmiyah lil Tiba'ah wa al-Nashr, 1966, p. 315.

23. Hitti, *Lebanon in History,* p. 505-506.

24. Hitti, *Lebanon in History,* p. 506.

25. Salibi, *The Modern History,* p. 193; Hudson, *The Precarious Republic,* p. 276; Malone, *The Arab States of West Asia,* pp. 21-22; Demejian, *Patterns of Political Leadership,* pp. 41-52.

26. Wade R. Goria, *Sovereignty and Leadership in Lebanon,* 1943-1967, London: Ithaca Press, 1985, pp. 36-38.

27. Salibi, *The Modern History of Lebanon,* p. 198.

28. Ephraim A. Frankel, "The Maronite Patriarch: An Historical View of A Religious Za'im in The 1958 Lebanese Crisis," in *The Muslim World,* vol. LXVI, no. 3, July 1976, pp. 213, 221.

29. Philip K. Hitti, *The Near East in History, A 5000 Year Study,* New York: Van Nostrand Reinhold and Co., 1961, p. 541.

30. Al-Badawi, *Siyasat al-Hukum fi Lubnan,* pp. 317-318.

31. Salibi, *The Modern History of Lebanon,* p. 201.

32. Nasser M. Kalawoun, *The Struggle For Lebanon, A History of Lebanese-Egyptian Relations,* London: I. B. Tauris, 2000, pp. 27-34, 36-37, 175-176. M. F. Ghuraiyib, *Al-Ta'ifiyah wa al-Iqta'iyah fi Lubnan,* Beirut: Samiya Press, 1964, p. 67.

33. Al-Sulh, *Ahtakim ila al-Ta'rikh,* p. 173; George E. Kirk, *Contemporary Arab Politics: A Concise History,* New York: Preager, 1961, pp. 126-127.

34. Al-Sulh, *Ahtakim ila al-Ta'rikh,* pp. 173-193.

35. Salibi, *The Modern History of Lebanon,* p. 201.

36. Qubain, *Crisis in Lebanon,* p. 72; Goria, *Sovereignty and Leadership in Lebanon,* p. 42.

37. Salibi, *The Modern History of Lebanon,* p. 201.

38. Malone, *The Arab Lands of West Asia,* p. 23.

39. Al-Tahiri, *Siyasat al-Hukum fi Lubnan,* p. 327.

40. Kirk, *Contemporary Arab Polities,* pp. 127-129; Malone, *The Arab Lands of West Asia,* p. 24.

41. Isma'il Musa al-Yusuf, *Thwrah al-Ahrar fi Lubnan,* Beirut: n.p., 1958, p. 47.

42. Al-Yusuf, *Thwrah al-Ahrar,* p. 55; Abd al-Rahman al-Sharqawi and Abd al-Halim Ibrahim, *Irfa'u Ayadikum 'Ann Lubnan,* Cairo: Dar al-Fikr, 1958, pp. 8-11.

43. Junblat, *Fi Majra al-Siyasah al-Lubnaniyah,* p. 46, 121.

44. Al-Sharqawi, *Irfa'u Ayadikum,* p.17; Ghuraiyib, *Al-Ta'ifiyah wa al-Iqta'iyah fi Lubnan,* pp. 67-69.

45. Camille Chamoun, *Crise au Moyen-Orient,* Paris: Gillimard, 1963.

46. Goria, *Sovereignty and Leadership in Lebanon,* p. 44; Salibi, *The Modern History of Lebanon,* pp. 203-204.

47. Salibi, *The Modern History of Lebanon,* p. 13.

48. Goria, *Sovereignty and Leadership in Lebanon,* pp. 59-60; Hudson, *The Precarious Republic,* pp. 313-315.

49. Goria, *Sovereignty and Leadership in Lebanon,* p. 60.

50. Hudson, *The Precarious Republic,* pp. 313-325.

51. K.S. Salibi, *Crossroads to Civil War, Lebanon 1958-1976,* New York: Caravan, 1976, p. 22.

52. Salibi, *Crossroads to Civil War*, p. 26.

53. Goria, *Sovereignty and Leadership in Lebanon*, p. 78.

54. Goria, *Sovereignty and Leadership in Lebanon*, pp. 89-90.

55. Salibi, *Crossroads to Civil War*, pp. 61-62.

56. Abraham, *Lebanon: a State of Siege*, pp. 19-26; Goria, *Sovereignty and Leadership in Lebanon*, pp. 117-145; Salibi, *Crossroads To Civil War*, p. 92; Al-Yusuf, *Thwrah al-Ahrar fi Lubnan*, p. 55.

57. Wazarah al-Anaba' fi Lubnan, *Qadiyat al Hizb al-Qawni*, Beirut, 1949, p. 16.

58. Abd Allah al-Qubrusi, *Nahnu wa Lubnan*, Beirut: Matba'at Lubnan, 1954, pp. 95-96.

59. *Moslem Lebanon Today*, pp. 12-13.

60. Kamal Junblat, *Fi Majara al-Siyasah al-Lubnaniyah*, p. 49; Kamal Junblat, *Haqiqat al-Thuwrat al-Lubnaniyat*, Beirut: Dar al-Nashr al-Arabiyat, 1959, p. 110.

61. Muhammad Ali al-Dannawi, *Al-Muslimun fi Lubnan, Muwatnun la Ra'aya*, Beirut: n.p., 1973, pp. 47-57.

62. Frank Stoakes, "The Supervigilantes: The Lebanese Kataeb Party as Builder, Surrogate and Defender of The State," *Middle Eastern Studies*, vol, 11, October, 1975, no. 3, p. 225, 231, 235.

63. Suleiman, *Political Parties in Lebanon*, p. 247; Meir Zamir, *Lebanon's Quest: The Road to Statehood, 1926-1939*, London: I, B. Tauris, 1997, p. 114.

64. Basim al-Jisr, *Ri'asah wa Siyasah wa Lubnan al-Jadid*, Beirut: Dar Maktabat al-Hayat, 1964, p. 64.

65. Yusuf Murad, *Fi Sabiel Lubnan*, n.p., n.d., introduction.

CHAPTER 10

THE WAR YEARS (1975-1985)

Almost as soon as the first shot of the Lebanese civil war was fired in April of 1975, scholars and specialists on Lebanon and the Middle East, as well as travelers, journalists and diplomats began as unending deluge, a "mishmash" or "hodgepodge," of books and articles blaming one side or the other for the conflict. Some studies described the obvious; while others delineated more complex causes and events; while still others predicted the outcome of the struggle. Yet, many of those accounts found their neatly pontificated scenarios upset by shifting alliances and foreign interventions.

Most of the scholarly studies of the conflict can be classified into one of two categories: those that see an external conspiracy behind the war, and those that blame the Lebanese and their social, political and economic system for the conflagration. There is, indeed, some truth in both perspectives.

The major academic studies on the war[1] have highlighted several of the sources of instability that contributed to the Lebanese civil war, at least to some significant degree. Those factors included "internal-external" linkages, "sub-national" identities, the "regional and extra regional" interference of foreign powers, the plight of the Palestinians, and foreign sponsored plots against Lebanon as a "Christian "Arab state. The war should also be seen in a fuller Arab context[2] involving pan-Arab ploys aggravated by class and civil unrest[3] and the conflict between liberal and conservative or radical and traditional regimes. And, it could also be seen as an extension and expansion of Iranian Islamic fundamentalism and, indeed, as a projection of the on-again, off-again Arab-Israeli conflict.

Lebanon's susceptibility to foreign influences can never be underestimated because of its strategic locale and as a bridge between eastern and western civilizations, cultures, and ideas. It has been a microcosm of the entire Near East, as eastern and western winds continually blow their conflicting ideas and political tensions over Lebanon's coasts, plains, valleys and mountains.

Also, the Arab World's animosities and internecine struggles have produced a regional "Arab Cold War" that remains on the periphery of world affairs. But unfortunately for Lebanon, almost every ideological contradiction finds a supporter among Lebanon's multi-religious, multi-communal social stratum and, thus, Lebanon has been and remains an ideological and sometimes violent battleground and hostage of everyone else's hot and cold wars.

The American role in the conflict, like the role of Europe, was low keyed, when it surfaced at all. To the eternal disgrace of the western alliance and the Free World, Lebanon was written off, until recently. As one European newspaper put it: "all the Christians (meaning the Maronites) of Lebanon are not worth a quart of oil." The struggle was falsely depicted in the West as religiously based, and the United States and the European nations did not want to offend Moslem sensitivities by supporting the predominantly pro-western Christian groups in Lebanon. That might have hampered the flow of oil to the West and Japan.

None of these conditions in Lebanon, however, were new or unknown to the traditional Lebanese politicians; and, it was possible, early in the conflict, to resolve all outstanding problems within the context of consensus and cooperation among the sects and groups. However, early in the war the Moslem traditional elite and leaders, with the notable exception of Kamal Junblat, were silenced or lost authority to younger men who lacked the spirit of compromise; while the Christian leaders became more fearful and isolated from their Moslem counterparts. And, as usual, each community envisioned its own "foreign policy" and future view of Lebanon, thereby isolating and rendering the Beirut government ineffectual. In fact, virtually all groups and leaders contributed to the prevailing instability and outbursts of hostility either by their action or inaction.

In reality, the conflict in Lebanon was far too complicated to be adroitly described by simply affixing labels to explain the groups of combatants. What may be said with a heightened degree of accuracy is that the war was not religious in origin or caused by the depravation, neglect, poverty, or the exploitation or victimization of any sect or group or community in Lebanon. Nor was it against the Palestine Liberation Organization or its goals or objectives. And religious hostility was not a major factor in the war; on numerous occasions the combatants were composed of both Moslems and Christians. (Only the Druze and the Maronites did not forge any alliance or take any common cause.) And, poverty in Lebanon was at an all time low at the start of the war. (According to the best available records, prior to the conflict, less than 1 percent of the population or 5 percent of the work force composed the Lebanese poor; and, the rate was dropping below accepted poverty limits.) The well known "Beirut slum belt" that grew during the war years was the result of the Arab-Israeli war. And, lastly, neither the Lebanese nor the Palestinians sought the conflict; the Lebanese civil war was not fought over the rights of the Palestinians, and no Palestinian leader called for Lebanon as a substitute homeland for the displaced Palestinians.

In general, we can say that the struggle was a "left" versus "right" conflict with other mitigating circumstances and groups coming into play at particular times, to achieve their own parochial aims. As always, the use of the terms "left" and "right' for lack of more accurate terminology, may seem unclear, and may need some additional explanation. By "right" we mean those groups that supported the status quo in Lebanese Moslem-Christian relations and those who wanted Lebanon to remain in the Free World; by "left" we mean those groups that were opposed to Lebanon as it existed and those who wanted Lebanon to be more strongly aligned with the Soviet Union and, particularly, Soviet foreign policy in the Arab-Israeli conflict. (For the most part, all the leftist groups believed that the Arab States, with few exceptions, were the lackeys of the West, and that only the Soviet Union truly supported the Arab cause in Palestine and the Palestine Liberation Organization (PLO).)

There was also another factor that enables us to use the generalization "left vs. right" in the Lebanese struggle, and that is that in each crisis juncture in the Lebanese conflict there was a concerted effort by the Lebanese or Palestinian left (the Rejection Front) to prevent any reconciliation effort among the Lebanese religious or political leaders from succeeding, for they believed that such a reconciliation might limit their guerrilla war against Israel.

The objective of the secular Lebanese left, composed of Christian Communists and Moslem Marxists, was simple and clear; to break down the Lebanese Formula which had absolutely no place in it for them. From the ashes of a pro-western Lebanon a new socialist leftist state would arise without any Confessional System, Lebanese Formula or National Pact. To achieve that objective and goal, the numerically small and politically weak,[4] but highly articulate and active Lebanese left enlisted the aid of any willing and like-minded domestic or foreign accomplice. One of these groups was the heavily armed PLO-left, called the Rejection Front, which believed that Lebanon was the only place left to them to wage their guerrilla war against Israel. If the new socialist Lebanon were to be aligned with the Soviet Union, as the State of Israel is aligned with the United States, then they believed that their chances for success would rise astronomically. Thus a marriage of convenience was forged between the Lebanese-left and the PLO left. By 1975, no force in Lebanon, governmental or private, was strong enough to police or control the new left wing alliance. The fabric of Lebanon was ready to be shorn at its seams.

Lebanon's political system can best be described as a set of three scales; each one perched atop the other in perfect balance. The first scale represents the Confessional System; the second represents the Lebanese Formula; and the third scale represents the National Pact. On each scale, one tray represents Muslim needs and aspirations while the other tray represents Christian hopes and desires. As long as no external or internal forces disrupted the balance, the system appeared to be working well. This political system represented the Lebanese "belief system" and its system of "checks and balances."

In retrospect, during the late 1940s and throughout the 1950s, Lebanon grew to maturity. Its political system became institutionalized and its old feudal aristocracy played the role of national leadership, jousting one another on key domestic and foreign issues, in the name of sect and nation. All seemed to be going well, but soon, two new forces that were unforeseen at the time of independence would rise and vie for political power and, thus, they would disrupt the scales of communal justice and balanced political relationships.

The first of these forces of instability arose from the 1948 clash between Palestinian and Jewish (Zionist) nationalisms which brought into being the Arab-Israeli conflict. Thousands of displaced Palestinians would enter Lebanon and seek refuge there, later becoming a unassimilable and disruptive force in Lebanese politics through the 1960s and 1970s.

Secondly, as Lebanon began to slowly industrialize in the late 1960s, a new political leadership emerged from the professional middle class; new challenges to the state began to coalesce. Locked out or frozen out of the political formula, a "democratic" left composed of Christian Communists and Moslem Marxist would challenge the Lebanese Formula and the existing institutions with their interlocking religious political ties and controls, in the name of the new working class and its interests. They blamed the "inflexible" Lebanese Formula for all communal, social, or labor unrest in the nation. Neither together nor apart, however, could these new forces win political recognition or accreditation from the Lebanese public, or from the government. They remained outside of the mainstream of Lebanese politics awaiting an opportunity to act. Locked out of the political arena, they worked to discredit the existing government.

In 1970, when the forces of King Husayn of Jordan clashed with the PLO-left in his kingdom, the king's forces drove several thousand Palestinian commandos into Lebanon where they became allies of the Lebanese left.[5] The state was now set for a violent conflict.

The initial clash of the "civil war" began with an attempt on the life of right-wing leader Shaykh Pierre Gemayel, on April 13, 1975, precipitating a larger clash between Gemayel's political party and its militia (the Phalangists/Kata'ib) and the PLO left (the Rejection Front). The issue in that crisis was the lack of control over PLO forces in Lebanon, and the damage done to the Shi'ite and Christian villages in South Lebanon resulting from Israeli counter attacks.

For the PLO, South Lebanon was the only place left for them to wage their war of liberation against Israel, because the other Arab States controlled them too tightly; for the Israelis, "hot pursuit" by land air and sea was totally justified. (Attempts to regulate the border war in Lebanon by the Cairo Agreement (1969) and, later, the Malkert Hotel Accord (1973) had failed and were later abrogated in 1987.) Meanwhile in the Lebanese cities, the various PLO groups intensified their battles against each other resulting in numerous casualties among the public, as Yasir Arafat, leader of al-Fatah, the largest group, tried in a limited way to stop the internecine conflict within his liberation movement. Nevertheless, by April of 1975, the Lebanese government was caught in the middle of a no win scenario.

These two factors, the rise of the "democratic" left and the injection of several thousand PLO commandos from the Rejection Front coalesced, eventually joining forces to overthrow the pro-western Lebanese government. Other than their hatred of the West and opposition to the Lebanese "Christian" government, they had no common plan or program for Lebanon or for the PLO resistance on Lebanese soil. This was largely a marriage of convenience. One thing, however, was still needed to give the illusion of a real civil war with Lebanese issues at the vortex, and to create some ideological or national coloration to the conflict. For the leftist alliance a Lebanese national figure was needed to reflect a national uprising and they found that person in the Ghandiesque figure of Kamal Junblat the Druze leader of the Progressive

Socialist Party.[6] With Junblat acting as a national figurehead, the leftist alliance called itself the National Movement.

No doubt, for the very small Druze community only a major upheaval, a revolution of sorts, could bring them greater power and prominence in the Lebanese state system; and, more importantly, very little was needed to prompt them to take up arms against their traditional enemies, the Maronites, who led the right wing political coalition known as the Lebanese Front and its combined militia, the Lebanese Forces, that was in the making at that time. In fact, the only consistent feature in the constantly shifting alliances and internal conflicts among the two alliances during the seventeen years of on-again, off-again battles was the Maronite-Druze animosity. The lines of battle were clearly drawn.

The first clash of the Lebanese civil war came on April 13, 1975. On that day, Shaykh Pierre Gemayel, the Phalangist leader,[7] was fired upon from a car with masked license plates which appeared to contain Palestinian commandos.[8] Gemayel was marked for assassination because he repeatedly called for a referendum on the PLO presence in South Lebanon to ascertain the wishes of the inhabitants of that region. The southern Lebanese had continually complained to the Beirut government about the uncontrolled "foreign" forces among them and the Israeli reprisal attacks which devastated their communities and the region.

Later that same day, a bus carrying PLO commandos from the Rejection Front came upon that scene and a fire fight ensued between them and Gemayel's security guards. When the smoke of battle cleared, twenty-one members of the PLO left lay dead or dying in the burned hulk that served as their military vehicle. (Photos of the dead commandos made the front pages of the Lebanese press.) The war was on!

Between the intermittent fighting, the street battles, and the outright open warfare, charges and counter charges between the PLO's Rejection Front and the Phalangist Party filled the air. The Beirut government, caught in the middle of the crisis, remained powerless to act, since it was split between its own pro and anti PLO factions. And no mediator was acceptable to either side. Thus, a military cabinet under Brigadier General Nur al-Din Rifai tried to calm the growing fears that the Lebanese government had lost its credibility to act as a mediator between the two factions, as fighting spread in late May into new districts of the capital. Meanwhile, a new premier, Rashid Karami, from Tripoli, was designated to replace Rashid al-Sulh; and President Franjieh met with his top aides to try to end the fighting. President Franjieh called upon Prime Minister Karami to use the army to stop the bloodshed, but the premier refused.[9] At the same time, north of the capital, in the city of Tripoli, a local clash deteriorated into an armed campaign between the predominantly Moslem city and the neighboring Christian town of Zgharta. The conflagration grew in intensity approximating a small battle forcing Karami to send the Lebanese Army into a peacekeeping role there. This was the Beirut government's one and only show of force. All eyes were fixed upon the army; it was Lebanon's last hope to restore order.

But the fighting persisted in Tripoli with the leftist groups gaining control of the city and siding with their allies in Beirut. Fearing that it might split along Moslem and Christian lines, the Lebanese Army was not committed to action.

During the outbreak of violence in Tripoli, Beirut experienced a few weeks of tenuous calm. Then, on September 18, 1975, a combined leftist PLO Rejection Front offensive blasted East Beirut, the Christian half of the city.[10] The war for the capital was on again in full force; and this time the spokesman for the anti-government forces was the renowned philosopher-politician Kamal Junblat. He called for the immediate implementation of his social program for Lebanon,[11] and a new National Pact. His main plan was to end the allocation of top posts by religion. Almost immediately, Pierre Gemayel, speaking for his party, responded to Junblat's challenge with a call to secularize the entire administration, top to bottom, as well as the legal system in personal law, calling the Druze leader's bluff.[12]

By the end of October, the PLO left and its allies had gained most of the coastal strip, West Beirut, and the hotel district. They were in no mood to negotiate any reforms, with part of East Beirut in their hands. By years end, the capital would be divided into two warring enclaves; a Christian East Beirut and a Moslem West Beirut. An imaginary "Green Line" would cut the city in half.

In the first nine months of combat, from April to December of 1975, the Lebanese government, the Lebanese Army, and the old line Moslem leadership, with exception of Kamal Junblat, had been completely discredited by younger and more violent militia leaders; with cold dispatch, the new warriors totally lacked any sense of compromise.

The New Year (1976), found the Lebanese Army hopelessly bogged down in Tripoli, a major factor that encouraged the Lebanese left and its PLO sympathizers to make their move on the capital. Rocket fire rained down on the eastern half of the city igniting massive artillery duels. By late January, it was painfully obvious that Yasir Arafat had lost control of the PLO left; now he could no longer straddle the fence. The fall of the Christian town of Damour, south of the capital, brought Camille Chamoun's National Liberal Party into the right wing alliance, in full force.[13] Thus, the conflict spread as Syrian mediation, by its foreign minister, unfortunately led nowhere. Kamal Junblat immediately rejected Syrian mediation or that of any other Arab State, in the conflict.

Meanwhile, in a last ditch effort to strengthen the Lebanese government, Brigadier General Abd al-Aziz al-Ahdab staged a military coup (the television coup) to save Beirut,[14] but it failed to stabilize the situation. By March of 1976, the leftists had made impressive gains in the capital, forcing the Phalangist forces against the wall. The end for them was near. And, finally, Arafat chose a side; after months of debate, the entire PLO would back the National Movement, for Arafat's credibility was at stake. The PLO's position was now crystal clear; the Jordanian debacle had been avoided, and victory by the left seemed near. Now, a leftist Lebanon allied to the Soviet Union could give the PLO a far better chance to liberate Palestine. Finally, a last minute meeting between President Assad of Syria and Kamal Junblat, to mediate the conflict, failed to produce any meaningful results.

By mid April, the right had lost the towns of Damour, Jiye, the port facilities in Beirut and the hotel district in the capital. They were totally blockaded in the Ashrafiyah district in East Beirut, their last major stronghold in the city. Consequently, Lebanon was clearly divided along the Beirut-Damascus Highway, into a Christian northern half and a Moslem southern half.

That division threatened Syrian interests in the region. Thus, in part, to prevent either a leftist victory or a PLO take over in Lebanon, Syria backed by the conservative oil-rich Arab regimes stealthily moved into Lebanon on April 9, 1976, in the vicinity of Masnaa. The Syrian occupation of Lebanon had begun; and it would eventually halt the PLO leftist drive northward; and it would stabilize the conflict within Syrian objectives and concerns.

Meanwhile, the Lebanese right, with Syrian consent, was busy ending the PLO leftist hold over the Jisr al-Basha and Tell al-Zaatar (Tel Zaatar) camps within an industrial park in East Beirut. The battle for those two PLO strongholds, a test of strength between the Lebanese Forces and the PLO, lasted about fifty-four days and proved to be one of the bloodiest battles.[15] But in the end, all hostages held there would be released unharmed through the efforts of Jean Hofliger and Edmond Cortesi of the International Red Cross.

Shortly thereafter, the remaining PLO forces north of the Beirut-Damascus Highway were contained by the Syrian Army and Lebanese Forces. Observing the dimensions of the conflict, the Arab League quickly approved an Arab Deterrent Force (the ADF) to enter and occupy parts of Lebanon,[16] to keep the peace. The ADF was seen by the Arab World as the last major effort to find an "Arab solution" to an "Arab problem" to avoid the internationalization of the war, by the United Nations.

In South Lebanon, however, the PLO was back to its own operations against the Jewish State. As the crescendo of violence between the PLO and the Israelis continued unabated in their on-again, off-again war, Israel decided on a major strike into Lebanon to silence the PLO. On March 15, 1978, the border war began with a powerful Israeli thrust into Lebanon,[17] to end a major PLO buildup near its northern border that had begun approximately a year earlier. In fact, that same year saw the assassination of Kamal Junblat (March, 1977)[18] when he began to close ranks with the Lebanese right, clearly opposing the Syrian presence in Lebanon thereby showing some national coloration to his usually socialist protestations.

The Israeli Defense Forces (the IDF) had its own agenda for Lebanon to "root out the terrorist bases."[19] They did, but only temporarily because the United States strongly pressed Israel to withdraw; and, the United Nations passed Security Council Resolution 425 (March 19, 1978) calling for an Israeli phased withdrawal. The following day, a United Nations Interim Force in Lebanon (UNIFIL) was created to patrol South Lebanon.

Meanwhile, Lebanon's new president, Elias Sarkis,[20] former governor of the Central Bank, tried his hand at ending the conflict, but Syria wanted to end the arrogance of the Phalangist militia as well. The Syrian rightist alliance or partnership had run its course. It had begun to unravel and would soon end on a sour note when the Gemayel-Chamoun alliance (known as the Lebanese Front/Lebanese Forces) called for an immediate Syrian departure from Lebanon.

The Syrian response came quickly. When a Phalangist and a National Liberal Party militiaman clashed over a personal problem in the town of Zahle, north of the Beirut-Damascus Highway, killing a Syrian soldier who was caught in the middle, Syria found an ideal opportunity to slap down its former allies and to consolidate its hold on Lebanon. The Battle for Zahle raged on for several weeks and, finally, it ended in a truce between the Lebanese Forces and the Syrians. Ninety-five Phalangist and National Liberal Party militiamen had held-off the Syrian Army; Syria had failed to capture the city and had incurred heavy losses.

With the end of the battle for Zahle, attention was refocused on South Lebanon where the Shi'ite community was caught once again between the PLO and the Israelis, as the blue helmeted United Nations forces stood by helplessly. The old-line Shi'ite political leadership had been discredited and replaced by Imam Musa al-Sadr,[21] an Iranian of Lebanese descent. He had taken over that community's affairs and had called for reconciliation with Lebanon's Christian leaders and the Beirut government, during a tour of the Arab States before leaving for Libya on August 28, 1978 to help celebrate the anniversary of the Libyan Revolution. Shortly after his arrival in Libya, a major disagreement, as reported in JANA (the Libyan news agency), occurred between the Shi'ite Imam and Muammar al-Qadhafi, over Sadr's refusal to blame the Christians of Lebanon for the problems his Shi'ite community faced. Qadhafi accused the Imam of using Libyan money to finance an Iranian Revolution, and not to help create an Islamic State in Lebanon. Soon afterwards, Imam Musa al-Sadr disappeared.

By August of 1981, the Lebanese state was quiet, at least for a while, abandoned by all the major powers with no militia strong enough to dominate the scene. During the second phase of the conflict, the Lebanese Forces had lost their Syrian ally and were increasingly isolated in East Beirut and northern Lebanon. The National Movement had lost its leader with the death of Karnal Junblat and was now only an adjunct to the PLO forces operating in Lebanon. More than ever, the conflict seemed to resemble a Lebanese war against a Palestinian intruder, trying to take over their land. At least that's how it was seen in the Arab World and its press. But, in reality, no PLO leader ever claimed Lebanon as a substitute homeland; and no Lebanese leader in the right wing alliance ever rejected the rights of the Palestinians. The only outstanding disagreement between the Lebanese and the PLO was over the uncontrolled, sprawling, and often chaotic presence of the PLO forces and the inability of the PLO to control its own commandos. Had the PLO been able to police its own forces, in the second phase of the conflict, many Lebanese writers believe the conflict would have never occurred, or it certainly would have not lasted as long as it did.

The year 1982 brought no relief to the embattled Lebanese state. Continued waves of violence involving all factions grew in intensity and the UNIFIL forces were unable to gain control of the Lebanese-Israeli border. In fact, the increased tempo of combat between the PLO and Israel began to worry all concerned.

The Begin government in Israel sent direct warnings to the Arab World regarding the intolerable situation on its northern frontier, as General Ariel Sharon and the Israeli Chief of Staff prepared for war.

When Israel's ambassador to London, Shlomo Argov, was shot and seriously wounded on June 6, 1982, Israel blamed the PLO and launched a massive full scale attack on Lebanon by land, sea and air.[22] Operation "Peace for Galilee" was to be the "final solution" to the Palestinian problem, according to either Sharon or Begin. Fierce battles raged along a thirty-five mile front; casualties were frighteningly high on all sides, but the PLO did not break and run. Nothing the PLO had, however, could stop the IDF's onslaught. Nor did the PLO secure any help from the Arab States. The Arab World sat this one out, hoping a muted PLO would survive and end the acrimonious relations that had developed between some Arab States and the Palestinian leadership (and, certainly, the Shi'ites of South Lebanon were only too happy to rid themselves of both the PLO and the leftists in their midst).

The dimensions of the war were devastating. Israeli tank columns and infantrymen fought their way into the vicinity of West Beirut, besieging the capital by land, sea and air, only to find themselves in a standoff with Arafat's forces. Expected help from the right-wing militia under Bashir Gemayel never materialized. Gemayel refused to commit the Lebanese Forces to battle. (While Bashir and his allies opposed the uncontrolled PLO presence on Lebanese soil, he always supported the rights of the Palestinian people and would not cooperate in their destruction at the hands of the Israelis.)

Throughout that long, hot summer, negotiations would start and stop, like the Lebanese cease-fires. But, finally, American intervention persuaded the Arab States to take in the PLO troops; under a United States evacuation plan to prevent Beirut from falling to the IDF and, thus, complicate further peace initiatives. The PLO had held off the Israelis longer then all the Arab States put together had ever done, and that was a victory of sorts for them. A Munti-National Force (the MNF)[23] would escort the Palestinian commandos, carrying their personal weapons, out of Lebanon. The Lebanese left was not consulted in those negotiations and were forced to make their way to safety in the PLO camps of Sabra and Shatila, in the capital.

On August 18, 1982 the Lebanese government officially requested the deployment of American, French and Italian troops to help withdraw the PLO forces from Beirut. By the end of the month, Yasir Arafat left Lebanon for Greece, his chosen place of exile, aboard the Atlantis.

With the departure of the PLO troops, the Lebanese citizens came out of their shelters and tried to piece together some semblance of normality. Bashir

Gemayel was quickly elected president on August 23, 1982, by a narrow margin; but before he could take office, he was assassinated on September 14, 1982, in his East Beirut office.[24] As a hero of the Lebanese resistance to foreign domination, he had made many enemies. The assassination, however, motivated the Israelis to move their troops into West Beirut, to keep order and prevent reprisals. A few days later, on September 18, 1982, the whole Arab World and the West awoke to horrific news that a massacre had taken place at the Sabra and Shatila camps.[25] The Arabs quickly blamed Israel as the occupying power for allowing the massacre to occur, but the culprits were renegade militiamen from the Damour Brigade who exacted revenge for the murders of their relatives after the siege of that village. Thus, the fall of the "democratic" left was completed in three days (September 16-18, 1982). The dead were identified, many of whom were foreigners from international leftist organizations in Europe and Asia; some were Palestinians whom they hid behind; and, others were Islamic fighters from around the Moslem World who came to help destroy the "Christian State." In March of 1997, the last of the leftists from the Japanese Red Army were captured in the Bekka Valley. In all, the Red Cross and the Red Crescent reported 327 deaths; photos of the dead were displayed in the Lebanese press.

In that gloomy atmosphere a ray of sunshine appeared in the election of Amine Gemayel to the presidency. In October of 1982, the Lebanese leader arrived in New York to address the United Nations and, then, he left for a meeting with President Reagan. Shortly thereafter, at the Lebanon Beach Hotel, withdrawal talks with Israel began. President Gemayel clarified the Lebanese position[26] on peace talks and other areas of concern indicating that all groups, parties, and factions in Lebanon recognized the rights of the Palestinians. Without a solution to the Arab-Israeli conflict, a return to the 1948 Lebanese-Israeli truce was all that Lebanon could offer, at that time. Consequently, the year ended on a downbeat, as negotiations dragged on. A peace treaty[27] was eventually hammered out at American insistence, only to be totally rejected by the Lebanese government. Thus, the American initiative to achieve Israeli objectives, long after Israel had abandoned them, proved to be a failure. But, more importantly, it hurt American goodwill efforts to act as an honest broker in the region and as a neutral arbitrator in Lebanon.

The third phase of the war in Lebanon saw an Israeli attempt to defeat the PLO; the eviction of the PLO forces from Beirut; and the fall of the "democratic" left in Lebanon. The rightist alliance appeared to have won their battles, but the Lebanon war would continue with new players. Peace had not been won!

As of 1984, the war in Lebanon entered its fourth and final phase; it began to approximate a civil war with Lebanese issues at its vortex.

With Lebanon in disarray, a new force the Islamic Movement, backed by Iran, sought to increase Shi'ite power in Lebanon. After the massacre at the Sabra and Shatila camps, an American military force entered Lebanon to act as a mediator in Lebanese governmental affairs, to help reconstruct the war ravaged country and to protect the Palestinians in the capital. But by October of 1983, the Shi'ites began to view the American presence as just another Christian militia which got caught in the middle of the fighting in Beirut. Finally, a suicide driver destroyed the U.S. Marines Battalion Landing Headquarters killing 251 American servicemen. Within a short period of time the United States evacuated its position in an orderly and secure manner, to ships offshore. Thus Lebanon's fate was, once again, cast into the stormy winds of change in the Middle East. The Israelis fared no better; they had stayed in Lebanon too long turning their Shi'ite friends into enemies by their occupation of South Lebanon. Consequently, Shi'ite extremists began suicide attacks against the IDF, forcing them back into a nine mile security zone in southern Lebanon across from their border.

With the Israelis restricted to South Lebanon, a combined Shi'ite-Druze force took over West Beirut in February of 1984, filling the vacuum left there by the withdrawal of both the Americans and the Israelis. By late 1985, the last of the PLO forces in northern Lebanon were disarmed. Meanwhile, the Shi'ite-Druze alliance broke up over religious and political issues and, by the end of the year, the Druze retreated to their mountain strongholds. In the long run, the Druze gained nothing. Some Shi'ites, supported by Iran, hardened their negotiating position calling for an Islamic Republic in Lebanon; and thus the Christians began to fear "Coptification." (This term refers to the Coptic Christians of Egypt, a powerless minority that faces constant humiliation and attack by Egypt's Moslem fundamentalists and their supporters.)

1. A. J. Abraham, *The Lebanon War,* CT.: Praeger, 1996; Lebanon: *A State of Siege,* Dilip Hiro, *Fire And Embers (A History of The Lebanese Civil War),* New York: St. Martin's Press, 1992; K. S. Salibi, *Crossroads to Civil War,* Edgar O'Ballance, *Civil War In Lebanon, 1975-1992,* New York: St. Martin's Press, 1998; P. E. Haley and L. W. Snider (eds.), *Lebanon In Crisis; Participants And Issues,* New York; Syracuse University Press, 1979; M. Deeb, *The Lebanese Civil War,* New York: Praeger, 1980; W. Khalidi, *Conflict And Violence In Lebanon: Confrontation In The Middle East,* MA.: Harvard University, Center for International Affairs, 1979; E. E. Azar (et.al.), *Lebanon And The World In The 1980's.* MD.: University of Maryland: The Center for International Development, 1983; Harold Vocke, The Lebanese War, New York: St. Martin's Press, 19Th; Thabita Petran, *The Struggle Over Lebanon,* New York: Monthly Review Press, 1978; Jean-Pierre Peroncel-Hugoz, *Une Croix sur le Liban,* Paris: Liew Comniun, 1984; Richard A. Gabriel, *Operation Peace For Galilee, The Israel-PLO War in Lebanon,* Toronto: Collins Publishers, 1984; Jean Said Makdisi, *Beirut Fragments, A War Memoir,* New York: Persea Books, 1990; Yair Evron, *War And Intervention In Lebanon, The Israeli-Syrian Deterrence Dialogue,* Baltimore: The Johns Hopkins University Press, 1987; A. J. Abraham, "The Lebanon War, In Retrospect And Prospect," *Journal of Third World Studies,* Fall, 1994, vol. XI, no. 2, pp. 117-150; Eric Rouleau, "Civil War In Lebanon," *SWASIA,* vol. II, no. 41, Oct., 1975, pp. 1-8; A. J. Abraham and Abmed Abdul Majid, " The Lebanese Labyrinth," *Transnational Perspectives,* vol. 12, no. 1, 1986, pp. 14-17; A. J. Abraham and Ahmed Abdul Majid, "The Lebanese Tangle," *Int'l. Journal on World Peace,* vol. IV, no. 2, Apr.-June, 1989, pp. 33-48; Paul Wilkinson, "The Lebanese Powder keg," *Contemporary Review,* Aug., 1983, vol. 243, no. 1411, pp. 64-71.

2. F. Moughrabi and N. Aruri (eds.), *Lebanon, Crisis And Challenge In The Arab World,* Special Report No. 1, Assoc. of Arab-American Univ. Graduates, January, 1977, p. 11.

3. P. L. Gabriel, *In the Ashes,* Penn.: Whitmore Pub., Co., 1978, p. 242.

4. B. C. Gordon, *Lebanon, the Fragmented Nation,* London: The Hoover Institution Press, 1980, p. 89.

5. Salibi, *Crossroads to Civil War,* p. 33; M. C. Hudson, "The Palestinian Role in The Lebanese Civil War," presented at the Annual Meeting of the Middle East Studies Association, New York, 9-11, November, 1977, p. 10.

6. Junblat, *Fi Majra al-Siyasa al-Lubmaiya;Haqiqat al-Thawra al-Lubnaniya.*

7. See: *Ta'rikh Hizb al-Kata'ib al-Lubnaniyah 1936-1940,* Beirut: Dar al-Amal lil Nashr, n.d.; John Entelis, *Pluralism and Party Transformation in Lebanon,*

Al-Kata'ib, 1936-1970, Leiden, The Netherlands; E. J. Brill, 1974; "Belief-System and Ideology Formation in The Lebanese Kata'ib Party," *IJMES,* vol. 4, no. 2, April, 1973, pp. 148-162.

8. Salibi, *Crossroads to Civil War,* pp. 97-98; Vocke, *The Lebanese War,* p. 39.

9. Karami's refusal was based upon his belief that the army should only be used to protect the state. He was also fearful that if it showed any partiality, it would split into Christian and Moslem halves, making the situation worse.

10. For differing views on who started the battles see: Petran, *The Struggle Over Lebanon,* p. 177: Salibi, *Crossroads to Civil War,* pp. 125-126; Vocke, *The Lebanese War,* p. 43; Odeh, *Lebanon, Dynamics of Conflict,* pp. 144-145; Gordon, *Lebanon,* p. 242.

11. For more on Karnal Junblat's ideology see: Junblat, *I Speak for Lebanon; Hadahi Wisayati,* Beirut; 1978.

12. The letters (Aug 23, 1975) were sent to the Lebanese President, the Maronite Patriarch, the Moslem clergymen, and leaders of the National Movement asking them to endorse the plan and to suggest ways to guarantee the secularization of the state for future generations. Gemayel received no response. Odeh, *Lebanon, Dynamics of Conflict,* p. 142; Petran, *The Struggle Over Lebanon,* p. 171; Khalidi, *Conflict and Violence in Lebanon,* p. 149.

13. Camille Chamoun, *Crise au Liban,* Beirut: 1977; Also see: *Memoire et Souvenirs du 17 Juillet 1977 au 24 December 1978,* Beirut: Impreme Catholique, 1979.

14. General al-Ahdab was a well known nationalist with no outstanding political ties. His coup on March 11, 1976 came a bit too late to succeed. For details on this "television coup" see: Petran, *The Struggle over Lebanon,* p. 191; Odeh, *Lebanon, Dynamics of Conflict,* pp. 161-162; Gordon, *Lebanon,* p. 247.

15. There are numerous accounts of the battle told from different ideological perspectives. See: Salibi, *Crossroads to Civil War,* pp. 149-151; Odeh, *Lebanon, Dynamics of Conflict,* p. 175.

16. The Arab League met on October 17-18, in Riyadh, Saudi Arabia, to expand the Syrian presence into the Arab Deterrent Force (the ADF), to enforce the Cairo Agreement of 1969.

17. This was a limited thrust into Lebanon to push the PLO forces away from the Israeli border.

18. Abraham, *Lebanon: A State of Siege.* p. 33; Odeh, *Lebanon; Dynamics of Conflict,* p. 189; Petran, *The Struggle Over Lebanon,* p. 220; David Gilmour, Lebanon: *The Fractured Country,* New York: St. Martin's Press, 1984, pp. 144-145.

19. Gilmour, Lebanon, *The Fractured Country,* pp. 147-150; Petran, *The Struggle Over Lebanon,* pp. 240-242; Khalidi, *Conflict and Violence in Lebanon,* pp. 123-143; Itamar Rabinovich, *The War For Lebanon,* Revised Edition, New York: Cornell University Press, 1985, p. 107.

20. Ghassan Tueni, *Kitab al-Harb,* Beirut: Dar al-Nashr lil Nashr, 1977; Karim Bakradouni, *Al-Salam al-Matqoud, Ahd al-Yas Sarkis, 1976-1982,* Beirut: TOP Press, n.d.; *La'nat al-Watan,* Beirut: n.p., n.d.

21. On Musa al-Sadr sees: Norton, *Amal and theShi'a,* pp. 38-58; Fouad Ajami, *The Vanished Imam,* New York: Cornell University Press, 1986; Musa al-Sadr, *Nukhba Min al-Muhadarat,* Beirut, n.p., n.d.

22. Z. Schiff and E. Ya'ari, *Israel's Lebanon War,* New York: Simon and Schuster, 1984; O'Ballance, *Civil War in Lebanon,* pp. 113-116. Rabinovich, *The War For Lebanon,* p. 134; David C. Gordon, *The Republic of Lebanon: Nation in Jeopardy,* Boulder, Co.: Westview Press, 1983, pp. 141-144; Gilmour, *Lebanon, The Fractured Country,* pp. 160-164; Odeh, *Lebanon: Dynamics of Conflict,* pp. 197-202; Petran, *The Struggle for Lebanon,* pp. 275-278; George W. Ball, *Error and Betrayal in Lebanon,* Washington, DC.; Foundation for Middle East Peace, 1984, pp. 36-38; Jacobo Timmerman, *The Longest War, Israel in Lebanon,* New York: Alfred A. Kompf, 1982.

23. Gilmour, Lebanon: *The Fractured Country,* p. 172; Abraham, *Lebanon: A State of Siege,* p. 37; Ball, *Error and Betrayal in Lebanon,* Pp. 49-52; *The Blue Helmets,* United Nations Publications, p. 144; Ramesh Thakur, *International Peacekeeping in Lebanon,* Boulder, Co. : Westview Press, 1987, pp. 79-107.

24. The explosion took place on September 14, 1982. On Bashir Gemayel and his ideology see: *Liberte et Securite,* Beirut: *La Resistance Libanaise,* 1980; Gordon, *The Republic of Lebanon,* p. 147; Gilmour, *Lebanon: The Fractured Country,* pp. 172-173; Petran, *The Struggle Over Lebanon,* pp. 283-284; Odeh, *Lebanon: Dynamics of Conflict,* p. 199; *The Blue Helmets,* p. 144; Rabinovich, *The War for Lebanon,* p. 144.

25. Petran, *The Struggle Over Lebanon,* pp. 386-388; *The Blue Helmets,* p. 145; Odeh, *Lebanon: Dynamics of Conflict,* p. 199; Gilmour, *Lebanon: The Fractured Country,* pp. 173-176.

26. See Amine Gemayel, *Peace and Unity,* Great Britain: Cohn Smythe Ltd., 1984.

27. Barry Rubin and Laura Blum, *The May 1983 Agreement Over Lebanon,* FPI Case Studies, no. 7, The Johns Hopkins University,1987; *The New York Times,* May 17, 1983, pp. A12- A13.

CHAPTER 11

POST-WAR LEBANON (1985-1996)

No doubt, Lebanon's many internal and external wars have left the state weak and in a no win scenario. But, the conflict of 1975 did, indeed, come to an end in 1985, when the actual battles stopped or were greatly reduced, with a no victor, no vanquished "cold peace." (Only the Palestinians were left to face the vengeance of the Shi'ites of South Lebanon. From June 1985 until January of 1988, the Amal militia with Syrian support and approval besieged and devastated the PLO camps in and around Beirut and Tyre, to root out any "returned fighters," remaining leftists hiding in the PLO camps, and to exact revenge for the alleged abuses that the Shi'ites suffered at the hands of the PLO leftist forces during the war years.[1] More than two thousand. Palestinians were reported killed and many more wounded. Palestinian power in Lebanon was permanently terminated.)

By themselves, the Lebanese politicians could have found a solution to their problems of power sharing, but outside interference prevented that. In the absence of meaningful negotiations among the Lebanese factions due to their constant bickering, Syria was the only force in the area among the Lebanese factions strong enough to deal with the heavily armed militia and their wily leaders.

On December 28, 1985, a Syrian sponsored initiative brought the Lebanese leaders to Damascus to sign a Tripartite Agreement calling for the "strategic integration of all major Lebanese institutions with their Syrian counterparts." The Lebanese Forces rejected the Syrian plan, but the plan won support at the Arab League summit in Casablanca on May 25, 1989. Thus, the Syrian hold over Lebanon was reinforced.

After the Casablanca conference, the Lebanese Front split into two factions: those led by Elie Hobeika who favored the Syrian option; and those led by Samir Geagea (*Jaja*) who called for a total Syrian withdrawal from Lebanon based upon a flexible timetable. Eventually Geagea's group won control of the Lebanese Forces.

The Islamic Front was also divided between a secular Amal led by Nabih Berri, and a smaller Islamic Amal backed by the militant fundamentalists of Hizb Allah (the Party of God) whose main objective has been to create an Islamic State in Lebanon, a clone of Iran. Hizb Allah and the Islamic Amal are allied and helped by several thousand Iranian Revolutionary Guards sent to Lebanon to fight the Israelis. They are financially supported by Iran through its embassy in Beirut.

As time passed on, this rather neat division was further complicated by General Michel Aoun's attempt to force all foreign troops from Lebanon. Meanwhile, the search for peace in Lebanon was likened to a blind man searching for a burned-out light bulb to replace a burned out light bulb, in a darkened room. Then, a new scenario was suggested to realign the forces at play.[2] The new psychological scenario set in motion a new peace effort to break the impasse that had developed over the years of struggle and, in the long run, it launched the Ta'if Accords, backed by both Syria and Saudi Arabia.

The Ta'if Accord of October 23, 1989 called upon Syria to disarm all militia in Lebanon and to establish a new "Lebanese Reconciliation Charter." That charter called for a redistribution of power between the Maronite Christians and the Sunnite Moslems, and for the expansion of the parliament to 128 members, equally divided between its Christian and Moslem delegates.

The Shi'ites and the Druze have gained little from the Ta'if Accord and, from their perspective, their enemies, the Maronites and the Sunnites, simply exchanged powers. Only Syria came out on top, having imposed a peace of subjugation with Lebanon tied to Syria, apparently forever. This was the price the Lebanese would pay for their political obstinacy, inter-group fears, hidden animosities, and the bloated egos of their leaders.

Under Syrian protection, the Lebanese legislature met to elect Rene Moawad to the presidency (November 5, 1989). Seventeen days later, on November 22, he was struck down by a car bomb. Immediately thereafter, on November 24, 1989, parliament elected Elias Hrawi to head the state. The Lebanese Forces supported Hrawi; and General Aoun and his nationalist supporters were defeated by a combined Syrian-Lebanese military force. General Aoun departed to the French Embassy and, later, left for France. With Aoun's departure, the "democratic right," or the Christian resistance to foreign domination was abruptly ended.[3]

The New Year of 1991 began with a governmental crisis. Walid Junblat, head of the Progressive Socialist Party, resigned from Prime Minister Omar Karami's cabinet and three Christian members of the cabinet, Samir Geagea, George Saadeh, and Michel Sassin representing the Lebanese Front refused to take their places over the worsening economic conditions and the plight of the Shi'ite refugees from the south.

Despite the problems the Lebanese government faced it remained in power, backed by Syria. Beirut became a unified city once again, but clashes continued between the Moslem parties in South Lebanon. By May of 1991, the Lebanese authorities sent the Lebanese Army south to disarm some of the militia. Only the Moslem fundamentalists of Hizb Allah, backed by Syria, remained armed and in power in parts of South Lebanon to oppose the Israeli presence on Lebanese soil. And, on the Lebanese-Israeli border, clashes were reported between the PLO, Israel and the South Lebanon Army under General Antoine Lahd. (The South Lebanon Army was a local force backed by Israel. Its main function was to prevent attacks across the southern border and to stabilize the region, in the absence of any control from the capital.)

Towards the end of May political attention was shifted and refocused on Damascus and Beirut as the presidents of both those states signed a Treaty of Brotherhood, Cooperation and Coordination, cementing the "special relationship" that exists between the two "sister" republics. However, there was no consensus on the treaty, for Lebanon lost sovereignty as the junior partner.[4] The treaty also violates the National Pact! Meanwhile, in South Lebanon, the Lebanese Army under the direction of Defense Minister Michel Murr (*al-Murr*) closed in on the remaining PLO bases and strongholds near the coastal city of Sidon, but it did not press the attack. General Murr warned the PLO leaders at the camps to obey Lebanese laws and control their forces.

Nevertheless, an upswing in the fighting in the south kept tensions high, for the remainder of the year. Then, on February 17, 1992, Shaykh Abbas al-Musawi, the Shi'ite leader of the anti-Israeli opposition forces, was killed in an Israeli air attack. He was, however, quickly replaced by Shaykh Hassan Naseallah, another militant, who sanctioned intensified raids into Israel. The Zionist State responded with lightning speed launching a twenty-four hour incursion into Lebanon, on February 21, 1992. By the end of the month both the Shi'ite militiamen and the IDF disengaged and returned to their former positions. In the capital, the middle of May saw the beginning of a new cabinet formed by an "old line" prime minister, Rashid al-Sulh. The new cabinet would include Nabih Berri, Walid Junblat, and Samir Geagea. Its aim was to be a balanced reconciliation cabinet.

Two months later, in July of 1992, the first act of the cabinet was to back President Hrawi's decision to return the Shi'ite and Christian refugees to their homes, a move that would affect approximately 116 villages and thousands of displaced persons from the south. Also, in that same month, the government announced plans to hold the first parliamentary elections since the war began some 17 years earlier.

To help secure a successful election, United States Secretary of State James A. Baker 3rd. visited Syria to hold talks with President Hafiz al-Assad on security for the elections and for a Syrian withdrawal from Lebanon. Then, Mr. Baker traveled to Zahle, Lebanon to meet with President Hrawi at his residence on July 22, 1992 to reaffirm Lebanon's sovereignty, independence and territorial integrity.

The elections were scheduled for September 22, 1992, after a Syrian withdrawal from the capital, to enable a free election to take place. But President Hrawi revised the schedule under Syrian pressure, and the Lebanese Front, led by Samir Geagea, and Maronite Patriarch, Nasr Allah (*Nasrallah*) Butrus Sfeir, wanted the Syrians out of the capital, before the elections took place to prevent the intimidation of anti-Syrian delegates or citizens. Prime Minister Sulh and minister Junblat wanted the elections to take place as soon as possible, under a Syrian security net to prevent any violence.

The crisis widened when the Lebanese Interior Minister, Major-General Sami al-Khatib, returned from a top level meeting in Damascus with Syrian Vice President Abd al-Halim Khaddam and announced that the elections would take place according to the new revised schedule; and that United Nations observers would not be allowed at the polling places. Only Syria would control the polling places. The Christian parties immediately called for a general strike on Election Day to block the vote, and quickly accused Syria of trying to influence the election with a strategy aimed at annexing Lebanon.

The first round of voting for the 128 legislative seats took place on August 23, 1992, in northern and eastern Lebanon, under stringent security. Few Christians voted and therefore the Iranian backed Hizb Allah candidates made substantial gains over the government backed candidates of the Speaker of the Parliament, Husayn al-Husayni. Due to the numerous "irregularities," and "vote-rigging," the speaker announced his resignation. Two Christian members of the Lebanese Cabinet, Foreign Minister Faris Bouez and Telecommunications Minister Georges Saadeh, handed in their resignations as well.

The second stage of voting began on August 30, 1992, in Beirut and the adjoining Christian and Druze mountain heartland. The turnout in Moslem areas was large; the Christians boycotted the election. Not surprisingly, the Iranian backed Hizb Allah won two seats in the capital and two Sunnite Moslem fundamentalists captured two other seats. The Deputy Speaker of Parliament, Michel Maalouli, called the election results inconclusive without the Christian population voting or running candidates. Only a Syrian "rubber stamp" parliament would emerge.

In the final round of balloting, on September 6, 1992, for delegates from the south, convoys of buses flying the black flag of Hizb Allah and the green flag of Amal trucked voters to the polls, to secure a fundamentalist victory. (No voting took place in the Israeli occupied security zone.)

No doubt, without Christian participation or with limited Christian participation in the voting, the election was invalid by any democratic standard. But more importantly, it threatened the structure of the state, the balance of communal power, and the democratic system in favor of the fundamentalists. The Lebanese nationalists of all sects were the losers by default.

To many, the election was a sham, a hoax. Syria, the Christian parties said, neutralized any popular or public figure that stood for Lebanese unity and independence, in favor of pro-Syrian candidates.[5] Ballot box stuffing and vote rigging were widespread. (Palestinians and Syrians voted using the names of dead Lebanese.) The results, translated into tangibles, gave Syria a new pro-Syrian Parliament until 1995 with a pro-Syrian president in power until 2001.

Had these elections taken place under United Nations auspice the results, obviously, would have been much different; and Lebanon might have truly begun to heal the wounds of war. Perhaps that was what Syria and the Iranian backed Hizb Allah feared the most, for it would have unified most of Lebanon against all outsiders. After the elections ended, calls for passive resistance were heard for the first time since the war had ended. And, some Christian extremists revived the idea of partitioning Lebanon into a Democratic Christian Republic north of the Beirut-Damascus highway, and an Islamic Republic south of that highway.

The elections were, however, an accomplished fact, and all parties had to acquiesce. By mid-September of 1992, Presidents Hafiz al-Assad and Elias Hrawi met in Latakia to discuss a Syrian withdrawal from Beirut. The following month, Nabih Berri won election to the parliament as its speaker, winning 105 out of 128 votes. His election was seen as a blow to the Hizb Allah candidates. The following day, on October 23, 1992, Rafiq al-Hariri, a Lebanese-Saudi businessman and billionaire, was named prime minister with a mandate to form a potent cabinet. In his acceptance speech Hariri set three goals for his term in office: to stem the economic crisis; to obtain investment capital for Lebanese reconstruction; and to lead a strong cabinet. A 500 million dollar investment fund was started in early December to help rebuild downtown Beirut, as a show of confidence in the prime minister and his program.

A month earlier, however, in an apparent nod to developments in Lebanon, Syria issued a statement saying that its withdrawal from Lebanon depended upon the implementation of the Ta'if Pact, conditions in South Lebanon, an end to sectarianism in Lebanese politics and an Israeli withdrawal from both the Golan Heights and southern Lebanon.

Meanwhile, in South Lebanon, the last three months of 1992 witnessed an Israeli build-up to stop rocket attacks across its border as well as hit and run attacks by the Islamic Resistance forces, the military wing of Hizb Allah, in the security zone. And, to complicate matters further, Israel deported 415 members of the Palestinian fundamentalist group Hamas to the Lebanese security zone. Lebanon refused to accept them; Israel refused to repatriate them; and, the United Nations was caught in the middle of a new crisis. In an attempt to stabilize conditions in South Lebanon, Lebanese Defense Minister Mohsin Dalloul sent an additional 2,000 troops south to maintain law and order, and to restrict the carrying of weapons in public.

Early January of 1993 saw a shift in focus from the reconstruction efforts in the capital to the deteriorating situation in the south. Despite Lebanese attempts to resolve the clashes between Israel and the Shi'ite fundamentalists, tensions grew. Thus, in February, United States Secretary of State Warren Christopher visited the Lebanese Defense Ministry complex in Beirut to try to defuse the situation in South Lebanon. His efforts were unsuccessful.

By July 1993, the Israelis began to use their jets and helicopter gun ships to keep Hizb Allah forces off-balance. This new and dangerous escalation in the fighting forced Lebanese Foreign Minister Faris Bouez to call for an urgent session of the United Nations Security Council, fearing another Israeli invasion of Lebanon, and perhaps a Syrian response.

Under extreme American pressure, Israel, in late July, announced that it would not invade Lebanon if the United States would broker a cease fire in which Hizb Allah would refrain from firing Katyusha rockets into Israel.[6] Soon after, an agreement was reached, and Lebanese civilians began returning to their homes in the south. Christopher, completing his meetings in Damascus in early August, made a quick, unscheduled, dash to Lebanon to meet with Hrawi, Hariri, and Bouez to try to induce Lebanon into participating in a newly proposed peace process. As Lebanese troops and personnel carriers deployed near Tyre, Israel and the Islamic fundamentalists traded fire within the security zone; while Israel, still under American pressure, agreed to take back the deported Palestinians.

By late August or certainly by early September, the situation in South Lebanon had calmed considerably as Hariri obtained a total of 74 million dollars in reconstruction aid from the Arab States. And, more importantly, the Arab-Israeli peace process began with Yasir Arafat and Israeli Prime Minister Shimon Perez at center stage. Lebanon's problems and interests seemed to be relegated to the back burners of Middle Eastern diplomacy and certainly to Israeli-Syrian negotiations.

Then, the pro-Iranian Party of God launched a new series of attacks in mid-September against Israeli forces camped in South Lebanon. It was the militia's response to the continued Israeli presence on Lebanese soil, the reconstruction initiative of the Beirut government, Israel's continued occupation of the Golan Heights, and the start of new Arab-Israeli peace talks. But the effort was futile! (On November 15, 1993, the United States had resumed issuing visas for travel to Lebanon, and as a result of that effort, air traffic to Beirut began in earnest; companies began to relocate back to Beirut, producing a sign of confidence in the Lebanese government and the peace talks.)

And, after several months of secret negotiations in Norway, Israel and the PLO agreed to a Declaration of Principles on Interim Self-Government Arrangements to be signed at the White House, on September 13, 1993. Ambushes, however, continued between the Israeli backed South Lebanon Army and Party of God forces well into February of 1994. Hizb Allah chief, Shaykh Hassan Nasrallah, called for Arafat's death as a traitor to the Arab cause in Palestine. In an attempt to ease the situation in South Lebanon and to prevent a full-scale Israeli invasion, President Elias Hrawi met with President Hafiz al-Assad of Syria, at the behest of United States Secretary of State Warren Christopher, to reign in Hizb Allah forces. But the battles continued, unabated.

By the end of March, the Lebanese government banned illegal broadcasts (from non-government stations) to end the verbal hostility from upsetting the growing peace effort.

The on again, off again border clashes, nevertheless, did continue well into April and May of 1994, with Syria now intensifying its demand not only for an Israeli withdrawal from South Lebanon, but also from all Syrian territory, before the legitimate resistance of the Party of God could end.

By early June, Israel's response was felt in the Bekka Valley when its war planes hit suspected Hizb Allah targets. Thus, President Hrawi called for an emergency United Nations meeting as United Nations Secretary General Boutros Boutros Ghali expressed concern over the escalation in the fighting. Lebanese Defense Minister Mohsin Dalloul warned all parties to the conflict that further attacks would jeopardize all peace initiatives in the region. The clashes, however, continued until the end of October when President Hrawi implied that he would set a timetable for the Lebanese Armed Forces to take over the south, after an Israeli pullout. By the end of the year, low level Israeli-

Syrian talks began in Washington, focusing on the Israeli occupation of the Golan Heights.

Despite the Israeli-Syrian peace talks that were in progress, Israel expanded its military operations in the north, towards Damour, and along the Lebanese coast, throughout the first two months of 1995. Lebanese Foreign Minister Faris Bouez called for United Nations intervention to end a new Israeli blockade that was affecting the economic life of South Lebanon's citizens, particularly its fishermen. On March 14, 1995, a nationwide strike and demonstration took place in the capital calling for an Israeli withdrawal from the south and the immediate implementation of United Nations Resolution 425 to get the Israelis out.[7] Throughout April, May and June, fighting intensified spiraling and spinning out of control; Israeli casualties mounted as did Hizb Allah's. Finally, in an appeal to Syria, General Antoine Lahad, commander of the South Lebanon Army (SLA), called on President Assad to help control the situation by restricting the activities of the Party of God. Israeli Foreign Minister Shimon Perez called on both Lebanon and Syria to try to prevent clashes along the northern Israeli border because they were becoming too dangerous to all parties concerned. He called for renewed negotiations in late October

The Israelis believed that Syria was the key to peace in Lebanon and, as an indication of that, Israel's new Foreign Minister Ehud Barak invited Syria to participate in joint peace efforts. Meanwhile, in Lebanon, President Hrawi began a new term in office, his old term extended with popular approval and Syrian backing. (The Constitution was amended on October 19, 1995 to initiate the change.)

The following month Prime Minister Perez called for a comprehensive peace that would involve Syria. Assad was to deliver security along the northern Israeli border in return for the Golan Heights. Finally Syria became a "prime time" player; but Lebanese independence would remain illusionary with Syria in charge of a "puppet" government in Beirut. In the Lebanese capital, people of all sects and groups mixed amid a friendly ambience (And as early as May of 1994, war damage began to disappear as a 1.8 billion dollar project called Solidere began to revive Beirut.) The year ended on a positive note.

But, peace did not come to South Lebanon; by mid-March, 1996, fighting resumed against the Israeli presence and the SLA, by the forces of Hizb Allah. Shaykh Hassan Nasrallah called for renewed attacks against the occupiers using a new "human bomb battalion" that was being trained.[8] By April, the fighting had escalated to a dangerous level, and Israel's right-wing leaders called for expanded operations into the eastern Bekka region. Syria implied that the hit and run tactics would continue because the Hizb Allah guerrillas were "within their rights to fight against Israeli troops occupying Lebanese territory."

On April 13, 1996 Israel penetrated Lebanese air space to hit the suburbs of Beirut, and Syrian anti-aircraft batteries. Israel intensified its raids against southern Lebanese villages producing a flood of refugees into Beirut. The Israelis called their military initiative: Operation Grapes of Wrath.[9] Fearing another all out invasion of Lebanon, Prime Minister Hariri met with President

Mubarak of Egypt and Jacques Chirac of France to try to get them to dissuade Israel. But, it was the United States that began talks with Israel led by Secretary of State Warren Christopher to try to stabilize the situation which had the potential for another mini-war. The talks revolved around two key issues: control of Hizb Allah by Syria in return for an Israeli withdrawal from the Golan Heights and an Israeli pullout from the entire buffer zone. The battles raged into late April, 1996.

Then, on April 20, Secretary of State Christopher flew to Damascus to meet with President Assad. His mission was to clarify the 1993 (oral) cease fire agreement by committing it to paper.[10] This would, in the American view, improve the still volatile atmosphere for direct talks to begin between Syria and Israel.

On the heels of the United States mediation effort, Iran sent its Foreign Minister Ali Akhbar Velayati to meet with President Assad and Shaykh Nasrallah to promise further aid to keep the situation unstable. (The Iranian budget to create a Shi'ite Islamic State in Lebanon was estimated to be 150 million dollars a year.) Despite a very generous offer, Syria stayed out of the fighting preferring to fight to "the last Lebanese Shi'ite," or until Syria was invited to the peace talks. Syria had been left out, isolated, from the Arab-Israeli peace process for too long, and it now felt that its prestige was on the line. But Syria would not intervene in open combat, unless Israel attacked the Syrian armed forces.

By the end of April, more than two weeks of fighting had resulted in yet another stalemate. President Hrawi met with President Clinton in Washington and called for a resumption of the Arab-Israeli peace talks to get Israel out of his country, and presumably frustrate Iranian attempts to destroy the peace process. Towards the end of April 1996, the United States obtained a preliminary written document for a cease-fire in South Lebanon with all parties agreeing to monitors to watch and record any cross border violations. All fighting would be restricted to Lebanese territory, the security zone, as "legitimate resistance to occupation." Members of the monitoring group would be drawn from the United States, Syria, France, Lebanon, and Israel. And, the agreement called for American, French and European Union aid to help reconstruct Lebanon, along with United States support for a resumption of direct Syrian-Israeli negotiations. By the end of the month, the Lebanese refugees began to return to their homes with the assistance of the Beirut government

The new cease-fire did not end the guerrilla warfare in South Lebanon, but it did become much more manageable. Over the next several months negotiations were resumed while clashes were monitored from a site in Naqura, using sophisticated satellite tracking equipment.

The peace talks between Syria and Israel faltered from the start when Prime Minister Benjamin Netanyahu called for two sets of negotiations,[11] one for the Golan Heights and the other for South Lebanon, with no promise of a complete withdrawal from either position. On August 8, 1996, Syria rejected the proposed change to the original agenda that had agreed upon the linkage.

Meanwhile, in Beirut, former right-wing leader Samir Geagea, surving a life term for the murders of Elias al-Zayek (1991) and Dani Chamoun (1990) was charged with the assassination of Prime Minister Rashid Karaini (1987).[12] The law and order government of President Hrawi was gaining confidence.

On Sunday, August 18, 1996, Parliamentary elections began in Mount Lebanon, North Lebanon, Beirut, South Lebanon and the Bekka Valley with a major victory for the government sponsored candidates,[13] although charges of irregularities were heard. Moderate candidates won 32 of the 35 contested seats. This was clearly a vote of confidence for Hrawi and his administration but, more importantly, it was a rejection of radicalism by the people of Lebanon. For the rest of the year stability would prevail and increase, with the sole exception of the southern security zone.

1. Elizabeth Picard, *Lebanon: A Shattered Country,* New York: Holmes and Meier Publishers, 1996, pp. 132-133; O'Ballance, *Civil War in Lebanon,* pp. 158-160.

2. A. J. Abraham, "A Psychological Approach to Conflict Resolution in the Third World," *Journal of Unconventional History,* vol. 9, no. 1, Fall, 1997, pp. 56-57.

3. Walid Phares, *Lebanese Christian Nationalism: The Rise and Fall of An Ethnic Resistance,* Boulder: Lynne Rienner Publishers, 1995, pp. 157-177; O'Ballance, *Civil War In Lebanon,* p. 187.

4. Fida Nasrallah, "Treaty of Brotherhood, Cooperation and Coordination: an assessment," in Youssef M. Choueiri (ed.), *State and Society in Syria and Lebanon,* New York: St. Martin's Press, 1993, pp. 103-111; Abraham, *The Lebanon War,* pp. 179-180; Dilip Hiro, *Lebanon, Fire And Embers,* New York: St. Martin's Press, 1992, pp. 241-245, 191-192.

5. William Harris, *Faces of Lebanon, Sects, Wars, And Global Extensions,* New Jersey: Markus Wiener Publishers, 1997, p. 281.

6. Hala Jaber, *Hizbollah, Born With a Vengeance,* New York: Columbia University Press, 1997, pp. 193-194.

7. Jaber, *Hizbollah,* pp. 195-196; Beate Hamiyrachi, *The Emergence of the South Lebanon Security Belt: Major Saad Haddad and The Ties With Israel 1975-1978,* New York: Preager Publishers, 1988.

8. Jaber, *Hizbollah,* pp. 186-187; Harris, *Faces of Lebanon,* p. 316.

9. Harris *Faces of Lebanon,* p. 318.

10. Jaber, *Hizbollah,* p. 203.

11. Harris *Faces of Lebanon,* p. 320.

12. Harris, *Faces of Lebanon,* p. 300; Phares, *Lebanese Christian Nationalism,* p. 218.

13. Harris, *Faces of Lebanon,* pp. 321-322; Jaber, *Hizbollah,* pp. 211-212.

CHAPTER 12

THE CONTEMPORARY SCENE (1997-2007)

By the end of 1996, post War Lebanon had reconstituted its government, its political leaders were back to a consensus and cooperation scenario, and most of Lebanon was back to business as usual, after successful reconstruction, leaving only South Lebanon in turmoil.

The first two weeks of January, 1997, however, saw an escalation in the fighting in southern Lebanon; by the end of the month, Prime Minister Netanyahu called for an end to the on-going proxy war; he agreed to reopen negotiations with Syria, under intense pressure from President Clinton. But Netanyahu wanted an end to all combat before any significant Israeli pull-out, adding a new condition for the peace talks to resume. Nevertheless, within Israel, some Israelis called for an immediate pull back from South Lebanon, since the security zone was no longer needed and had become "Israel's little Vietnam." Instead of the security zone protecting Israel, Israel was protecting the security zone!

In the Bekka Valley, a mid-February sweep of the region by Lebanese troops detained several members of the Japanese Red Army still hiding there. Lebanese Foreign Minister Faris Bouez said that Lebanon would hold them, the last of numerous leftist groups that had come to Lebanon to overthrow its pro-western "Christian" government. Those arrested were: Kozo Okamato, Kazuo Tohira, Hisashi Matsuda, Masao Adachi, Mariko Yamamoto, and Haruwo Wako, all trained and supplied by the Iranian Revolutionary Guards, and supposedly sent to Lebanon to fight Israel and its supporters. The heavily armed Iranian Revolutionary Guards continued to influence large areas of eastern Lebanon backed by millions of dollars shuffled to them through the Iranian Embassy in Beirut and with arms sent through Syria. With those resources available to the warriors of Hizb Allah, clashes continued with increasing frequency in South Lebanon throughout early May of 1997.

Despite the recurring confrontations and reprisal raids, Lebanon was a much safer place than it was before. Early in May, the Beirut government indicated that the famous Baalbek Festival would return with its pageantry: opera and modern music; ballet and Jazz; theater and plays; and music from around the world.

Furthermore, it was announced that Pope John Paul II would visit Lebanon to prop up the new spirit of reconciliation among all groups and sects. On May 10, 1997, the Pope arrived in Beirut for a two day visit; he was received at the airport by President Hrawi; and, he received a warm welcome from various Christian leaders and best wishes for a successful visit from notable Moslems including Shaykh Muhammad Hussayn Fadl Allah. He met with Maronite Patriarch Nasr Allah (Cardinal) Butros Sfeir calling for Lebanese independence and sovereignty, and the Pope discussed the Syrian and Israeli presence in

Lebanon. The Holy Father said that the Vatican was opposed to foreign troops (meaning Syrian or Israeli) in Lebanon. He called for a "dialogue of compromise" among all Lebanese sects. The presence of the pope in Lebanon for the first time was a tremendous boost for the Christians of Lebanon, particularly for the Maronites. It took place without a hitch, even though some Islamic fundamentalists had vowed to blow up the pope's plane upon its arrival. The threat proved to be hollow; more than half a million people, Christians and Moslems, attended a mass calling for all faiths to "live together in peace, brotherhood, and co-operation." The pope called Lebanon more than a country or nation but, rather, "a message of tolerance" to the troubled region. He was, later, to meet with several Moslem leaders who welcomed his message of peace and reconciliation.

In the capital, Beirut's government was more concerned with avoiding a diplomatic problem with Japan over the arrest and trial of several members of the Japanese Red Army. On June 10, five guerrilla leaders were brought to trial and admitted to illegal entry into Lebanon where they were recruited by leftist groups to "bring down the predominantly Christian pro western government." (One of the leaders, Kozo Okamato, had been captured by the Israelis and exchanged in a PLO prisoner swap.) They also claimed responsibility for an attack on the American consulate in Kuala Lumpur, Malaysia, and for the hijacking of a Japanese airliner. They were trained in the Bekka Valley by Iranians to kill Jews and Christians. Lastly, they admitted that many other "foreign nationals" had been trained there. To avoid a diplomatic incident or crisis, the Lebanese court sentenced the men to three years in jail with a reduced sentence on the charge of using forged passports, and illegal entry, on August 1, 1997.

While attention was focused on the capital for a while, the end of July saw the ban on travel to Lebanon from the United States lifted, as Dr. Madeleine K. Albright, the United States Secretary of State, called for increased cooperation between the two nations, and the complete independence of Lebanon. Throughout the month of August, the United States called for "maximum restraint" from both sides in South Lebanon, but violence continued to spread, with Israeli air strikes near Sidon, and Hizh Allah rocket fire hitting Qiryat Shemona. Prime Minister Hariri called the Israeli strikes "state terrorism." (The five nation monitoring group proved to be as useless as its UNIFIL predecessor.)

With increased Israeli losses becoming a problem to the Netanyahu government, new debates in Israel on the value of the security zone, from mid-September until years end, continued with no conclusion in sight. For the Israelis, the key issue in the debate was how to extract themselves from South Lebanon without looking as if they were defeated or that they had abandoned their allies.

By early March, 1998, opinion in the Jewish State was strongly divided between those who called for an immediate withdrawal and those who wanted security established in northern Israel first. Lebanon called for unconditional withdrawal; and Syria said all this activity was just another Israeli ploy to cut a separate deal with Lebanon and avoid any pull out on the Golan Heights. Over the next four months fighting continued with each side claiming that the other side started it first. No progress was made. Then the Lebanese authorities began a search for a stronger leader who might influence the situation without opposing Syrian wishes or aggravating the Israelis.

Their candidate was General Emile Lahoud. He enjoyed a broad base of support among all Lebanese factions; Lahoud was neutral in the recent conflict; and, he had pledged to reform the public administration to end the endemic corruption and inefficiency, if elected. The Lebanese Parliament, once again, amended the constitution to achieve his election in October of 1998.

Meanwhile, a new crisis was brewing in South Lebanon. Apparently, in the security zone, Israel had been carting away Lebanese top soil for use in Israel to make the desert bloom. "Hundreds of tons" had been taken, loaded on to trucks by earth moving equipment, (Once again, Israel was accused of "stealing" Arab land.) Lebanese Parliament Speaker Nabih Berri and, shortly afterwards, Lebanese Foreign Minister Faris Bouez, called upon the United Nations and the European Union to pressure Israel to stop the theft of a Lebanese national resource. After the United Nations confirmed the theft of soil, Israel ordered its army to stop further plundering and to apprehend the suspects. However, they were never caught, nor were any soil returned.

By the end of November, 1998, Emile Lahoud was sworn in as president but the joy of the moment diminished when George Saade, who had helped in negotiating an end to the 1975 civil war, died. In early December of 1998, Lahoud backed Salim al-Hoss' candidacy for prime minister, and Rafiq al-Hariri resigned his post. Political instability increased.

Then, Israeli aircraft was seen over Beirut and sonic booms rattled windows to demonstrate that Israeli patience was thinning. Israel had demanded, in early December, that all attacks on the IDF be ended to facilitate a rapid withdrawal from Lebanon. When no response was forthcoming, Israeli jets hit targets in eastern Lebanon, fourteen miles south-west of Baalbek. Hizb Allah quickly responded with Katyusha rocket fire aimed at Qiryat Shamona. The year ended on a sour note.

In the capital, Prime Minister Salim al-Hoss won parliamentary approval to revive some public services, and the ban on all demonstrations was lifted, thereby showing increased confidence in the state.

The New Year began on a positive note when the Lebanese government ended the requirement to obtain visas to return to Lebanon, thus strengthening the forces of normalization in early 1999; only the south remained outside the grasp of the authorities. Prime Minister al-Hoss articulated the view that negotiations with Israel remained deadlocked; no further contacts had been made since the New Year began. In fact, fierce battles raged between the IDF and Hizb Allah well into February.

By early May, the Israeli death toll was reaching alarming proportions; and some Israelis in Prime Minister Netanyahu's government pressured him to negotiate a way out of South Lebanon. Netanyahu's response to the deteriorating situation was to send war planes over Beirut again rattling windows, and to send a small force to occupy the village of Armoun from which Hizb Allah forces ambushed the IDF. Shortly afterwards, Syria broke its long silence on South Lebanon saying that the new provocation would be resisted. The situation remained stalemated throughout April of 1999, as the international monitoring committee argued among themselves as to weather the occupation of Armoun violated the 1996 cease-fire agreement.

Netanyahu's policies, however, were soon rebuffed when Israel backed Ehud Barak for prime minister on a platform to make the withdrawal of Israeli forces from the security zone his top priority. By June 1, Israeli advisors and SLA troops began to pullout of Jazzin (*Jezzin*), an area they had held since 1985. General Lahad said that holding the town made casualties intolerable, but Israel was the force behind the departure of all the troops stationed there. It was, according to the Zionist State, a test to see the response of Hizb Allah to a limited pullback. Shaykh Nasrallah replied quickly saying that his forces would not enter the vacated area. Only Lebanese Army troops would he acceptable. Prime Minister Hoss confirmed the fact that only the legitimate authorities (the LAF) would patrol the town to avoid problems with any party; but, he refused amnesty for about two hundred members of the South Lebanon Army that gave up their weapons and stayed in Jazzin with their families. (By late August, a military court sentenced 83 members of the SLA to jail terms from 6 months to two years for "collaborating" with the enemy; in mid-September another seventeen militiamen were sentenced to terms ranging from one year to eighteen months. But, under the circumstances, this may prove to be a major error of the administration.) Most of the citizens of Jazzin were overjoyed to see the Beirut authorities reestablished. Israel called the phased withdrawal an "inconsequential" and "isolated" incident of no concern.

Both Prime Minister Hoss and President Lahoud visited Jazzin to bolster the government's authority in the south. Retaliatory raids, however, continued well into August; the blood letting continued to keep South Lebanon in turmoil maintaining its normal level of combat and instability. In mid-August, the situation took a turn for the worse when Shaykh Ali Hassan Deeb (*Dib*), also known as Abu Hassan, a Hizb Allah leader, was killed by a road side bomb blast aimed at the Israelis. Hizb Allah blamed the IDF, but Israel said it was Shaykh Ali's internal enemies that had murdered him. Fighting intensified and Israeli air power hit the Shi'ite forces in the security zone near Rihan, in late August of 1999.

Despite the new intensity in combat, the peace process between Arabs and Israelis continued. Yasir Arafat met with Georges Habash of the Popular Front for the Liberation of Palestine in Damascus and with Nayef Hawatmeh of the Democratic Front for the Liberation of Palestine in Cairo, to prepare for upcoming talks with Israel.

On the fourth of September, 1999, Madeleine K. Albright arrived in Beirut for talks with Salim al-Hoss in the hopes of getting Lebanon to participate with Syria and Israel in the future peace initiative. The main concern for Israel was to end Hizb Allah attacks along its northern border, before its troops departed. Syria, in addition, insisted that the talks start where they had left off in 1996. At that time President Assad maintained that then Prime Minister Rabin had pledged a total Israeli withdrawal from the Golan Heights in exchange for a peace treaty and the normalization of relations between both nations. And, more importantly for Lebanon, they had agreed to the disarming of Hizb Allah by Syria before its departure from Lebanon.

After Albright's discussions with Prime Minister Hoss and President Lahoud, the month of October witnessed a change of tactics by the Israelis, in their twenty-one year old, low intensity, war with the Shi'ites of Lebanon. Israel began to tone down its responses to Hizb Allah attacks; relying on new surveillance technology, Israel began pulling out some of its troops, as promised in the campaign of its new Prime Minister Ehud Barak. Barak's pledge to bring home the troops began to change the style of combat in the contested area. Increased air strikes were launched to reduce ground-force casualties.

Ground attacks against the Israeli backed South Lebanon Army continued throughout November with an increase in mortar and rocket fire. But the Israeli troops and the Hizb Allah forces took advantage of the lulls in the fighting to sound out each other and state some additional initiatives to end their confrontation. Most of the Lebanese population believed that Syria should be a major player in any new scenario.

Syria had been slighted in talks thus far and she wanted to be invited by the United States to negotiations with the Jewish State. Thus, peace along the Israeli-Lebanese border remained the "trump card" in any future negotiations. The "trick" to successful peace talks remained an exchange of the Golan Heights (all of it) for a Syrian-Israeli peace treaty and an end to all attacks along Israel's northern border. For Lebanon, the reward would be the disarmament of Hizb Allah, and both a Syrian and Israeli departure from all Lebanese territory. These two issues would dominate Lebanese politics well into the new millennium!

Early in December, President Lahoud struck a note of caution for any upcoming talks between Israel and Syria. He clearly stated that there would be no independent Lebanese-Israeli talks. Lebanon and Syria would act jointly; but Syria would lead the discussions for both of them, hence Lebanon's presence at the preliminary negotiations in Washington was deemed unnecessary. But, if asked, Lebanon would accept an American invitation to the talks.

By mid-December, peace talks were under way in the American capital. President Clinton acted as a go between and mediator to the representatives-Prime Minister Ehud Barak and Syrian Foreign Minister Farouk al-Shara. Clinton's main concern, at that time, was the upsurge in fighting in South Lebanon which could upset the talks or bring them to a halt. Syria, in a show of good faith to the Clinton administration, held back a Hizb Allah response to an Israeli barrage that injured about fifteen to twenty school children in the village of Arab al-Salim. Thus peace talks would not be derailed. A cease fire would prevail, at least for a while; and, in another gesture aimed at Hizb Allah, Israel released five of its prisoners from that group. The good will gesture was in anticipation of a second round of talks with Syria on substantial issues. Clearly the year ended on an optimistic note.

The next round of negotiations was set for the Clarion Hotel in Shepherdstown, West Virginia with an American "working paper" to maintain the momentum of the talks on a variety of concerns. Meanwhile, Lebanon remained an outside observer, while her destiny, once again, would be decided by foreign powers.

CONCLUSION

Lebanon has risen from its own ashes. The war, the violence, fanaticism, and political intrigues, has long subsided under the watchful eyes of the Syrian occupation forces. And, the Lebanese political and religious leaders have resumed their historic role as guardians of "consensus and cooperation."

The Lebanese economy is booming with ample initiative and financing. The prognosis for continued economic revival seems quite positive. As of November 1993, the Lebanese government launched a 650 million dollar financial plan to rehabilitate Beirut's commercial district.[1] Money for the reconstruction of war damaged Lebanon was plentiful with funds including loans, grants, and foreign credits coming from a wide variety of sources including the World Bank and the Arab Fund for Economic and Social Development.

The blueprint for rebuilding Lebanon, originally called Plan 2000, later changed to Horizon 2000, was an ambitious three phase program that included rehabilitation, recovery, and new developments. The Lebanese Council for Reconstruction and Development set a ten year, ten billion dollar goal to accomplish its task; and a subsequent plan called Horizon 2002 was projected to aid education. Funds for the program will be financed from the private sector by a joint-stock company called Solidere (The Lebanese Company for The Development and Reconstruction of The Beirut Central District), brought into being by an act of parliament.

At present, Lebanese business interests are seeking additional funds and know how from the United States Export-Import Bank and the United States Investment Corporation; investment possibilities for the United States in Lebanon abound.

Economic know how and incentive has never been a problem for the Lebanese and, certainly, opportunity has never been a problem in Lebanon. The time honored, and worn out, theories of economic "victimization" or "neglect" of some communities at the hands of the others has been over-rated, for opportunity existed and still exists for all but, perhaps, for some groups a bit more than others. But that is not unusual, for any nation. Indeed, there was, and still is to some small extent, the exploitation of the poor by the rich within each community, for Lebanon continues to have some "hidden or phantom" feudalism. But, Lebanon has never been nor is it now a Third World nation.

Lebanon's religious strife has also been tremendously over exaggerated in some analysis of the nation's recurring instability. Contrary to popular myth and misconception, religion has never been the cause of political problems or conflicts and wars in Lebanon. Organized religion has acted, more often than not, as a source of stability in a land of religious minorities with little or no true secularism.[2] However, in a highly religious atmosphere, there are always religious extremist like Hizb Allah (on the Moslem side) and the Guardians of The Cedars (on the Christian side). These groups only represent a minority of the population, but they are extremely vocal and ambitious. Hizb Allah is armed and supported by Syria and Iran; the Guardian of The Cedars are an alliance of pro-Christian Maronites who believe that Islam is more of a political religion seeking the establishment of an Islamic state under only Islamic law inLebanon.[3] And, that, they believe would be detrimental and would impact negatively upon the Christian population and Moslem minorities. Thus, religious fears and aspirations tend to blend together to produce some religious flavor to every political problem; but it is the political problem that manifests itself in Lebanese communal relations.

Lebanon's communal organization has produced an identity problem in the tiny republic. Each community or sect sees itself as a proto-national group, under its own leadership, and to protect themselves they band together for their own good. Each group or sect has its own version of what Lebanon should be like, and how to enhance their own pride, prestige and power. This has led to a powerful psychological predisposition among most communities to maintain autonomy or seek independence from the neighboring states, while other communities sought allies outside of Lebanon to further their goals. In fact, each community or sect has its own "foreign policy" that diminishes the strength of the central government's authority and often places the Lebanese communities in conflict with one another. Thus, they act as independent mini-nations within a larger national entity called Lebanon making it very difficult for a citizen to be "just Lebanese." (The Lebanese communities act like the many Third World communities living among the modern nations of the West. They seek to preserve their own parochial interests, identities and cultural peculiarities while trying to avoid assimilation into a large whole.).

The recent struggle (1975-1982) is just another example of the external and internal linkages in Lebanon that propels communal strife.

It is now clear to all observers of the Lebanese scene that the mixed marriage between the PLO and the "democratic left" in Lebanon is no longer a viable factor. Each group used the other unsuccessfully to achieve an illusionary goal; and they both failed in the long run.

On the domestic scene, since 1984, the rise of an Islamic fundamentalist movement has kept Lebanon unstable. It is primarily supported by Iranian Revolutionary Guards who train and equip fundamentalist Shi'ites who feel cheated by the Ta'if Accord (1989). For them, one of the largest communities in Lebanon, they have gained nothing from the peace agreement and, hence, they oppose it in favor of an Islamic State. But not all Shi'ites agree, and certainly, the Druze oppose any religious state in Lebanon.

To a great extent, the Shi'ites and Druze communities want a greater share of the pie. And, no doubt, they have some justification in that the Shi'ite population has grown and the Druze deserve a position of greater prestige in the government. The Ta'if Accord, to them, was only seen as an exchange of power among their enemies: the Maronites and the Sunnites. They gained nothing from it. During the horrific years of bloody conflict, many well intentioned scholars and diplomats have contributed to the deluge of books and articles attempting to resolve the conflict in Lebanon.[4] International conflict resolution such as the

Ta'if Accord and international economic development are not enough to stabilize Lebanese communal relations. More is needed.

Most of the studies on the Lebanese civil war agree that the United States should support the return of all of the Golan Heights to Syrian sovereignty upon the complete withdrawal of Syrian forces from all Lebanon and the total disarming of Hizb Allah forces. This was agreed upon in talks between Prime Minister Rabin and Hafiz al-Assad, same time ago. Recently Hafiz al-Assad's successor Bashar al-Assad, his son, offered the Israeli government a chance to renew or continue negotiations from that agreement, with other side issues or concerns to be discussed and dealt within side letters.

It would also auger well for the United States to adopt an interventionalist posture on Lebanon to give it a degree of priority in American Foreign Policy. Some scholars and diplomats have argued that there are no strategic benefits for the United States in Lebanon, such as oil or military bases. But, since when did the United States need physical tangibles to support its own principles over sees. Lebanon has always been supportive of Western ideals; and it is the Arab World's only functional democracy of any kind. For many Lebanese of all sects, the United States is "more than just an arms merchant to whom they (the Arabs) pay cash." There is a meaningful identity between the Western World and Lebanon, an identity rooted in the ideas of human dignity, human values, and individualism; in freedom of thought and religious belief; and in a commitment to liberalism and social justice. A stable, democratic and prosperous Lebanon is in the best interest and global strategy of the United States.

Lebanon must be declared neutral territory to all parties. Lebanon and its people have already paid an exorbitant price in the Arab-Israeli conflict; all foreign forces must leave Lebanon and stay out. Otherwise, Lebanon may be divided and "gobbled up" by its neighbors and, perhaps, lost forever. Further more, Lebanon and Syria: must end their "special" relationship; they are not "sister republics," but rather very different entities, at present. They are independent states with some similarities, perhaps like the United States and Canada. But, they have been independent entities for more than a century, and should arrange an ambassadorial exchange and terminate all other special ties by treaty or otherwise.

Lebanon's survival remains paramount to the entire region; it is the main source of progress and freedom in a troubled region of the world. It still radiates a modern culture with humane values worldwide. It is still an example and symbol of tolerance to the Third World and a missionary of hope for a better future in the Arab World. Lebanon is truly a Temple of Janus.

1. See: Sainir Khalif and Philip S. Khoury (eds.), *Recovering Beirut*, Leiden: E.J. Brill, 1993; for another perspective see: Hassan N. Diab, *Beirut, Reviving Lebanon's Past*, Conn.: Praeger, 1999.

2. A. J. Abraham, "Maronite Culture, Lebanon, and The Arab World," *In Transnational Perspectives*, vol. 15, no. 1, 1989, reprinted in *The Challenge*, June 10, 1990.

3. Abul-Husn, *The Lebanese Conflict, Looking Inward*, pp. 96-97.

4. For example see: D. Ignatius, "How to Rebuild Lebanon," *Foreign Affairs*, vol, 61, no, 5 (Summer, 1983), pp. 1141, 1150-1151; G. Tueni, "Lebanon: A New Republic," *Foreign Affairs,* vol. 61, no. 1, (Fall, 1982), pp. 96-97; Farid Khazin, "The Lebanese Economy After A Decade of Turmoil, 1975-1985," in *American-Arab Affairs*, Spring, 1985, no. 12, pp. 72-84.

EPILOGUE

In the two years since the beginning of the new millennium, Lebanon has undergone renewed tension resulting from the rapidly changing situation in the Middle East.

The war of attrition along the Lebanese-Israeli border intensified in late January of 2000, with increased exchanges of artillery fire and Israeli air strikes. But, amid the rise in tensions, Prime Minister Ehud Bank promised to withdraw the 1,100 Israeli soldiers from South Lebanon, leaving the SLA to defend the Israeli border. Despite the announcement, Israel lost three more men of the IDF and, then, several influential Israelis called for an immediate "unilateral, non-negotiated," withdrawal, while holding Syria responsible for the upswing in the fighting. But, Israel escalated its own response to Hizb Allah, hitting Lebanese power stations. Radio Damascus accused Israel of sabotaging the negotiation process which was still in limbo. Hizb Allah launched new attacks across the contested border to drive home their point- all Israeli forces must go, with or without negotiations!

But any withdrawal of Syrian forces would remain contingent upon an Israeli departure from the Golan Heights. Israel refused to negotiate any further on the issue of the Golan Heights, and United States Secretary of State Albright rushed to Syria to meet with Syrian Foreign Minister Al-Shara, unfortunately to no avail; but, Albright instructed United States Ambassador to Lebanon, David Satterfield, to write to Prime Minister Salim al-Hoss expressing "sorrow and regret" on behalf of the United States for the Israeli attack upon the Lebanese infrastructure, the power plants. Then, the United States pressured Israel to keep the July 7, 2000 deadline for a "unilateral" exit from Lebanon.

Israel had no choice but to get out of Lebanon. It had stayed too long in a hostile situation with nothing left to gain from its presence in South Lebanon. Escalating attacks were its only option and, in the long run, that would not protect northern Israel. After eighteen years of occupation and involvement, Israel had to make a decision to leave. (The Lebanese were fighting on their own soil to get the Israelis out of their country and they had Arab World support; and the United States no longer considered the PLO in Lebanon a threat to Israel and also wanted the Israelis out.)

Fighting continued throughout much of March. The Beirut government, however, was more concerned with its "tug of war" with Japan over the Japanese Red Army prisoners held in Lebanon. Eventually, Kozo Okamoto, a convert to Islam, was granted asylum while the others were deported to Jordan where they were handed over to Japanese officials.

No doubt, anxiety among the SLA members began to reach new heights when the Lebanese government, prodded by Shaykh Nasrallah, called for "collaborators" to be tried; He rejected all amnesty pleas on behalf of the SLA.

On April 18, 2000, Israel informed the United Nations command that it intended to withdraw all its forces by July 7, 2000. Meanwhile, fighting continued in southern Lebanon; Hizb Allah kept up the pressure to prevent

Israeli "hawks" from upsetting the timetable. Israel asked the United Nations to protect the SLA members while its leader, General Antoine Lahad, asked for complete amnesty for his troops. The United Nations said they could not intervene on behalf of the SLA; all they could do was to send additional troops to South Lebanon until the Beirut government could assume authority over the area.

On May 23, 2000, the long awaited Israeli pullout began in the buffer zone. All posts in the central sector were quickly abandoned, equipment was hauled out; and the Lebanese soldiers went home. Clearly, both Hizb Allah and Syria were caught by surprise; the Israelis left as quickly as they had come; within hours, all Israeli forces were out of Lebanon. Hizb Allah immediately sent its forces into the area to maintain order; and President Lahoud praised Hizb Allah for its role in achieving Lebanese objectives. Prime Minister Barak received Israeli congratulations for a safe withdrawal, but Ariel Sharon called it a "disgraceful retreat."

Complete peace, however, did not come to Lebanon. The new confrontation site would be at the Fatima Gate, and in an area called the Shebaa Farms, a four mile strip at the base of Mount Hermon near the Golan Heights that were capture by the Israelis in 1967. Israel has maintained that the Shebaa Farms are not covered in United Nations Resolution 425; and, that it had completed its departure from Lebanon in accordance with resolution 425. (The United Nations would eventually verify Israel's pullout; and, soon afterwards, the Lebanese Armed Forces would enter the south.)

In Syria, President Hafiz al-Assad had died and his son, Bashar al-Assad, took over and Lebanon quickly deployed an additional 500 soldiers and 500 policemen to the South, for security duty which apparently held without any Syrian aid.

By mid-June Israel began to encroach upon the Shebaa Farms area which both Lebanon and Syria claimed. In response, Hizb Allah said that it would fight for the liberation of the region. Meanwhile, the Lebanese public was distracted from both South Lebanon and the Shebaa Farms controversy by new elections for parliament which would run from August 20, 2000 to September 3, 2000, for a total of 128 seats. In the capital the Lebanese government announced that a military tribunal had sentenced several hundred SLA members to jail terms for their collaboration with the enemy, to satisfy Hizb Allah demands. But, Amnesty International called the trials a "show" and a "parody of justice," whose only purpose was to deflect anti-Christian feeling among some Shi'ites. Furthermore, in August, the United Nations clearly stated that border security was the sole responsibility of the Lebanese government, not the United Nations, and that UNIFIL's end was near.

But, the Lebanese were more concerned with the impending vote for parliament. A clash of interests had developed between the former prime minister, Rafiq Hariri (1992-1998) and President Emile Lahoud; both men were once backed by Syria but were now locked in a struggle for power. Rafiq

Hariri's political machine proved to be stronger than President Lahoud's and, thus, he won a sweeping victory for his parliamentary candidates at the polls (about 100 out of 128 seats); consequently his reappointment as prime minister by President Lahoud, in late October, was inevitable. Prime Minister Hariri's first act after appointment was to slash import duties to stimulate the economy. Thus, Lebanon ended the year politically stable; however, Maronite Patriarch Nasr Allah Sfeir raised a strong note of caution against over optimism in a message calling upon Syria to remove its troops from Lebanon, now that the IDF had departed; and, for Syria to seek a more "honest" partnership with Lebanon, in the New Year.

But the New Year opened on a familiar note: the Shebaa Farms dispute. The United Nations said that the Lebanese and the Syrians should decide whose property Shebaa Farms belonged to before any United Nations investigation could be made over Israeli claims. By mid-February 2001, Hizb Allah launched new military strikes in the Shebaa Farm region. Israel retaliated with air strikes against Syrian positions. Thus, the United Nations issued its own statement implying that the disputed territory was Syrian, not Lebanese. And, Israel hit Syrian radar stations in mid-April to underscore the point. Hizb Allah, however, defied both the United Nations and Syria saying that the region was, indeed, Lebanese territory, further complicating the situation.

By mid-June, 2001, Syria began to withdraw its troops from Beirut. The Maronite Patriarch along with several other Moslem and Christian political and religious leaders expressed some satisfaction while most of the Lebanese population supported them, in accordance with the Ta'if Accords. Walid Junblat, speaking for the Druze community, strongly supported the patriarch's initiative. And, the Lebanese government said that a complete Syrian pullout would greatly improve Syrian-Lebanese relations. By the end of June, six thousand Syrian soldiers had left Lebanon while others were deployed to less sensitive areas.

All Lebanese groups supported Hizb Allah's efforts to expel the Israelis and, therefore, they strongly refused to associate the movement with terrorism; for the Lebanese it was resistance to occupation. And, in fact, Hizb Allah acted in a more responsible way towards the people of South Lebanon than the Beirut authorities could; however, by December of 2001, Hizb Allah had become a state within a state with strong foreign ties and its own "foreign policy."

At noon on January 24, 2002 a powerful car bomb took the life of Elie Hobeika, a Christian leader many held responsible for the Sabra and Shatila massacre. Shortly after the blast an anti-Syrian Lebanese group, "Lebanese for a Free and Independent Lebanon," claimed responsibility.

By early April, the Israeli-Lebanese confrontation over the Shebaa Farms area had flared up once again when Hizb Allah fired mortars and anti-tank missiles into Israel. Moments later, Israeli jets struck several Lebanese villages. Tensions continued to mount into mid-June prompting a visit from United States Secretary of State Colin Powell to Lebanon and Syria to pressure both states to "crack down" on Hizb Allah and its leader Shaykh Nasrallah. Over the next few months Hizb Allah was determined to maintain its largely symbolic resistance to Israel hoping to force Israel out of the Shebaa Farms region and the Syrian Golan Heights.

The unstable conditions in Lebanon induced a return visit by Powell to Beirut seeking support for a new peace initiative called the "road map." He met with President Lahoud, Prime Minister Rafiq Hariri, and Parliamentary Speaker Nabih Berri. Hizb Allah leader Nasrallah was not consulted and, consequently, Hizb Allah issued a statement that it would not end its resistance to the Israeli occupation of the Shebaa Farms or the Golan Heights.

Nevertheless, the United States reopened its consulate in Beirut on May 30, 2003 indicating a normalization of relations between the two nations- a confidence building gesture. But, the border situation remained problematic. Negotiations over the Shebaa Farms region and the Golan Heights remained deadlocked despite all American efforts. Israel rebuffed an American call for talks with Syrian President Bashar al-Assad leading to renewed attacks by Hizb Allah on Israeli territory in mid-January 2004.

Meanwhile, negotiations between the two states have remained frozen with Prime Minister Sharon demanding new talks while Assad wanted to continue from previous agreements that were made between his father and Prime Minister Rabin. To punctuate his point, President Assad pushed for a Lebanese constitutional amendment, opposed by all Lebanese but Hizb Allah his surrogate in Lebanon, to keep President Lahoud in office after his term has expired. The bill was presented to the Lebanese Parliament, but expected support for it from Rafiq Hariri and Walid Jumblat failed to materialize. Both men rejected Syria's heavy handed dictation of that scenario, and overt interference in Lebanon.

These events led to a coordinated effort by both the United States and France calling upon Syria to withdraw its 14,000 troops and personnel from Lebanon by August 31, 2004. (The new American initiative bolstered President Bush's Syrian Accountability and Lebanese Sovereignty Restoration Act of 2003.)

Faced by this extraordinary course of events, the Maronite Patriarch and the Lebanese Prime Minister closed ranks after an attempted reconciliation with Syria had failed. Then, Walid Junblat's Progressive Socialist Party joined the opposition. Lahoud quickly responded by rejecting American and French meddling in Lebanese affairs.

At United Nations headquarters, the Security Council passed resolution 1559 (September 2, 2004), with nine votes in favor and six abstaining, calling upon Syria to stop interfering in Lebanese politics and for all foreign forces to leave Lebanon.

No doubt, Syria held all the cards in Lebanon; the Lebanese Parliament "rubber stamped" Syria's instructions to amend its constitution in a 96 to 29 vote; but the heavy handed effort failed in the long run. Syria had miscalculated Lebanese opposition to its military presence and secret agents.

In an attempt to head off a major international crisis in Lebanon, The Gulf Cooperation Council appealed to Syria to "respect" the Security Council Resolution in its own time and way. President Assad's reply said that Syrian troops were in Lebanon "by mutual agreement" and he voiced concern for Lebanese stability if the Syrians departed.

Hariri replied that the "mutual agreement" had ended, and he resigned from office on October 20, 2004 dissolving the Lebanese Cabinet bringing the crisis to a head. The president responded by quickly appointing Omar Karami, a pro-Syrian politician from Tripoli, as the new prime minister with a mandate to form a new cabinet.

On February 14, 2005, an enormous car bomb destroyed the motorcade of former Prime Minister Rafiq Hariri instantly killing him and eleven other persons. Syria immediately condemned the attack calling it the work of "criminals;" Hariri may have had many personal enemies, but the nature and extent of the blast left little doubt that Syrian agents were behind it. The explosion at mid-day demolished a large building and killed or wounded about one hundred persons. President Lahoud called Hariri a martyr for a united Lebanon.

Hariri supporters rejected notions that "rogue" warriors were behind the attack implying that the culprits were the Syrian security services. They called for an immediate Syrian pull out from Lebanon and for Syrian compliance with resolution 1559. And, they called for an international investigation into the event.

The Bush administration condemned the assassination and called for a United Nations investigation and, then, withdrew its ambassador from Syria in protest. The United States asked Secretary-General Kofi Annan to investigate the circumstances to pinpoint the culprits.

Hariri's funeral, near an unfinished mosque that he had supported, became the rallying point for thousands of Lebanese protesters from all walks of life. Posters and signs read: "Syria Out" and "We Don't Want You". At Martyr's Square traffic came to a complete halt. Lebanese people of all sects and groups, with the exception of Hizb Allah, clamored for an independent investigation into Hariri's death and an end to the Syrian presence in Lebanon. This was a unified uprising by a hastily formed coalition; but this was also a revolution in the making!

By the end of the day, the Lebanese nationalists had won the support of the Maronite Patriarch, Nasr Allah Pierre Sfeir, and Druze leader Walid Junblat. Only the Shi'ites of South Lebanon backed Syria calling for restraint and to keep foreigners out of Lebanese affairs.

By the end of February, Syria was still in the hot seat. The intensity of the opposition to Syria was far too powerful to be neglected and, therefore, Syria agreed to withdraw its forces from Lebanon. Bashar al-Assad made that pledge to the Arab League's General Secretary on February 21, 2005, but with no specific timetable. In a face saving gesture Assad said that he would implement the final stage of the Ta'if Accords.

Europe responded strongly to what was being called the "Cedar Revolution," named after the symbolic tree on the Lebanese flag. The European Union supported the call for the Syrian's to pull out of all Lebanon; and President Bush and President Chirac, in a rare moment of unity, demanded a quick Syrian evacuation.

The crowds at Martyr's Square marched for freedom numbering in the tens of thousands from all sects, acting jointly, peacefully, and joyfully amid the fluttering of thousands of Lebanese flags. Prime Minister Omar Karami resigned as the Beirut government was quickly losing the confidence of the people, and Lebanese nationalism was rising. Lahoud's pro-Syrian loyalists were in jeopardy.

As the Cedar Revolution grew in intensity, United States Secretary of State Dr. Condolezza Rice and French Foreign Minister Michel Barnier called for the immediate exit of all Syrian troops and their intelligence services from Lebanon so that free elections could be scheduled for May of 2005. And, both the United States and France demanded a "full, credible, and transparent" investigation into the death of Rafiq Hariri. At the same time Crown Prince Abd Allah of Saudi Arabia met with Assad and counseled a quick departure of all Syrian forces from Lebanon. On the heels of that statement, Egypt called for the "quickest" possible withdrawal with "dignity" to occur.

Syria was isolated in the world. Both Russia and Germany added their voices to the riding crescendo calling for Syria's departure saying "leave Lebanon for the Lebanese."

Under increasing "worldwide" pressure to withdraw from Lebanon, President Asad had only one card left to play and that was his Hizb Allah supporters. On Sunday, March 6, 2005 Hizb Allah leader Shaykh Hassan Nasrallah, standing in front of a Lebanese flag, not his party banner, declared full support for President Assad, rejecting United Nations Resolution 1559 and all foreign plots, ploys and interference in Lebanon. Two days later, buses brought hundreds of thousands of Shi'ite supporters to the capital to back Shaykh Nasrallah; the crowd swelled to half a million.

Speaking at the rally in Riyad al-Sulh Square, the Shi'ite leader called for Lebanese unity but, in reality, this was a "thank you" or "goodbye" party for the Syrians.

Meanwhile, the United Nations had already designated an observer or envoy and investigator, Terje Roed-Larsen of Norway, to implement United Nations objectives in Lebanon. He met with President Assad in Mid-March to extract a timetable far Syria's departure. The date was set for the end of March.

During the Shi'ite demonstration, Lahoud orchestrated Karami's return to power as the only person who could form a national unity cabinet while Washington acknowledged Hizb Allah's legitimate claims and supported its transformation into the political sphere.

Then, on March 15, 2005, the largest anti-Syrian, pro-Lebanon, demonstration transpired drawing an estimated one million people calling for "freedom" and "sovereignty" for the republic. A sea of humanity converged on Martyr's Square; the crowd overflowed into almost all the streets of the capital and produce a festive all day affair. Signs read "long live the Syrians in Syria." Soon afterwards, Syrian intelligence officers evacuated their Ramlet al-Baida headquarters in the capital; as they departed ordinary Lebanese citizens hoisted Lebanese flags where Syrian flags once stood. But the Lebanese government remained deadlocked; Karami's influence railed to establish a national unity government. And by late March, the United Nations issued its findings on the Hariri murder citing Syrian "interference" and "flawed" police work, concluding that Syria bears primary responsibility for the assassination.

On Sunday, April 3, 2005, United Nations envoy Roed-Larsen said that Syria's Foreign Minister Farouk al-Sharaa promised to remove all Syrian troops, military assets, and intelligence apparatus from Lebanon and that Syria would fulfill the terms of the Ta'if Accord and United Nations Resolution 1559, but that close ties with its "sister republic" would remain.

In New York, at the United Nations Headquarters, the Security Council unanimously passed a joint United States, British, and French resolution to order another independent investigation into Hariri's death since the previous investigation was "vague" or inconclusive.

Within Lebanon there was no doubt that most of the Lebanese people were overjoyed at Syria's departure; they expressed the view that Syria had "over stayed their welcome" which had become "pernicious and overbearing" at times. Lebanon's prime minister stepped down once again; his attempt to form a new government was hopelessly dead ended. Thus, President Lahoud appointed a compromise candidate to form a new administration. Najib Mikati (Miqati) formed a new cabinet and set the new Parliamentary election date for the end of May or the beginning of June.

On April 23, 2005, Syria completed its evacuation from an area near Balbek in a highly ornate military show. Meanwhile, in the capital, Mikati received a strong vote of confidence and May 29, 2005 was set for the start of the parliamentary elections. At the same time house cleaning continued to dismiss or remove all Syrian appointees and supporters.

With a clean sweep in progress, former General Michel Aoun returned to Lebanon from exile in France hoping to throw his hat into the political arena. Despite his great popularity with young Lebanese men and women, he still faced opposition from the Maronite Patriarch who was quite uncomfortable with Aoun's secular tendencies. He focused his future role on parliamentary power and saw his major opposition in the person of Saad Hariri, the son of the slain Lebanese leader.

As May drew to a close, Lebanese voters were preparing for a historic vote, a landmark election for the 128 member chamber. This was a serious event lacking the usual glitz or any outreach program from the candidates.

Parliamentary elections began on May 30, 2005 in the capital where Saad Hariri's list of candidates clinched all nineteen available seats. His success was seen by some as the result of a financial "Tsunami" and as an "appointment by another name," but the election was both open and clean.

Amid the outward gaiety, a new tragedy struck Lebanon in early June when a Lebanese opposition leader, Samir Kasir, was killed by a car bomb. President Lahoud deplored the incident, and United States Secretary of State Rice called the murder a "heinous act" demanding immediate justice. Kasir had called for the president's resignation citing Lahoud's complacency in dealing with Syrian agents. A candle light vigil was held for the fallen national hero at a local Greek Orthodox Church in the capital; his flag draped coffin was held high by the mourners.

June 6, 2005 focused attention on the second round of the parliamentary elections in the Shi'ite south with strong campaigning between Hizb Allah and Amal candidates, in two districts. By the time the polls closed, Hizb Allah held the Majority of the twenty-three available seats.

At the United Nations, Kofi Annan supported an American initiative to block the return of Syrian agents to Lebanon trying to interfere in the elections and sent envoy Roed-Larsen back to Syria. Meanwhile, in the mountains above Beirut, the third round in the elections began in a hotly contested race between Michel Aoun's supporters and an anti-Syrian coalition of onetime "civil War" enemies led by Walid Junblat and Shaykh Hassan Nasrallah. Aoun's allies included a strong list of powerful Maronite Christian personalities such as Sulayman Franjieh, grandson of the former president, and Talal Arslan whose Druze clan opposed Junblat's clan. Later, they were joined by former defense and interior minister Michel Murr. In that region, thirty-four Christian posts and twenty-four Moslem seats were up for grabs. The vigorous campaign gave fifteen out of sixteen seats to Aoun's list of candidates; and only one of the opposition leaders, Pierre Gemayel, won a victory. Junblat's nominees obtained eight of the available Moslems positions.

The last phase of the four part election took place on June 14, 2005 and, clearly, Syrian influence was felt in several e-mails and faxes sent in support of some pro-Syrian candidates. Syrian agents were spotted in some parts of Lebanon trying to influence the vote that could keep Lahoud in office, if Aoun's candidates did indeed win the round. Of the twenty-eight seats reserved for the mixed northern districts, fifteen were assigned to Christian candidates and thirteen for the Moslems, Hoping for a clean sweep of the Christian slate, Aoun allied himself with the Franjieh and Karami clans.

When the votes were counted in the final round, the results favored Saad Hariri's men. They took twenty-one of the twenty-eight seats. Thus, the anti-Syrian alliance would hold the majority of seats in the Parliament, but probably not enough votes to oust President Lahoud from office.

The first anti-Syrian, Lebanese Parliament convened in June of 2005 and elected Nabih Berri as its speaker, and Fuad Siniora as Prime Minister. The

Moslem opposition and the Christian reformers did not have the majority vote. Lahoud would remain in office.

Clearly, by late June, the anti-Syrian coalition swept the voting with Saad Hariri and Walid Junblat's parties taking a strong position. And, on June 21, 2005 the anti-Syrian leader of the Lebanese Communist Party was assassinated. Two days earlier, on July 19, 2005 right wing leader Samir Geagea was granted a pardon. The following day, Prime Minister Fuad Siniora formed Lebanon's first independent government in decades.

Detlev Mehlis continued his United Nations sponsored investigation into Rafiq Hariri's murder and, on September 2, 2005 Mehlis indicated that he believed that Syria was behind the assassination indicting Mustafa Hamdan (Commander of the Lebanese Republican Guard); Jamil al-Sayyid (Head of General Security); Ali al-Hajj (Chief of Police); and Ramond Azar (Chief of Military Intelligence).

The Mehlis Report entitled: *Report of the International Independent Investigation Commission Established Pursuant to Security Council Resolution 1595 (2005)* is 53 pages long. It includes a PREFACE, BACKGROUND, THE CRIME, THE LEBANESE INVESTIGATION, THE COMMISSION'S INVESTIGATION and a CONCLUSION. The report concludes that "many leads point directly towards Syrian security officials" being involved in the assassination, but it remained "inconclusive" as to Syria's role in the murder. (The Mehlis report was later supplemented by a second report from Serge Brammertz, of the International Court, which came to the same conclusion.)

By mid-December, the powerful and prestigious anti-Syrian lawmaker and journalist, Gebran Tueni, was killed in a car bombing incident; at his funeral at St. Nicolas Church, anti-Syrian feelings reverberated among mourners of all faiths and sects.

By July of 2006, attention to the Israeli-Hizb Allah cross border attacks was on the rise. The State of Israel ruled out any negotiations with Hizb Allah or its leader Shaykh Hassan Nasrallah. The Zionist State continued to hold several Hizb Allah men; and that prompted Hizb Allah to capture two Israeli soldiers, Ehud Goldwasser and Eldad Regev, after an Israeli ground assault on July 3, 2006. That action was followed up by an Israeli naval blockade; Hizb Allah's response came quickly with rocket attacks deep into Israeli territory. Israel held the Lebanese government responsible and sent its army into South Lebanon.

The Beirut government and most of the world, with the exception of the United States, considered the Israeli invasion "disproportionate" and "collective punishment" but President Bush backed Israel calling Hizb Allah a "terrorist group," yet Hizb Allah did not break or run as Israeli forces pounded Lebanon and sent thousands of fresh troops into South Lebanon and attacked the capital.

On July 18, 2006, United Nations Secretary General Kofi Annan called on Israel to halt its offensive; and Prime Minister Tony Blair of England pleaded for international peacekeepers. However, America's ambassador to the United Nations, John Bolton, found himself "confused" about how to establish "a cease fire with a terrorist organization;" thus delaying any action on a cease-fire. When the Bush administration agreed to the Israeli request for "cluster bombs and "precision guided bombs" to be used against the civilian population, the United States lost all credibility in the Arab and Moslem world.

The United States now totally isolated in the world finally agreed to an international force to be sent to Lebanon and pressured Israel to accept the United Nations action. Then, the Lebanese government and Hizb Allah presented their conditions for peace:

1. Release of 3 Lebanese POWs
2. Return of the Shebaa Farms to Lebanon
3. An end to Israeli flyovers
4. And, finally, for Israel to provide a map indicating the location of land mines and cluster bombs.

The United Nations and the European Union called for an immediate cease-fire; meanwhile, the tide of public opinion in the Arab World supported Nasrallah and proclaimed him an Arab hero. The Maronite Patriarch along with other Christian and Moslem leaders condemned the Israeli aggression and hailed the Shi'ite resistance. Hizb Allah, once again, called for an Israeli pullout from both the Shebaa Farms and the Syrian Golan Heights.

Human Rights Watch issued a report that United States cluster bombs and M-25 multiple launch rockets were deployed against Lebanese civilians; and Amnesty International reported that Lebanon suffered 1,183 deaths (1/3 of whom were children), and 4,054. wounded; 970,000 persons were displaced and 4 million dollars in property damage occurred after 34 days of war. Israel suffered 150 civilian casualties from rocket fire. By August of 2006, the Israeli cabinet, under American pressure, voted 24 to 0 to approve a new Security Council Resolution (1701) and began a slow withdrawal from Lebanon. By late August, the United Nations had assigned General Alain Pelegrini of France to implement the full deployment of 6,900 European troops into South Lebanon as peace keepers.

Meanwhile, in the Lebanese capital, the March 14 Coalition composed of Christians, Sunnite Moslems and the Druze, endorsed the United Nations action, but Druze leader Walid Junblat, speaking for the group, said that Hizb Allah wanted to topple the pro-French, pro-American Lebanese government: and he implied that Hizb Allah was a "puppet" of Iran. Junblat's Progressive Socialist Party called for disarmament of that party because it started a conflict between itself and the Lebanese government. Shortly after that statement, in early November, the Lebanese authorities released the leader of the Lebanese Forces from prison. At about the same time, five Shi'ite members of the Lebanese Cabinet resigned making it "illegitimate".

On the 19th of November, in a Sunday broadcast, Shaykh Hassan Nasrallah called for a peaceful demonstration to bring down the government of Fuad Siniora and replace it with a "national unity" cabinet and government under President Lahoud. In response, the March 14 Coalition made a new effort at compromise. Three days later, Pierre Gemayel, the son of former President Amine Gemayel and the grandson of the founder of the Phalangist Party was gunned down in his car. He was the fifth anti-Syrian politician to be killed raising the anti-Syrian fury to new heights. Germayal's funeral mass at St. Georges Cathedral, presided over by the Maronite Patriarch, reached huge proportions similar to Hariri's, with all sects attending the funeral. Speaking on the Hizb Allah television station, *al-manar,* Skaykh Nasrallah called the March 14 Coalition "a failure" and puppets of the West. The following day, December 2, 2006, thousands of Shi'ites descended on Beirut in a festive atmosphere calling on Siniora to "step down." Tensions remained high through the last month of the year, as Nasrallah escalated his demands calling for veto power over all government decisions, thus ending the balanced Lebanese Confessional system and probably all ties to the West.

Prime Minister Siniora quickly lashed out at Hizb Allah's leader saying, "you are not our Lord, and your party is not our Lord," heightening the personal animosity between the two men. Siniora, however, remained held-up in his office, as the Lebanese government asked Hizb Allah to reconsider its position and join the Lahoud administration to prevent "outsiders" from gaining an advantage in Lebanon. Hizb Allah responded immediately calling the Lebanese government "ineffectual" and "powerless" every time Israel invaded its territory.

The year ended with a standoff in the capital; Hizb Allah called for Siniora's resignation to be followed by a trial for treason and corruption, ratcheting up Nasrallah's demands. Saudi Arabia and the United States, meanwhile, backed Siniora and the Lebanese government, as Arab League Secretary General Amr Moussa's negotiations between the parties resulted in another stalemate. The impasse, now backed by mixed sectarian support, would continue into the new year.

As of New Years Day 2007, almost all of the non Shi'ite Lebanese believe that Hizb Allah's objective is to take over Lebanon and to create a clone of Iran. To that end, it is supported by Iran whose stated objective is to establish itself as a nuclear power to protect and expand Shi'ism in the Arab and Moslem World.

Syria has its own agenda for Lebanon. It backs Hizb Allah hoping to regain the Golan Heights and the Shebaa Farms areas from the Israelis, but, more importantly, Syria wants to help install Hizb Allah in power so that it can invite Syrian troops back into Lebanon to "restore order" and, consequently, undo the French-American effort to secure Lebanese independence from Syria's grip.

Iran and Syria consider Hizb Allah and its leader Nasrallah as a "tool" or "puppet" for their own purposes. But Nasrallah is no fool; thus he continues to play them off against each other, hoping to come out on top as the Arab and Moslem World's new charismatic leader for the new century.

The Cedar Revolution has succeeded but it remains in jeopardy. In Lebanon's complex society, with long term sectarian, group, clan, and family tensions as well as some local feudal leaders, the road ahead is extremely unstable. To a great extent, confused loyalties, an ongoing identity crisis, and the differing foreign policy concerns between the Beirut government and religious Sects has survived into the twenty-first century. But even-with all these foreign and domestic problems and tensions, there is no doubt about it; Lebanon remains the sole column of progress for the Arab World and well beyond.

SELECT BIBLIOGRAPHY

ARCHIVES

The United States: Archives of the United States of America, Documents and Dispatches, Alexandria, Egypt, 1835-1873.

United States, Treaty Series, No. 695, Convention between the United States and The Lebanon, Signed at Paris, April 4, 1924, Washington, 1924.

France: Ministere Des Affairs Etrangeres, Documents Diplomatiques, Paris, 1860-1928.

Ministere Des Affairs Etrangeres, Rapport Sur La Situation De La Syrie et Liban, 1924-1931 and 1934-1936, Paris, 1925-1932, 1935-1937.

Great Britain: Accounts and Papers, no. 17, Affairs of the Levant 1841, vol.29, Correspondence Relative to The Affairs of The Levant, part I and part II, 1841.

Accounts and Papers, vol. 51, 2/4-8/9, 1845, Correspondence Relative to The Affairs of Syria, part I and part II, 1843-1845.

Accounts and Papers, vol. 69, 1860, State Papers:

I. Dispatches From Her Majesty's Consuls in The Levant, respecting past or apprehended disturbances in Syria, 1858-1860, 1860.

II. Papers Relating to the Disturbances in Syria 1860, 1860.

III. Correspondence Relating to the Affairs of Syria. 1860-1861, 1861.

IV. Further Correspondence, With Maps, 1861, 1861.

Great Britain, Foreign Office (F.O.), Turkey, 1883, no.1,

Correspondence Respecting the Affairs of Lebanon, and the

Appointment of a Governor-General, Presented to both Houses of Parliament by Command of Her Majesty, 1883, vol. 82, pp. 735-770, London: Harrison and Sons, 1883.

Hansard's Parliamentary Debates, London: T. C. Hansard, 1860.

Lebanon: The Maronite Patriarchal Archives, Bkirki, Lebanon.

Collections: Documents, Dispatches, Correspondence, Special Studies,unpublished Works.

Al-Khazin, P. and F., *Ma jmu'at al-Muharrarat al-Siyasiyah wa al-Mufawada al-Duwaliyah*, (The Collection of the Political Documents and International Negotiations), 3 vol., Lebanon: Djounieh, n.p., 1910.

Al-Nusuli, Anis, *Rasa'il al-Amir Fakhr al-Din min Tuskana*, (The Letters of Prince Fakhr al-Din from Tuscany), Beirut: n.p., 1946.

Al-Qadiya al-Lubnaniya, (The Lebanese Case), 20 vol., Lebanon: Kaslik University Press, 1976.

American Lebanese League Publications: *Issues Confronting Lebanon Today*, October, 1983.

Anon., "La Syrie Et Le Liban Au Parlement," *Revue Politique et Parlementaire*, vol. 126, Paris, 1926, pp. 90-109.

Arab-American University Graduates; Publications. Meo, Leila and Edward Said, *Lebanon: Two Perspectives*, 1975.

Attie, Caroline, "The Lebanese Greek Orthodox Community: Historical and Contemporary Perspectives," presented to the Middle East Studies Association Conference, 1990.

Beirut College for Women, *Cultural Resources in Lebanon*, Beirut: Librairie du Liban, 1969.

Browne, Walter L., ed., *The Political History of Lebanon*, vol. I and II (1920-50). Documents on the French Mandate and World War II, 1936-1943, North Carolina: Documentary Publishers, 1977.

---, *Lebanon's Struggle for Independence*, part I and II, 1943-1944, 1944-1947, North Carolina: Documentary Publishers, 1980.

Farah, Caesar E., *The Problem of the Ottoman Administration in Lebanon, 1840-1861*, Unpublished Ph.D. Dissertation, Princeton University, 1957.

France: Haut Commissariat en Syrie et au Liban, *La France En Syrie et Au Liban, Le Mandat Devant Les Faits*, Paris: E. Larose, 1921.

France: *Haut Commissariat de la Republique Francaise En Syrie et Au Liban En 1922* Paris; E. Larose, 1922.

France: Haut Commissariat de la Republic Francaise en Syrie et au Liban, *Ce Que Tout Francais Doit Savoir de la Syrie et du Liban*, Paris; E. Larose, 1922.

France: Haut Commissariat en Syrie et au Liban, *Monsieur Henri Ponsot Haut Commissaire de la Republique Francaise a son excellence Monsieur Aristide Briand Ministre des Affairs Etrangeres: statute organique des etats sous mandate francais*, Beirut, 1930.

Rapport sur la situation De La Syrie Et Du Liban, 1924-1931 and 1934-1936, Paris: 1925-1932, 1935-1937.

Dix Ans Du Mandat, L'Oeuvre Francaise en Syrie et au Liban, Paris: C.G.P. editions, 1931.

Quinze Ans De Mandat, L'Oeuvre Francaise en Syrie et au Liban, Beirut: Imprimerie Catholique, 1936.

Freedman, Robert O. *"The Soviet Union and the Civil War in Lebanon"*, presented to the Middle East Studies Association Conference, November, 1977.

Labaki, Georges T., *The Lebanon Crisis (1975-1985), A Bibliography*, Maryland: University of Maryland Press, 1986.

Lebanese Information and Research Center, Publications Division, Washington D.C.: Aoun, Rashid and Elias El-Hayek, *Syria's Design for Lebanon*, January, 1979; Malik, Charles H., *The Problem of the West*, April, 1979; *A Better Understanding of Syria*, April, 1984; *White Paper, Discussion of the Syrian Sponsored Peace Agreement for Lebanon-Full Text of the Agreement*, February, 1986.

The Missionary Herald, Mission's Council of the Congregational and Christian Churches for the American Board of Home Missions, Boston: 1841-1860.

Moslem Lebanon Today, n.p., 1953.

Nawwar, Abd al-Aziz, *Wathaiq Assasiyah Min Ta'rikh Lubnan al-Hadith, 1517-1920*, (Fundamental Documents From the History of Contemporary Lebanon, 1517-1920), Beirut: Arab University, Press, 1974.

Rabbath, Pere Antoine, *Documents Inedits Pour Servir A L'Histoire Du Christianisme en Orient*, 2 vol., Paris: A. Picard et Fils, 1905-1907, 1910-1911.

Rustum, A. J., *The Royal Archives of Egypt and the Origins of the Egyptian Expedition to Syria, 1831-1841*, Beirut: American Press, 1936.

---, A   *Calendar of State Papers from the Royal Archives of Egypt Relating to The Affairs of Syria*, 4 vol., Beirut: American Press, 1940-1943.

Societe Des Nations, *Mandat pour la Syrie et le Liban*, August, 1922.

---, *La Syrie et le Liban sous l'Occupation et le Mandat Francais, 1919-1927*, Nancy: Berger-Levrault, 1927.

Ta'rikh Hizb al-Kata'ib al-Lubnaniyah, 1936-1940, (A History of the Lebanese Kata'ib Party, 1936-1940), Beirut: Dar al-Amal.

The Blue Helmets, United Nations Publication.

Wathiqat Harb Lubnan, (Lebanese War Documents), Beirut: Sayyid Press, 1977.

Wazarah al-Anaba fi Lubnan, (The Lebanese Ministry of Information), *Qadiyat Al-Hizb al-Qawmi*, (The Issue of the National Party), Beirut, n.p., 1949.

Yazbak, Y. I., ed, *Awraq Lubnaniyah*, (Lebanese Documents), 3 vol., Beirut, 1955-1957.

BOOKS AND ARTICLES (in Arabic)

Abu Khalil, J., *Qissat al-Mawarinah fi al-Harb* (The Story of the Maronites During the War), Beirut: Sharikat al-Tiba'a, 1990.

Abu Khattar, A., "Mukhtasar Ta'rikh Jabal Lubnan," (A Summary of the History of Mount Lebanon), *A1-Mashriq* vol. XLIV, 1952, part II, pp. 309-334, part IV, pp. 433-446, part V, pp. 525-570.

Abu Shaqra, Hussayn Ghadban and 'Arif Abu Shaqra, ed., *Al-Harakat fi Lubnan ila 'Ahd al-Mutasarrifiyah*, (The Movements (Events) in Lebanon Until the Time of the Mutasarrfiyah), Beirut: Matba'at al-Ittihad, 1952.

A1-Ahdab, Aziz, *Fakhr al-Din, Muasses Lubnan al-Hadith*, (Fakhr al-Din, Founder of Modern Lebanon), Beirut: Dar al-Kitab al Lubnani, 1984.

Al-'Aqiqi, Antun Dahir, *Lebanon in the Last Years of Feudalism, 1840-1868*, trans. by Malcolm H. Kerr, Beirut: Catholic Press, 1959.

Al-'Aynturini, A., "Kitab Mukhtasar Ta'rikh Jabal Lubnan," (A Book Summarizing the History of Mount Lebanon), *Al-Mashriq*, vol. 47, 1953, pp. 26-65, 172-203.

Al-Bustani, U., "Tarjamat al-Batrik Bulus Mas'ad," (A Biography of Patriarch Bulus Mas'ad), *Al-Mashriq*, vol. XXVIII, 1930, pp. 721-733.

Al-Dannawi, Muhammad Ali, *Al-Muslimun fi Lubnan, Muwatnun La Ra'aya*, (The Muslims in Lebanon, Citizens Not Subjects), Beirut: n. p., 1973.

Al-Dimishqi, M. "Ta'rikh Hawadith al-Sham wa Lubnan," (A History of the Happenings (Events) in Syria and Lebanon), *Al-Mashriq*, vol. XV, 1912, pp. 102-115.

Al-Duwayhi, Istifan, "Silsilat Batarikat al-Ta'ifa al-Maruniyah," (The Chain of The Patriarchs of the Maronite Sect), *Al-Mashriq* vol. 1898, pp. 247-252, 308-313, 347-353, 390-396.

---, "Ta'rikh al-Azminah, 1095-1699 A.D.", (A History of the Times, 1095-1699 A.D.), *Al-Mashriq*, vol. XLIV, 1951, pp. 303-311.

---, *Ta'rikh al-Ta'ifa al-Marruniyah*, (The History of the Maronite Sect), Beirut: Matba'at al-Kathulikiyah, 1890.

Al-Hajj, Kamal Yusuf, *Al-Qawmiya al-Lubnaniyah*, (Lebanese Nationalism), Beirut, n.p., 1970.

Al-Hakim, Yusuf, *Beirut wa Lubnan fi 'Ahd al-Uthman*, (Beirut and Lebanon in The Ottoman Age), Beirut: Matba'at al-Kathulikiyah, 1964.

Al-Hattuni, Mansur Tannus, *Nubdhah Ta'rikhiyah fi al-Muqata'at al-Kisrawaniyah*, (A Historical Note on the Kissrawani Districts), Beirut: n.p., (first published in 1884), 1956.

Al-Huss, Salim, *Lubnan 'ala al-Muftaraq*, (Lebanon on the Crossroads), Beirut: Al-Markaz al-Islaimi lil 'Alam wa al-Tammiya, 1984.

Al-Jisr, Basim, *Ri'asa wa Siyash wa Lubnan al-Jadid*, (Presidency and Politics and The New Lebanon), Beirut: Dar Maktabat al-Hayat, 1964.

---, *Mithaq 1943*, (The National Pact of 1943), Beirut: Al-Nahar, 1978.

Al-Khalidi, A., (Al-Safadi), *Lubnan fi 'Ahd al-Amir Fakhr al-Din al Ma'ni al-Thani*, (Lebanon in the Time of Prince Fakr al-Din al-Ma'ni the Second), Beirut: Matba'at al-Kathulikiyah, 1969.

Al-Khazin, Philippe, *Lamahat Ta'rikhiyah*, (Historical Glances), Cairo: Matab'at al-Fajjalah, 1910.

Al-Khuri, Bishara, *Haqa'iq Lubnaniyah*, (Lebanese Realities), 3 vol., Beirut: Manshurat Awraq Lubnaniyah, 1960.

Al-Madani, H. and M. al-Zi'bi, *Al-Islam wa al-Masihiyah fi Lubnan*, (Islam and Christianity in Lebanon), Beirut: Matba'at al-Insaf, 1952.

Al-Mallah, Abd Allah, *Mutasarrifiyat Jabal Lubnan fi 'Ahd Muzaffar Basha, 1902-1907*, (Mount Lebanon during the Time of Muzaffar Pasha, 1902-1907), Beirut: Muassassa Khalifa, 1985.

Al-Masudi, Bulus, *Al-Dawlah al-'Uthmaniyah fi Lubnan wa Suriyah, 1517-1916*, (Ottoman Government in Lebanon and Syria, 1517-1916), n. p., 1916.

Al-Munaiyyir, H.," Al-Durr al-Marsuf fi Ta'rikh al-Shuf," (The Arranged Pearls in the History of the Shuf), *Al-Mashriq*, 1954-1957, vol. 48, pp. 671-695, vol. 49, pp. 257-274, vol. 50, pp. 193-214, 415-448, vol. 51, pp. 443-486.

Al-Qubrusi, Abd Allah, *Nahnu wa Lubnan*, (We and Lebanon/Lebanon And Us), Beirut: Matba'at Lubnan, 1954.

Al-Rayyes, Riad, *Al-Massihiyun wa al-Uruba*, (The Christians and Arab Nationalism), London: Riyad al-Rayyes Books, 1988.

Al-Sadr, Musa, *Nukhba Min al-Muhadarat*, (A Selection of Prepared Speeches/Lectures), Beirut: n. p., n.d.

Al-Sammak, Muhammad, *Al-Aqaliyat Bayna al-Uruba wa al-Islam*, (The Mentality (Mental Understanding) Between Arabism and Islam), Beirut: Dar al-Ilm lil Malayin, 1990.

Al-Sawda, Yusuf, *Fi Sabil Lubnan*, (In The Interest of Lebanon), Alexandria: Matba'at Madrasat al-Frair 1919.

---, *Fi Sabil al-Istiqlal*, (For the Sake of Independence), Beirut: Dar al-Rihani lil Tiba'ah wa Nashr, 1967.

Al-Sharqawi, Abd al-Rahman and Ibrahirm Abd al-Halim, *Irfa'u Aydikum' an Lubnan*, (Take Your Hands off Lebanon), Cairo: Dar al-Fikr, 1958.

Al-Shidyaq, Tannus, *Kitab Akhbar al-A'yan fi Ta'rikh Jabal Lubnan*, (A Book of Information on the Notables of Mount Lebanon), Beirut: Al-Jami'at al-Lubnaniyah, 1970.

Al-Shihab, Amir Haidar Ahmad, *Lubnan fi Ahd al-Umara' al-Shihabiyin*, (Lebanon in the Time of the Shihabi Amirs), Beirut: Al-Jami'at al-Lubnaniyah, 1969.

Al-Sulh, Sami, *Ahtakim ila al-Ta'rikh*, (I Seek Judgement in History), Beirut: Dar al-Nahar lil Nashr, 1970.

Al-Tahiri, Hamid Badawi, *Siyasat al-Hukum fi Lubnan*, (The Politics of Rule In Lebanon), Cairo: Al-Dar al-Qawmiyah lil Tiba'ah wa al-Nashr, 1966.

Al-Yaziji, Ibrahim Nasif, *Al-Arab wa al-Turk*, (The Arabs and the Turks), Pub. in No. America,1910.

Al-Yusuf, I. M., *Thwrah al-Ahrar fi Lubnan*, (The Liberal Revolution in Lebanon), Beirut: n. p., 1958.

Al-Zaila, Na'im, *Shamoun Yatakallam*, (Chamoun Speaks), Beirut: Matba'at al-Jihah, 1959.

Arslan, Shakib, *Muzaffar Basha fi Lubnan*, (Muzaffar Pasha in Lebanon), Alexandria, n.p., 1907.

Ashkuty, Raji, *Mihnat al-Massihyin fi Lubnan*, (The Trial/Ordeal of the Christians in Lebanon), Beirut: n.p., 1991.

Bakradouni, Karim, *Al-Salam al-Mafqud, Ahd Ilyas Sarkis 1976-1982*, (The Lost/Missing Peace, the Administration of Elias Sarkis 1976-1982), Beirut: Ibr al-Sharq, 1984.

---, *Lant al-Watn, Min Harb Lubnan ila Harb al-Khalij*, (The Curse of a Nation, From the Lebanese War to the Gulf War), Beirut: TOP, Ibr al-Sharq lil Manshurat, 1991.

Bayhum, Muhammad Jamil, *Lubnan Bayna Mushriq wa Maghrib, 1920-1969*, (Lebanon Between East and West, 1920-1969), Beirut: 1969.

Urubat Lubnan, (Lebanon's Arab Nationalism), Beirut: 1969. *Suriyah wa Lubnan*, (Syria and Lebanon), Beirut: Dar al-Tabi'ah, 1968.

Daghir, Yusuf As'ad, *Batarikiyah al-Maruniyah*, (The Maronite Patriarch), Beirut: Matba'at al-Kathulikiyah, 1958.

Dahir, Masoud, *Ta'rikh Lubnan al-Ijtima'i, 1914-1967* (A Social History of Lebanon, 1914-1967), Beirut: Dar al-Matba'at al-Sharqiyat, 1974.

Daryan, Yusuf, *Nubdhah Ta'rikhiyah fi Asl al-Ta'ifa al-Maruniyah*, (A Historical Note on the Origins of the Maronite Sect), Beirut: Al-Matba'ah al-'Ilmiyah, 1919.

Daww, Butrus, *Ta'rikh al-Mawarnah al-Dini wa al-Siyasi wa al- Hadari*, (The Religious, Political and Cultural History of The Maronites), Beirut: Dar al-Nahar lil Nashr, 1977.

Daww, Istifan, *Kitab Hadiqat al-Jinan fi Ta'rikh Lubnan*, (The Book of the Garden of Paradise in the History of Lebanon), Lebanon: Al-Matba'ah al-Jami'ah, 1911-1913.

Fadl Allah, Muhammad Husayn, *Al-Islam wa Muntaq al-Quwah*, (Islam and The Logic of Power), Beirut: Dar al-Ma'arif lil Matbu'at, 1978 (1985).

Ghuraiyib, M. F., *Al-Ta'ifiyah wa al-Iqta'iyah fi Lubnan*, (Sectarianism and Feudalism in Lebanon), Beirut: Samiya Press, 1964.

Hamali, H., *Jamahir wa Kawarith*, (Throngs and Disasters), Beirut: Dar al-Tiba'ah wa Nashr, 1968.

Hanna, G., *Al-'Uqdah al-Lubnaniyah*, (The Lebanese Problem), Beirut: Dar al-'Im, 1957.

Haqqi, Ismail Bey, ed., *Lubnan*, (Lebanon), Beirut, n.p., n.d.

Haroun, Georges, Yusuf-*ai-Sawda, A'lam al-Qawmiyah al-Lubnaniyah*, (Yusuf Al-Sawda: Leading Scholar of Lebanese Nationalism), Lebanon: University of Kaslik Press, 1979.

Hilu, Charles, *Mudhakkirati*, (My Memoirs), Araya: Matba'at al-Kathulikiyah, 1984.

Junblat, Kamal, *Fi Majra al-Siyasah al-Lubnaniyah*. (In the Course of Lebanese Politics), Beirut: Dar al-Tali'ah, 1958.

---, *Haqiqat al-Thawarah al-Lubnaniyah*, (The Truth about the Lebanese Revolution), Beirut: Dar al-Nashr al-Arabiyah, 1959.

Kautharani, Wajih, *Al-Ittijahat al-Ijtima'iya-al-Siyasia fi Jabal Lubnan wa al Mashriq al-Arabi, 1860-1920*, (The Political and Social Trends in Mount Lebanon and the Arab East, 1860-1920), Beirut: 1976.

Khalid, H., *Al-Muslimun fi Lubnan*, (The Moslems in Lebanon), Beirut: Dar al-Kindi, 1978.

Khalifa, Isam, *Abhath fi Ta'rikh Lubnan al-Mu'asir*, (Studies on the Contemporary History of Lebanon), Beirut: n.p., 1985.

Khalil, K. A., *Lubnan Yasaran*, (Lebanon Towards the Left), Beirut: Matba'ah al-Amal, 1972.

Khatir, Lahd, *Ahd al-Mutasarrifin fi Lubnan, 1861-1918*, (The Reign of the Mutasrrifs in Lebanon, 1861-1918), Beirut: Matba'ah al-Katulikiyah, 1967.

Khazin, Sim'an, *Yusuf Bey Karam, Qaim-maqam Nasara Lubnan*, (Yusuf Bey Karim, Christian Sub-governor of Lebanon), Juniyah: n.p., 1954.

---, *Yusuf Bey fi al-Manfa*, (Yusuf Bey in Exile), Tripoli: n.p., 1950.

---, *Al-Harb fi Sabil al-Istiqlal, aw Yusuf Bey Karam wa Daud Pasha*, (The War In the Cause of Independence or Yusuf Bey Kararn and Daud Pasha), Juniyah: N.P., 1957.

Khoueri, Antoine, *Lubnan Tahta al-Intidab*. (Lebanon under the Mandate), Lebanon: Dar al-Jadiyah lil Sihafah, 1981.

Ma'luf, Isa Iskandar, *Ta'rikh al-Amir Fakhr al-Din al-Thani*, (The History of Prince Fakir al-Din, The Second), Juniyah: Matba'at al-Risalah al-Lubnaniyah, 1934.

Mughaizal, Joesph, *Lubnan wa al-Qadiyyah al-Arabiyah*, (Lebanon and the Arab Cause/Case), Beirut: Manshurat Queidat, 1959.

Murad, Said, *Al-Harakat al-Wataniiyah fi Lubnan*, (National Movements/Action In Lebanon), Beirut: n.p., 1986.

---, *Fi Sabil Lubnan*, (For The Sake of Lebanon), New York: n.p., n.d.

Naoum, Sarkis, *Michel Aoun: Hilm aw Wahm*, (Michel Aoun: Dream or Illusion), Beirut: Matba'at al-Mutawassit, 1992.

Nassar, Ghalamiyya, *Asbab wa Asrar al-Harb al-Lubnaniyah*, (Causes and Secrets of the Lebanese War), Beirut: n.p., 1976.

Nawfal, Nasim, *Kitab Batal Lubnan*, (A Book on Lebanon's Hero), Alexandria: A1-Matba'at al-Watiniyah, 1896.

Phares (Faris), Walid, *Al-Ta'adoudiya fi Lubnan*, (Pluralism in Lebanon), Lebanon: University of Kaslik Press, 1979.

---, *Al-Fikr al-Massihi al-Dimuqrati al-Lubnani*, (Lebanese Christian Democratic Thought), Beirut: Dar al-Sharq al-Massihi, 1981.

Qara'li, Bulus, ed., *Ta'rikh Amir Bashir al-Kabir*, (A History of Prince Bashir,The Great), Lebanon: n.p., 1922.

---, *Fakhr al-Din al-Mani al-Thani Hakim Lubnan*, (Fakhr al-Din al-Mani, The Second, Governor of Lebanon), vol. 2, Rome: Realte Accademia d'Italia, 1928.

Rihani, A. F., *Al-Nakabat*, (The Disasters), Beirut: Matba'at Sadr Rihani, 1948.

Rustum, Asad J., *Lubnan fi Ahd al-Mutasarrifiya*, (Lebanon in the Era of the Mutasarrifs), Beirut: Dar al-Nihar, 1973.

---, *Bashir Bayna Al-Sultan wa al-'Aziz*, (Bashir between the Sultan and the Mighty Governor of Egypt), 2 vol., Jubayl: Manshurat al-Jami'ah al-Lubanaiyyah, 1966.

---, *Dhikra al-Batal al-Fatih Ibrahim Basha*, (Recollections of the Conquering Hero Ibrahim Pasha, Cairo: n.p., 1948.

Saghye, Hazem, *Ta'arib al-Kata'ib al-Lubnaniyah*, (The Arabization of the Lebanese Kata'ib Party), Beirut: Dar al-Jadid, 1992.

Saliba, Maurice, ed. /trans., *Lubnan fi Zaman al-Harb: Min Inhiyar al-Dawla ila Inbi'ath al-Umma*, (Lebanon in Time of War: From the Collapse of the State to the Awakening of the Nation), Paris: Center for European Arab Studies, 1994.

Sayegh, Anis, *Lubnan al-Ta'ifi*, (Sectarian Lebanon), Beirut: Dar al-Sira al-Fikri, 1955.

Sfeir, Butrus, *Al-Amir Bashir al-Shihabi*, (Prince Bashir Shihab), Beirut: Dar al-Tiba'ah wa al-Nashr, 1950.

Sharara, Waddah, *Fi Usul Lubnan al-Ta'ifi*, (On the Origins of Sectarianism in Lebanon/Lebanese Sectarianism), Beirut: n.p., 1975.

Sulh, Sami, *Mudhakkirat*, (Memoirs), Beirut: Maktabat al-Fikr al-Arabi, 1960.

Taqi al-Din, Munir, *Wiladat Istiqlal*, (The Birth of Independence), Beirut: Dar al-Ilm lil Malaiyn, 1953.

Tarabayn, Ahmad, *Azmat al-Hukum fi Lubnan Mundhu Suqut al-Usrah al-Shihabiyah Hatta Ibtida' Ahd al-Mutasarrifiyah, 1842-1860*, (The Governmental Crisis in Lebanon from the fall of the Shihabi Dynasty Until the Beginning of the Period of the Mutasarrifiyah, 1842-1860), Damascus: n.p., 1966.

---, *Lubnan Mundhu Ahd al-Mutasarrifiyah ila Bidayat al Intidab 1861-1920*, (Lebanon from the Origin of the Muta-sarrifiyah to the Beginnings of The Mandate, 1861-1920), Cairo: Matba'at Nahdat Misr, 1968.

Tarrazi, P. *Asdaq Ma Kan An Ta'rikh Lubnan*, (The Most Truthful Narration Concerning the History of Lebanon), Beirut: Matba'at Joseph Salim Sayqali, 1948.

Uwaydat, Abdu, *Ba'd Amrad al-Dawlah fi Lubnan*, (Some of the Diseases of The Nation/Government in Lebanon), Beirut: Manshurat Uwaydat, 1968.

Yamin, Antun, *Lubnan fi al-Harb, 1914-1919*, (Lebanon during the War, 1914-1919), Beirut: Matba'at al-Adabiyah, 1919.

Yazbek, Yusuf I., *Tarikh Lubnan Min 1841 ila al-Intidab*, (The History of Lebanon from 1841 until the Mandate), Beirut: n.p., 1967.

Ziadeh, N. A., *Ab'ad al-Ta'rikh al-Lubnani al-Hadith* (Aspects of Modern Lebanese History), Cairo: n.p., 1972.

Zubian, Sami, *Al-Harakah al-Wataniyah al-Lubnaniyah*, (The Lebanese National Movement), Beirut: Dar al-Masira, 1977.

BOOKS AND ARTICLES (in Western Languages)

Abdel-Malek, Anounar, ed., *Contemporary Arab Political Thought*, London: Zed Press, 1983.

Abraham, Antoine J., "Lebanese Communal Relations," *Muslim World*, LXVII, no. 2, 1977, pp. 91-105.

Abraham, A. J., *The Lebanon War*, Connecticut: Praeger, 1996.

---, *Lebanon: A State of Siege (1975-1984)*, Indiana: Wyndham Hall Press, 1984.

---, "Maronite Culture, Lebanon and the Arab World," *Transnational Perspectives*, vol. 15, no. 1, 1989, pp. 14-16.

---, *Lebanon at Mid-Century, Maronite-Druze Relations in Lebanon 1840-1860: A Prelude to Arab Nationalism*, MD.: University Press of America, 1981.

---, "The Lebanon War, In Retrospect and Prospect," *Journal of Third World Studies*, Fall, 1994, vol. XI, no. 2, pp. 117-150.

---, "A Psychological Approach to Conflict Resolution in the Third World", *Journal of Unconventional History*, vol. 9, Fall, 1997, pp. 54-59.

Abraham, A. J. and Ahmed Abdul Majid, "The Lebanese Labyrinth," *Transnational Perspectives*, vol. 12, no. 1, 1986, pp.14-17.

---, "The Lebanese Tangle," *International Journal on World Peace*, vol. VI, No. 2, APR-JUN, 1989, pp. 33-48.

Abraham, A. J. and George Haddad, *The Warriors of God: Jihad (Holy War) And The Fundamentalists of Islam*, Indiana: Wyndham Hall Press, 1989.

Abouchdid, E. E., *Thirty Years of Lebanon and Syria 1917-1947*, Beirut: The Sader-Rihani Printing Co, 1948.

Abu Manneh, Butrus, "The Christians Between Ottomanism and Syrian Nationalism: The Ideas of Butrus al-Bustani," *International Journal of Middle East Studies*, vol. 11, no. 3, May 1980, pp. 187-304.

Abul-Husn, Latif, *The Lebanese Conflict, Looking Inward*, Boulder: Lynne-Rienner Publishers, 1998.

Adams, Michael, ed., *The Middle East*, New York: Facts on File Publishers, 1988.

Adib, August Pasha, *Le Liban Apres La Guerre*, Paris: E. Leroux, 1918.

Ajami, Fouad, "Lebanon and Its Inheritors, *Foreign Affairs*, Spring, 1985, pp. 778-799.

---, *The Vanished Imam*, New York: Cornell University Press, 1986.

Ajay Jr., Nicholas Z., "Political Intrigue And Suppression in Lebanon During World War I," *International Journal of Middle East Studies*, vol. 5, no. 2, April, 1974, pp. 140-160.

Akarli, Engin, *The Long Peace, Ottoman Lebanon 1861-1920*, Berkeley: University of California Press, 1993.

Alem, Jean-Pierre, *Le Liban*, Paris: Presses universitaires de France, 1963.

Amoun, Iskander, *Alliance Libanaise D'Egypt, Memoire sur la Question Libanaise*, Cairo: Al-Ma'aref Neguib Mitri, 1913.

Anderson, Rufus, *History of the Missions of the American Board of Missions to the Oriental Churches*, 2 vol., Boston: Congregational Publishing Society, 1872.

Anno, *Memoire of Lady Hester Stanhope*, 3 vol., London: H.. Colburn, 1845.

Antonius, George, *The Arab Awakening*, New York: Capricorn Books, 1946.

Azar, Edward E. and Robert F. Haddad, *Seminar on the Reconstruction of The Lebanese Economy: Plans for Recovery–abstract*, MD.: University of Maryland: Center for International Development and Conflict Management. 1985.

Azar, E. E., et.al, *Lebanon and the World In The 1980's*, MD.: University of Maryland: Center For International Development, 1983.

Baaklini, Abdo I., *Legislative and Political Development: Lebanon, 1842-1972* No. Carolina: Duke University Press, 1976.

Ball, George W., *Error and Betrayal in Lebanon*, Washington D.C., Foundation For Middle East Peace, 1984.

Barakat, Halim, "Social and Political Integration in Lebanon: a Case of Social Mosaic," *Middle East Journal*, vol. 27, no. 3, Summer, 1973, pp. 301-318.

---, *Lebanon in Strife. Student Preludes to the Civil War*, Austin: University of Texas Press, 1977.

Baudicour, Louis de, *La France au Liban*, Paris: E. Dentu, 1879.

Baz. J., *Etude Sur La Nationalite Libanaise*, Jounieh, Liban, 1969.

Binder, Leonard, ed., *Politics in Lebanon*, New York: John Wiley and Sons, 1966.

Bliss, Frederick J., *The Religions of Modern Syria and Palestine*, New York: C. Scribner's Sons, 1912.

---, *The Reminiscences of Daniel Bliss*, New York; Fleming H. Revell Co., 1920.

Bouron, Narcisse, *Les Deuze: Histoire du Liban et la Montagne Haouranaise*, Paris: Berger-Levrault, 1930.

Bruce, I., *The Nun of Lebanon*, London: Collins, 1951.

Bruneau, A., *Traditions et Politique de la France au Levant*, Paris: F. Alcan 1932.

Burckhard, Charles, *Le Mandat Francais En Syrie Et Au Liban*, Nimes: Courrouy, 1925.

Burckhardt, J. L, *Travels in Syria and The Holy Land*, London: J. Murray, 1922.

Burke, E., "A Comparative View of French Native Policy in Morocco and Syria, 1912-1925," *Middle Eastern Studies*, vol. 9, no. 2, (May, 1973), pp. 175-186.

Cadalvene, E. de and E. Barrault, *Histoire de la Guerre de Mehmed-Ali contre la Porte Ottomane en Syrie et en Asie-Mineure, 1831-1833*, Paris: Arthus Bertrand, 1837.

Carali, P., *Fakhr ad-Din II Principe del Libano e La Corte di Toscana, 1605-1635*, vol. I, Rome: Reale Accademia d' Italia, 1936.

Carnarvon, Henry Howard Molyneaux Herbert, (The Earl of), *Recollections of The Druze of the Lebanon*, 2nd. ed., London: J. Murray, 1860.

Catafago, J., "Histoire Des Emirs Maan, Qui ont Gouvernee le Liban Despuis l'annee 1119 de J. C. Jusqu'a 1699," *Journal Asiatique*, sixieme serie, vol. III Paris 1964, pp. 267-287.

Catroux, Georges, *Deux Missions en Moyen-Orient*, Paris: Plon, 1958.

Chamie, Joseph, "Religions Groups in Lebanon: A Descriptive Investigation," *International Journal of Middle East Studies*, vol. 11, April 1980, no. 2, pp. 175-187.

Chamoun, Camille, *Crise au Moyen-Orient*, Paris: Gillimard, 1963.

---, *Memoire et Souvenirs Du 17 Juillet 1977 au 24 December 1978*, Beirut: Impreme Catholique, 1979.

Chasseaud, George W., *The Druze of the Lebanon: Their Manners Customs and History*, London: R. Bentley, 1855.

Chebli, M., *Une Histoire du Liban L'epoque des Emirs, 1635-1841*, Beirut: Imprimerie Catholique, 1955.

Chevallier, Dominique, "Aux origines des troubles agraires libanais en 1858," *Annales: Economics, Societes, Civilizations*, vol. 14, no. 1, (Janvier-Mars), 1959, pp. 35-64.

---, *La Societe du Mont Liban a l'epoque de la Revolution Industrielle en Europe*, Paris: Genthner, 1971.

Chiba, M., *Liban Aujourd'hui (1942)*, Beiruth: Editions du Trident, 1949.

Choueiri, Youssef, ed., *State And Society in Syria and Lebanon*, New York: St. Martin's Press, 1993.

Churchill, Colonel Charles Henry (Spencer), *The Druze and the Maronites Under Turkish Rule: From 1840-1860*, London: Bernard Quaritch, 1862.

---, *Life of Abdel Kadir*, London: Chapman and Hall, 1867

---, *Mount Lebanon: A Ten Years' Residence 1842-1852*, 3 vol., London: Saunders and Otley, 1853.

Cioeta, Donald J., "Ottoman Censorship in Lebanon and Syria, 1876-1908," *International Journal of Middle East Studies*, vol. 10, no. 2, May 1979,pp. 167-186.

Cleveland, William L., *Islam against the West, Shakib Arslan and The Campaign for Islamic Nationalism*, Austin: University of Texas Press, 1985.

Coury, Alfred, *Le Martyre Due Liban*, Marseille: Imprimeree Nouvelle, 1919.

Cuinet, V., *Syrie, Liban et Palestine*, Paris: E. Leroux, 1896- 1901.

Dahdah, Najib, *Evolution Historique Du Liban*, Beyrouth: Librairie du Liban, 1967.

Dahdah, S., "Le I[er] Voyage du L'Emir Bechir en Egypt Recit de Salim Dahdah," *Al-Mashriq*, XVIII, 1920, pp. 682-697, 732-739.

D'Alaux, M. G., "Le Liban et Davoud Pasha," *Revue Des Deux Mondes*, XXXV[e] Annee Second Periode, vol. 58, (July, 1865), pp. 139-168.

---, "Le Liban et Davoud Pasha," *Revue Des Deux Mondes*, XXXVI[e] Annee Second Periode, vol. LXIII, (May, 1866), pp. 5-49.

D'Armagnac, M. Le Baron, *Nezib et Beyrouth*, Paris: J. Laisne, 1844.

Davis, Helen M., *Constitutions, Electoral Laws, Treaties of State in the Near and Middle East*, No. Carolina: Duke University Press, 1953.

Davison, Roderic H., *Turkey*, New Jersey: Prentice Hall, 1968.

---, "Turkish Attitudes Concerning Christian Muslim Equality in the Nineteenth Century," *The American Historical Review*, vol. LIX, no. 4, July, 1954, pp. 844-864.

Dawisha, Adeed I., *Syria and the Lebanese Crisis*, New York: St. Martin's Press, 1980.

De Binos, Abbe, *Voyage au Mont Liban*, 2 vol., Paris; 1908.

Deeb, Marius, *The Lebanese Civil War*, New York: Praeger, 1980.

---, *Militant Islamic Movements in Lebanon:* Origins, Social Basis, and Ideology, Occasional Papers, Center for Contemporary Arab Studies, Georgetown University, 1986.

Dekmejian, R. Hrair, *Patterns of Political Leadership: Lebanon, Israel, Egypt*, New York: State University of New York Press, 1975.

De Lamartine, A., *Souvenirs, Impressions, Pensees et Paysages Pendant un Voyage en Orient, 1832-1833*, 2 vol., Paris: Hachette et Cie-Furne, 1835.

Denis, A., "Etudes Sur le Liban," *Revue De L'Orient*, vol. 3, pp. 345-356; vol.4, pp. 52-76, 180-190, 305-340, Paris, 1844.

Deringil, Selim, *The Anglo-French Clash in Lebanon and Syria, 1940-1945*, New York: St. Martin's Press, 1987.

De Tott, F., *Memoirs*, 4 vol., London: G. G. J. and J. Robinson, 1786.

Diab, Hassan, *Beirut, Reviving Lebanon's Past*, CT.: Praeger, 1999.

Dib, Pierre, *History of the Maronite Church*, (trans, by Seely Beggiani), Washington, D.C., The Maronite Seminary, 1962.

Dilip, Hiro, *Fire and Embers (A History of the Lebanese Civil War)*, New York: St. Martin's Press, 1992.

Dishon, Daniel, "The Lebanese War-An All Arab Crisis," *Mainstream*, January 1977, pp. 25-32.

Donon, Jean, "L'Organisation De La Federation Des Etats De Syrie Et Du Grand Liban Sous Le Mandat Francaise," *Revue Des Sciences Politique*, vol. 47, Paris, 1924, pp. 345-373.

D'Orleans, P. A. (Comte de Paris), Damas et Liban, Londras: W.Jeffs, 1861.

Douin, Georges, *La Premiere Guerre De Syrie*, 2 vol., Cairo: L' Institute Francais d'archealogie orientale du Caire pour la societe royal de geographie d'Egypte, 1931.

---, *La Mission Du Baron De Boislecomte -L'Egypte et la Syrie en 1833*, Cairo: Imprime. . .pour la societe royal de geographie d' Egypte, 1927.

Entelis, John P., *Pluralism and Party Transformation in Lebanon. Al-Kata'ib*, 1936-1970 Leiden: E. J. Brill, 1974.

---, "Party Transformation in Lebanon: Al-Kata'ib as a Case Study, *Middle East Studies*, vol. 9, no. 3, (October, 1973), pp. 325-340.

---, "Belief-System and Ideology in the Lebanese Kata'ib Party," *International Journal of Middle East Studies*, vol. 4, no. 2, April 1973, pp. 148-162.

Etinoff, N. S., *Thirty Years in Lebanon and the Middle East* Beirut: n.p., 1969.

Evron, Yair, *War and Intervention in Lebanon. The Israeli-Syrian Deterrence Dialogue*, Baltimore: The Johns Hopkins University Press, 1987.

Fabre-Luce, Alfred, *Deuil Au Levant* Paris: Fayard, 1950.

Farah, Caesar E., *The Politics of Interventionism in Ottoman Lebanon*, 1830-1961 London: I. B. Tauris, 2000.

---, "The Lebanese Insurgence of 1840 and the Powers," *Journal of Asian Studies*, vol. 1, no. 2, 1967, pp. 105-132.

Farley, James L., *Massacres in Syria*, London: Bradbury and Evans, 1861.

Favre, Rene, *Les Problems Politiques Dan Les Etats Du Levant Sous Mandat Francais*, Paris: Societe d'etudes et d'informations economiques, 1936.

Fawaz, Leila Tarazi, *Migrants and Merchants in Nineteenth Century Beirut*, Mass.: Harvard University Press, 1983.

---, "The City and the Mountain: Beirut's Political Radius in the Nineteenth Century as Revealed in the Crisis of 1860," *International Journal Of Middle East Studies*, vol.16, n.p., 4, November 1984, pp. 489-495.

Fedden, Robin, *The Phoenix Land*, New York, n. p., 1965; also published as *Syria and Lebanon*, London; J. Murray, 1965.

Feriet, Rene de, *L'Application D'Un Mandat*, Beyrouth, 1926.

Frankel, Ephraim A., "The Maronite Patriarch: An Historical View of A Religious Za'im in The 1958 Lebanese Crisis," *The Muslim World*, vol. LXVI, no. 3, July 1976, pp. 213-225.

Gabriel, Philip L., *In The Ashes*, Penn.: Whitmore Pub. C., 1978.

Gabriel, Richard A., *Operation Peace for Galilee, the Israeli-PLO War in Lebanon*, Toranto: Collins Pub., 1984.

Ganem, Chekri, *Comite Libanais De Paris, Memoire Sur La Question Du Liban*, Paris: C. Pariset, 1912.

Gates, Carolyn L., *The Merchant Republic of Lebanon, Rise of an Open Economy*, Center for Lebanese Studies and I. B. Tauris & Co., 1998.

Gelvin, James L., *Divided Loyalties: Nationalism and Mass Politics in Syria at The Close of Empire*, Los Angeles: University of California Press, 1998.

Gemayel, Amine, *Peace and Unity*, Gt. Britain: Colyn Smythe, 1984. "The Price and the Promise," *Foreign Affairs*, Spring1985, pp. 359-777.

---, *Lebanon: Struggle for a Lasting Peace*, Washington D. C., Embassy of Lebanon, April, 1986.

Gemayel, Bashir, *Liberte et Security*, Beirut: La Resistance Libanaise, 1980.

Gemayel, Pierre, "A Call from Christian Lebanon," *Al-Amal*, Beirut, 1954, pp. 5-19.

Gemayel, Maurice, *Le Pari Libanaise*, Beyrouth: Dar An-nahar, Liban, 1970.

Gendzier, Irene L., *Notes from the minefield: United States Intervention in Lebanon and the Middle East, 1945-1958*, New York: Columbia University Press, 1997.

Gheerbrandt, J. L., "Syria and Lebanon," *The Asiatic Review*, New Series, vol. 23, no. 75, (July, 1927), pp. 393-400.

Gibb, H. A. R. and H. Bowen, *Islamic Society and the West*, part I and II, New York: Oxford University Press, 1950; 1957.

Gilmour, David, Lebanon: *The Fractured Country*, New York: St. Martin's Press, 1984.

Godard, J., *L'Oeuvre Politique, Economique, Et Sociale De La France Combattants En Syrie Et Au Liban*, Beyrouth, 1943.

Gordon, David C., *Lebanon: The Fragmented Nation*, London: Croom Helm/Hoover Press, 1980.

---, *The Republic of Lebanon: Nation in Jeopardy*, Colorado: Westview Press, 1983.

Goria, Wade R., *Sovereignty and Leadership in Lebanon, 1943- 1967*, London: Ithaca Press, 1985.

Guys, Henry, *Beyrouth et le Liban, Relation d'un Sejour de Plusieurs Annees Dans Ce Pays*, 2 vol., Paris: Imprimerie de W. Remquet et Cie, 1850.

---, *La Nation Druze*, Paris: Chez France, 1863.

Haddad, George, *Fifty Years of Modern Syria and Lebanon*, Beirut: Dar al-Hayat, 1950.

Hagopian, Elaine and Samih Farsoun, ed., *South Lebanon*, special report no. 2, Arab-American University Graduates publication August, 1978.

Haley, P. Edward and Lewis W. Snider, ed., *Lebanon In Crisis, Participants and Issues*, New York: Syracuse University Press, 1979.

Halland, Thomas E., *The European Concert and the Eastern Question*, Oxford, 1985.

Hamiyrachi, Beate, *The Emergence of The South Lebanon Security Belt: Major Saad Haddad and the Ties with Israel, 1975-1978*, New York: Praeger, 1988.

Harik, Iliya, "The Iqta' System in Lebanon: A Comparative Political View," *Middle East Journal*, vol. 19, no. 4, 1965, pp., 405-421.

---, *Politics and Change in a Traditional Society: Lebanon 1711-1845*, New Jersey: Princeton University Press, 1968.

Harris, William, *Faces of Lebanon: Sects, Wars and Global Extensions*, New Jersey: Markus Wiener Pub., 1997.

Hess, C.G. and H. L. Bodman Jr., "Confessionalism and Feudality in Lebanese Politics," *Middle East Journal,* vol. 8, no. 1, 1954, pp. 10-26.

Hitti, Philip K. , *Lebanon in History*, New York: St. Martin's Press, 1967.

A Short History of Lebanon, New York: St. Martin's 1965.

History of Syria Including Lebanon and Palestine, New York: The Macmillian Co., 1951.

---, "The Impact of the West on Syria and Lebanon in the Nineteenth Century," *Cahiers D'Histoire Mondiale*, vol. II, no. 3, Paris, 1955, pp. 608-633.

---, *The Origins of the Druze People and Religion*, New York: Columbia University Press, 1928.

---, *The Near East in History: A 5000 Year Study*, New York: Van Nostrand, Reinhold & Co., 1961.

Holt, P. M., *Egypt and the Fertile Crescent, 1516-1922*, London: Longman's, Green and Co., 1966.

Hottinger, A., "Zu'ama and Parties in the Lebanese Crisis of 1958," *Middle East Journal*, vol. 15, no. 2, Spring 1961, pp. 127-140.

Hourani, Albert H., *Syria and Lebanon: A Political Essay*, London: Oxford University Press, 1946.

---, *Arabic Thought in the Liberal Age, 1798-1939*, London: Oxford University Press, 1962.

---, "Lebanon from Feudalism to Modern State," *Middle East Studies*, vol. 2, no. 3, April 1966, pp. 256-263.

---, *A Vision of History, Near Eastern and Other Essays*, Beirut: Khayats, 1961.

Hudson, Michael C., *The Precarious Republic, Political Modernization in Lebanon*, New York: Random House, 1968.

---, "The Electoral Process and Political Development in Lebanon," *Middle East Journal*, vol. 20, no. 2, Spring 1966, pp. 173-186.

---, The Palestinian Role in the Lebanese Civil War," Given at the Annual Meeting of the Middle East Studies Association, in New York, 9-11, November, 1977.

Hurewitz, J. C., "Lebanese Democracy in Its International Setting," *Middle East Journal*, vol. 17, 1963, pp. 487-506.

Huxley, Frederick C., *Wasita in a Lebanese Context: Social Exchange Among Villagers and Outsiders,* Anthropological Papers: Museum of Anthropology, no. 64, Michigan: University of Michigan, 1978.

Ignatius, David, "How to Rebuild Lebanon," *Foreign Affairs*, Summer 1983, pp. 1140-1156.

Ismail, Adel, *Histoire du Liban du XVII ᵉ Siecle a Nos Jours*, 5 vol., Paris: G. P. Maisonneuve, 1955-1958.

---, *Lebanon, History of a People*, Beirut: Dar al Makchouf, 1972.

Issawi, Charles, British Trade and The Rise of Beirut, 1830-1860, *International Journal of Middle East Studies*, vol. 8, no. 1, January, 1977, pp. 103-116.

Jaber, Hala, *Hizbollah, Born With A Vengeance*; New York: Columbia University Press, 1997.

Jalabert, Louis, *Syrie Et Liban, Reussite Francaise*, Paris: Librairie Plon, 1934.

---, "L'Amitie Francaise Au Liban," *Etudes*, Apr.-June, 1919, vol. 159, Paris, pp. 235-242.

---, "Dix Ans De Politique Mandataire En Syrie Et Au Liban," *Etudes,* 20 Fevrier, 1934, Paris, PP. 454-475.

Jandora, John W., "Butrus al-Bustani, Arab Consciousness and Arabic Revival," *The Muslim World*, vol. LXXIV, no. 2, April, 1984, pp. 71-84.

Jessup, Henry Harris, *Fifty Three Years in Syria*, New York: Fleming H. Revell Co., 1910.

Joffre, Alphonse, *Le Mandat de la France sur La Syrie et le Grand-Liban*, Lyon: L. Bascou, 1924.

Jones, J. M., *La Fin Du Mandat Francais En Syrie Au Liban*, Paris: Editions A. Pedone, 1938.

Joumblatt, Kamal, *I Speak for Lebanon*, London: Zed Press, 1982.

Jouplain, M. (Paul Noujaim/Njaym), *La Question du Liban*, Paris: A. Rousseau, 1908.

Kalawoun, Nasser M., *The Struggle For Lebanon: A History of Lebanese-Egyptian Relations*, London: I. B. Tauris, 2000.

Kedourie, Eli, *The Chatham House Version and Other Middle Eastern Studies* London: Weidenfeld & Nicolson, 1970.

---, *Islam in the Modern World and Other Studies*, New York: Holt, Rinehart and Winston, 1980.

Khadduri, Majid, *Arab Contemporaries: The Role of Personalities in Politics*, Baltimore: The Johns Hopkins University Press, 1973.

Khairallah, K. T. *Le Probleme du Levant, Les Regions Arabes Liberees*, Paris: E. Leroux, 1919.

Khairallah, S., *This is Lebanon*, Beirut: Khayats, 1965.

Khalaf, S., "Primordial Ties and Politics in Lebanon," *Middle Eastern Studies*, vol. 4, no. 3, April 1968, pp. 243-269.

Khalidi, Rashid I., "Lebanon in the Context of Regional Politics," *Third World Quarterly*, vol. 7, no. 3, July, 1985, pp. 495-514.

Khalidi, W., *Conflict and Violence in Lebanon: Confrontation in the Middle East*, MA: Harvard University Center for International Affairs, 1979.

Khalif, Samir and Philip S. Khoury, eds., *Recovering Beirut*, Leiden: E. J. Brill, 1993.

Khashan, Hilal, *Inside the Lebanese Confessional Mind*, Lanham: University Press of America, 1992.

Khazin, Farid, "The Lebanese Economy after a Decade of Turmoil, 1975-1985," *Arab-American Affairs*, no.12, Spring, 1985, pp. 72-84.

Khoury, Enver M., *The Crisis in the Lebanese System, Confessionalism and Chaos*, Washington: American Enterprise Institute for Public Policy Research, 1976.

Kilot, N., "The Collapse of The Lebanese State," *Middle Eastern Studies*, vol. 23, no; 1, January 1987, pp. 54-74.

Kirk, George E., *Contemporary Arab Politics: A Concise History*, New York: Praeger, 1961.

Labaki, Georges, *La Fiscalite Et Le Financement De L'Habitat Au Liban*, Paris: Librairie Generale De Droit Et De Jurusprudence, 1987.

Lammens, Pere Henri, *La Syrie: Precis Historique*, 2 vol., Beyrouth: Imprimerie Catholique, 1921.

Laurent, Achille, *Relation Historique des Affaires De Syrie Despuis 1840 Jusqu'en 1842*, 2 vol., Paris: Gaume Freres, 1846.

Lenczowski, George, ed., *Political Elites in the Middle East*, Washington: American Enterprise Institute for Political Research, 1975.

Lenormant, Francais, *Histoire des Massacres de Syrie en 1860*, Paris: L. Hachette et Cie, 1861.

Levantine, H., "Quarante Ans D'Autonomie Au Liban," *Etudes*, July-Sept.1902, Paris, Annee 39, vol. 92, pp. 31-52; 157-169.

Lontet, E., *Expedition de Syrie: Beyrouth, le Liban, et Jerusalem, 1860-1861*, Paris: Amyot, 1862.

Longrigg, Stephen H., *Syria and Lebanon under French Mandate*, London: Oxford University Press, 1958.

Lortet, Louis, *La Syrie D'Aujourd'hui*, Paris: Librairie Hachette et Cie, 1884.

Maamoun, Seiffedine, *Le Pouvoir Executif en droit constitutionel libanais et Syrien*, Lyon: Imprimerie Bosc freres E. Rion, 1930.

Mac Callum, E. P., *The Nationalist Crusade in Syria*, New York: The Foreign Policy Association, 1928.

Makdisi, Jean Said, *Beirut Fragments, a War Memoire*, New York: Persa Books, 1990.

Mallison, Sally and W. Thomas Mallison, *Armed Conflict in Lebanon, 1882*, London: American Educational Trust, 1985.

Malone, J. J., *The Arab Lands of Western Asia*, New Jersey: Prentice-Hall, Inc., 1973.

Ma'oz, Moshe, *Ottoman Reform in Syria and Palestine, 1840-1861*, London: Oxford, Clarendon Press, 1968.

Mariti, Giovanni, *Voyages Dans L'Isle de Chypre, La Syrie et La Palestine*, 2 vol. London: Cambridge University Press, 1791.

Masson, P., *Histoire du Commerce Francais Dan Le Levant, au XVIIIe Siecle*, Paris: Librairie Hachette, 1896.

Mc Dermott, Anthony and Kjell Skjelsbaek, ed., *The Multinational Force in Beirut*, 1982-1984 FL.: Univ. Press of Florida, 1991.

Meo, Leila, Lebanon, *Improbable Nation*, Indiana: Indiana University Press, 1965.

Michaud, M. et J. J. Poujoulat, *Correspondance D'Orient 1830-1831*, 6 vol., Bruxelles: Meline, 1835.

Mishaqa, Mikhayil, *Murder, Mayhem, Pillage and Plunder*, (Trans. by W. M. Thackston), N.Y.: State Univ. of N.Y. Press, 1988.

Mokarzel, N.A., "Les Voeux Du Liban," *L'Asie Francaise*, Annee 18, no. 175, Fevrier-Juillet, 1919, pp. 189-190.

Monterde, Rene, *Precis D'Histoire de Syrie et du Liban*, Bayrouth Imprimerie Catholique, 1939.

Moughrabi, Fouad and Nasser Aruri, *Lebanon: Crisis and Challenge in the Arab World*, special report no. 1, Arab-American University Graduates, January, 1977.

Nantet, Jacques, *Histoire Du Liban*, Paris: Editions de Minuit, 1963.

Napier, Sir Charles, *The War in Syria*, 2 vol., London: Parker, 1862.

Nasr, Nafhat and Monte Palmer, "Alienation and Political Participation in Lebanon", *International Journal of Middle East Studies*, vol. 8, no. 4, October 1977, pp. 493-516.

Neale, F. A. (esq.), *Eight Years in Syria Palestine and Asia Minor, From 1842-1850*, 2 vol., London: Colburn & Co., 1852.

Nehme, Michael J., "Lebanon: Open Arena for Regional Feuds," *Journal of Third World Studies*, vol. 12, no. 1, Spring, 1995, pp. 120-150.

Nimri, N. N., "The Warrior People of Djebel Druze: A Militant Minority in the Middle East," *Journal of the Middle East Society*, vol. 1, part 1, 1946-1947, pp. 47-62; no. 2, part II, 1947, pp. 90-96.

Noradoughian, Gabriel, ed., *Recueil d'actes internationaux de l'Empire Ottoman,* Paris: 3 vol., 1897-1902.

Norton, Richard Augustus, "Israel and South Lebanon," *American-Arab Affairs* Spring 1983, no. 4, pp. 23-31.

---, *Amal and the Shi'a, Struggle for the Soul of Lebanon,* Austin: University of Texas Press, 1987.

O'Ballance, Edgar, *Civil War in Lebanon, 1975-1992,* New York: St. Martin's Press, 1998.

Odeh, B.J., *Lebanon: Dynamics of Conflict,* London: Zed Books, 1985.

Oliphant, Lawrence, *The Land of Gilead with Excursions in the Lebanon,* London: W. Blackwood and Sons, 1880.

Olson, Robert, *The Ba'th And Syria, 1947-1982,* New Jersey: The Kingston Press, 1982.

Owen, Roger, ed., *Essays on the Crisis in Lebanon,* London: Itheca Press, 1976.

O'Zoux, R., *Les Etats Du Levant Sous Mandat Francais,* Paris: Larose, 1931.

Patai, Raphael, ed., *The Republic of Lebanon,* 2 vol., New Haven: Human Relations Area Files Inc., 1956.

Peroncel-Hugoz, Jean-Pierre, *Une Croix sur le Liban,* Paris: Liew Commun, 1984.

Perrier, Ferdinand, *La Syrie sous le gouvernment de Mehemet Ali jusqu'en 1840,* Paris: Arthus Bertrand Librairie, 1842.

Persen, William, "Lebanese Economic Development," *Middle East Journal,* vol.12, no. 3, Summer, 1958, pp. 177-294.

Petran, Thabita, *The Struggle over Lebanon,* New York: Monthly Review Press, 1978.

Phares, Walid, *Lebanese Christian Nationalism: The Rise and Fall of an Ethnic Resistance,* Boulder: Lynne Rienner Pub., 1995.

Picard, Elizabeth, *Lebanon: A Shattered Country,* New York: Holmes and Meier pub., 1996.

Pipes, Daniel, *The History of an Ambition,* New York: Oxford University Press, 1990.

Poliak, A. N., *Feudalism in Egypt, Syria, Palestine and The Lebanon, 1250-1900,* London: The Royal Asiatic Society, 1939.

Polk, William R., *The Opening of South Lebanon, 1788-1840,* Massachusetts: Harvard University Press, 1963.

Polk, William R. and Richard L. Chambers, *Beginnings of Modernization In the Middle East, the Nineteenth Century,* Chicago: Chicago University Press, 1968.

Poujade, E., "La Turque et Les Population Du Liban," *Revue Contemporaine,* 2^e Serie, Tome Onzieme, Paris, Sept-Oct, 1859, pp. 466-492.

---, "La Turque et Les Population Du Liban," *Revue Contemporaine,* 2^e Serie, Tome Treizieme, Paris, Jan-Feb. 1860, pp. 5-23; 677-693.

---, "Le Liban Et La Syrie En 1860," *Revue Contemporaine,* Neuvieme Annee, 2^e Serie, Tome Seizieme, Paris, 1860, pp. 508-527.

Poujoulat, Baptistin, *La Verite sur la Syrie*, Paris: Gaume Freres et Duprey, 1861.

Puaux, Gabriel, *Deux Annees au Levant*, Paris: Hachette, 1952.

Qubain, Fahim I., *Crisis in Lebanon*, Washington D. C. The Middle East Institute Press, 1961.

Rabbath, Edmond, "Constitution et independance au Liban: Un cas de genese conjointe," *Orient*, no. 47/48, 1968, pp. 9-71.

Rabinovich, Itamar, *The War For Lebanon*, Revised Edition, New York: Cornell University Press, 1985.

Rahall, Nick J. III, "Lebanon and U.S. Foreign Policy Toward The Middle East, *American-Arab Affairs*, Fall 1982, no.2, pp. 40-50.

Richani, Nazih, *Dilemmas of Democracy and Political Parties in Sectarian Societies: The Case of the Progressive Socialist Party of Lebanon*, 1949-1996 New York: St. Martin's Press, 1998.

Ristelhueber, Rene, "Les Maronites," *Revue des Deux Mondes*, XXV, January, 1915, LXXXVe Annee, Sixieme Periode, pp.187-215.

---, *Tradition francaise au Liban*, Paris: F. Alcan, 1918.

---, "Liban, Cher Liban 1908! (Souvenirs)," *Revue D' Histoire Diplomatique*, soixante-Quatorizieme Annee, Jan- Mars, 1960, pp. 9-32.

Rondot, Pierre, "Lebanese Institutions and Arab Nationalism," *Journal of Contemporary History*, vol. 3, no. 3, 1968, pp. 37-51.

---, *Les Institutions Politiques Du Liban*, Paris: Imprimerie nationale, 1947

---, "L'experience du Mandat francaise en Syrie et au Liban (1918-1945)," *Revue Generale de Droit International Public*, nos. 3-4, vol. 52, serie XIX, Juillet-December, 1948, pp. 387-409.

Rouleau, Eric, "Civil War in Lebanon, "*South West Asia*, vol. II, no. 41, October 1975, pp. 1-8.

Rubin, Barry, "Lebanon Who's Failure?" *FPI Policy Briefs*, Washington D. C.: The Johns Hopkins University Press, 1987.

Rubin, Barry and Laura Blum, *The May 1983 Agreement Over Lebanon, FPI Case Studies*, no. 7, Washington D.C.: The Johns Hopkins University Press, 1987.

Rustum, Asad J., "Bashir Shihab," E.I.^{2} pp. 1078-1079.

---, "A New Page on the History of the Druze Revolt," *Al-Mashriq* vol. XXXV, 1937, pp. 475-490.

---, ed., *Les Campagnes D'Ibrahim Pacha en Syrie et en Asie Mineure, 1831-1840*, Cairo, n.d.

Saab, Ann P., "English and Irish Reactions to the Massacres in Lebanon and Syria, 1860," *The Muslim World*, vol. LXXIV, no. 1, January 1984, pp. 12-25.

Salem, Elie A., "Cabinet Politics in Lebanon," *Middle East Journal*, vol. 21, no. 4, Autumn, 1967, pp. 488-502.

---, *Modernization without Revolution, Lebanon's Experience*, Indiana: Indiana University Press, 1973.

Salibi, Kemal S., *The Modern History of Lebanon*, New York: Praeger, 1965.

---, "Fakhr Al-Din," *E.I².*, pp. 749-751.

---, *Maronite Historians of Mediaeval Lebanon*, Beirut: AUB Publications of the Faculty of Arts and Sciences, 1959.

---, The Secret of the House of Ma'an," *International Journal of Middle East Studies*, vol. 4, no. 3, July, 1973, pp. 272-287.

---, *Crossroads to Civil War, Lebanon 1958-1976*, New York Caravan Press, 1976.

---, *A House of Many Mansions, the History of Lebanon Reconsidered*, Berkeley: University of California Press, 1988.

Samne, G., "L'Organisation de la Syrie et le statue du Liban," *Correspondance D'Orient*, 14 Annee, no. 269-270 (Sept., 1921), pp. 625-637.

---, La Question du Liban ou la Quadrature du Cercle," *Correspondance D'Orient*, 14 Annee, no. 261 (May, 1921), pp. 385-390.

---, "Le Grand Liban et la Syrie," *Correspondance D'Orient*, 14 Annee, no. 260 (April, 1921), pp. 337-344.

Scheltema, Johann Friederich, *The Lebanon in Turmoil: Syria and the Powers in 1860*, New Haven: Yale University Press, 1920.

Schiff Ze'ev and Ehud Ya'ari, *Israel's Lebanon War*, New York: Simon and Schuster, 1984.

Sfer, Abdallah (Pasha), "Le Mandat Francaises En Syrie et Au Liban," *La Revue Hebdomadaire*, Auguste, 1922, Annee 31, Tome 8, pp. 131-154, 295-314, 434-447; Tome 9, pp. 83-98, 223-235.

---, *Le Mandat Francais Et Les Traditions Francais En Syrie Et Au Liban*, Paris: Plon-Nourrit et Cie, 1922.

Shaw, Stanford J., "The Origins of Representative Government in the Ottoman Empire, an Introduction to the Provincial Councils, 1839-1876," *Near East Round Table*, New York: 1969, pp. 53-142.

---, "The Central Legislative Councils in the Nineteenth Century Ottoman-Reform Movement before 1876," *International Journal of Middle East Studies*, vol. 1, January, 1970, no. 1, pp. 51-84.

Shehadi, Nadim and Dana Haffar Mills, *Lebanon: a History of Conflict and Consensus*, London: I. B. Tauris 1992.

Simon, James J., "The Role of the Administrative Council of Mount Lebanon in the Creation of Greater Lebanon, 1918- 1920," *Journal of Third World Studies*, vol. XIII, no. 2, Fall, 1996, pp. 119-171.

Sorel, Jean-Albert, *Le Mandat Francais t L'Expansion Economique de la Syrie et du Liban*, Paris: Marcel Giard, 1929.

Spagnolo, John P., *France and Ottoman Lebanon, 1861-1914*, London: Ithaca Press, 1977.

---, "Constitutional Change in Mount Lebanon: 1861-1864," *Middle East Studies*, vol. 7, no. 1, (January, 1971), pp. 25-48.

---, "Mount Lebanon, France, and Daud Pasha," *International Journal of Middle East Studies*, vol. 2, no. 2, (April, 1971), pp. 148-167.

Spencer, W., *Political Evolution in the Middle East*, Philadelphia: Lippincott, 1962.

Stewart, D., *Turmoil in Beirut*, London: A. Wingate, 1958.

Stoakes, Frank, "The Supervigilantes: The Lebanese Kataeb Party as Builder, Surrogate and Defender of the State," *Middle Eastern Studies* vol. 11, no. 3, October, 1975, pp. 215-236.

Suleiman, Michael, W., *Political Parties in Lebanon*, New York: Cornell University Press, 1967.

---, "Crisis and Revolution in Lebanon," *Middle East Journal*, vol. 26, no. 1, Winter 1972, pp. 11-24.

Tanenbaum, Jan Karl, *France and the Arab Middle East, 1914-1920*. Philadelphia: The American Philosophical Society, October, 1978.

Thakar, Ramesh, *International Peacekeeping in Lebanon*, CO: Westview Press, 1987.

Tibawi, Abd Al-Latif, *A Modern History of Syria Including Lebanon and Palestine*, London: Macmillan & Co., 1969.

---, "The American Missionaries in Beirut and Butrus Al-Bustani," *St. Anthony Papers*, no. 16/Middle Eastern Affaris no. 3, 1963, pp. 137-182.

Timmerman, Jacob, *The Longest War, Israel in Lebanon*, New York: Alfred A. Knopf, 1982.

Touma, Toufic, *Paysans et institutions feodales chez les druses et les maronites du Liban du XVIIe siecle a 1914*, 2 vol., Beirut: L'Universite Lebanaise, 1971-1972.

Tueni, Ghassan, "Lebanon: A New Republic?"*Foreign Affairs*, Fall, 1982, pp. 82-99.

Urquhart, David, *The Lebanon: (Mount Souria) A History and A Diary*, 2 vol., London: T. C. Newly, 1860.

Van Leeuwen, Richard, *Notables and Clergy in Mount Lebanon, the Khazin Sheikhs and the Maronite Church (1736-1840)*, The Netherlands: E. J. Brill, 1994.

Van Lennep, H. J., *Bible Lands: Their Modern Customs and Manners*, New York: Harper Bros., 1875.

Verney, Noel and George Dambmann, *Les Puissances Etrangeres dans le Levant, en Syrie et en Palestine*, Paris: Guillaumin et Cie, 1900.

Vincent, Jack E., *International Relations*, vol. 2, Lanham: University of America Press, 1983.

Vocke, Harold, *The Lebanese War*, New York: St Martin's Press, 1978.

Wetterle, Abbe E., *En Syrie avec le general Gouraud*, Paris: E. Grevin-Imprimere de Lagnt, 1924.

Wilkinson, Paul, "The Lebanese Powder keg." *Contemporary Review*, August, 1983, vol. 243, no 1411, pp. 64-71.

Zamir, Meir, *The Formation of Modern Lebanon*, New York: Cornell University Press, 1985.

---, *Lebanon's Quest. The Road to Statehood, 1926-1936*, London: I. B. Tauris, 1997.

Zeine, N. Z., *The Struggle for Arab Independence*, Beirut: Khayat's, 1060.

---, Arab-Turkish Relations and the Emergence of Arab Nationalism, Beirut: Khayat's, 1968.

---, *The Emergence of Arab Nationalism*, Beirut: Khayat's 1966.

Ziadeh, Nicola A., *Syria and Lebanon*, London: Ernest Benn Ltd., 1957.

---, "The Lebanese Elections of 1960," *Middle East Journal*, vol. 4, no. 4, Autumn 1960, pp. 367-381.

Zisser, Eyal, Lebanon: *The Challenge of Independence*, London: I. B. Tauris, 2000.

NEWSPAPERS:

The Times (London): June 5, 1845; July 5, 6, 12, 21, 23, 27, and 1860.

The New York Times; May 17, 1983, pp. A12-A13.

Le Moniteur Universal: Sept. 4, 1841, Dec. 14, 23, 1841; Jan. 13, 1842; July 21, 29, 1860; Aug. 4, 12, 1860.

Al-Sayyar (Ar.), *Kitab Fad'ih Lubnan* (A Book on the Shame of Lebanon), Alexanderia, Egypt, 1901, pp. 9-55.

About the Author

A. J. Abraham is professor of history and international relations at John Jay College (CUNY) and New York Institute of Technology. He received his B.A. and M.A. from Hunter College (CUNY) and his Ph.D. from New York University.

A World Class Scholar, Professor Abraham has served as a consultant to several governments, as well as to international agencies and organizations. He is the author of numerous articles and books on the Near and Middle East and the Third World.